The Chinese People at War

The Chinese peoples' experience of war during World War II, as it is known in the West, was one of suffering and stoicism in the face of dreadful conditions. China's War of Resistance began in 1937 with the Japanese invasion and ended in 1945 after eight long years. Diana Lary, one of the foremost historians of the period, tells the tragic history of China's war and its consequences from the perspective of those who went through it. Using archival evidence only recently made available, interviews with survivors, and extracts from literature, she creates a vivid and highly disturbing picture of the havoc created by the war, the destruction of towns and villages, the displacement of peoples, and the accompanying economic and social disintegration. Her focus is on families torn apart – men, women, and children left homeless and struck down by disease and famine. It is also a story of courage and survival. By 1945, the fabric of China's society had been utterly transformed, and entirely new social categories had emerged. As the author suggests in a new interpretation of modern Chinese history, far from stemming the spread of communism from the USSR, which was the Japanese pretext for invasion, the horrors of the war and the damage it created nurtured the Chinese Communist Party and helped it to win power in 1949.

DIANA LARY is Professor Emerita in the Department of History at the University of British Columbia. She has spent many years working on modern Chinese history, teaching the subject to thousands of students and writing or editing six books and numerous articles.

New Approaches to Asian History

This dynamic new series will publish books on the milestones in Asian history, those that have come to define particular periods or mark turning points in the political, cultural, and social evolution of the region. The books in this series are intended as introductions for students to be used in the classroom. They are written by scholars whose credentials are well established in their particular fields and who have, in many cases, taught the subject across a number of years.

Books in the Series
Judith M. Brown, *Global South Asians: Introducing the Modern Diaspora*
Diana Lary, *China's Republic*
Peter A. Lorge, *The Asian Military Revolution: From Gunpowder to the Bomb*
Ian Talbot and Gurharpal Singh, *The Partition of India*
Stephen F. Dale, *The Muslim Empires of the Ottomans, Safavids, and Mughals*

The Chinese People at War
Human Suffering and Social Transformation, 1937–1945

Diana Lary

University of British Columbia, Vancouver

CAMBRIDGE
UNIVERSITY PRESS

CAMBRIDGE UNIVERSITY PRESS
Cambridge, New York, Melbourne, Madrid, Cape Town,
Singapore, São Paulo, Delhi, Tokyo, Mexico City

Cambridge University Press
32 Avenue of the Americas, New York, NY 10013-2473, USA

www.cambridge.org
Information on this title: www.cambridge.org/9780521144100

First published 2010
Reprinted 2011

A catalog record for this publication is available from the British Library.

Library of Congress Cataloging in Publication Data

Lary, Diana.
The Chinese people at war : human suffering and social transformation, 1937–1945 /
Diana Lary.
    p.   cm. – (New approaches to Asian history)
Includes index.
ISBN 978-0-521-19506-5 (hardback)
1. China – Social conditions – 1912–1949. 2. Sino-Japanese War, 1937–1945 –
Social aspects. 3. China – History – 1937–1945. I. Title. II. Series.
HN733.L37   2010
940.53´51–dc22   2010015143

ISBN 978-0-521-19506-5 Hardback
ISBN 978-0-521-14410-0 Paperback

Dedication

For my beloved mother, M. M. E. Lainson, who died just as this book was finished.

And for my friend since childhood, Jenni Calder. We did Latin together at the Perse (Cambridge) and learnt the phrase for the Aeneid, '*lacrimae rerum*', 'the tears of things'. The tears are for the sadness and anguish war produces, and the waste it causes.

Contents

Illustrations

Maps

Preface

This book was written to help explain the awful impact of the Resistance War (1937–45) on Chinese society. It is written in the hope that readers will come to see this war as one of the pivotal events in modern Chinese history and not just a murky prelude to the communist advent to power in 1949.

I grew up in the shadow of the two world wars. World War I was the overwhelming event in the lives of my grandmothers. Mabel Symmes mourned all her long life for her husband, killed on Easter Sunday 1917, along with almost 4,000 Canadians. Margaret Lainson kept two scrapbooks filled with three-line death announcements from the *Times* of men from her small part of Suffolk who had been killed in the war. World War II was my parents' war. It was close to us as children. The adults in our world talked about the war constantly. We lived with post-war shortages, and we understood the losses war had brought to a 'victorious' country. My mother, M. M. E. Lainson, taught us how painful and wasteful war was. The human costs to the West can be magnified many times for China. I have wanted to bring some understanding of the trauma and also of the heroism of the Resistance War.

In writing this book, I have relied on help from people beyond the field of Chinese history. One of the people who has helped me most, with her enthusiasm and her clear insight, is Martha Carroll of New York. She insisted on the importance of my topic, and she brought her wide-ranging knowledge to move me from my rather narrow academic world to a much broader one.

I thank my colleagues at the University of British Columbia who have helped me so much over the years of writing this book: Alison Bailey, Timothy Brook, Gu Xiong, Liu Jing, Steven Lee, Tsao Hsing-yuan, Alexander Woodside, and Eleanor Yuen.

Beryl Williams (Sussex) helped me with the European literature on the impact of World War II on Europe. My colleagues in a collaborative project on the Resistance War have been very helpful. My thanks go to Ezra Vogel (Harvard), Hans van de Ven (Cambridge), Stephen MacKinnon (Arizona State), Yang Tianshi (Beijing), and Yamada

Tatsuo (Tokyo). My former students have helped me enormously: Colin Green (Kwantlen University College) and Chu Shao-kang (UBC Okanagan). Current UBC students collected research materials for me: Yang Wu, David Luesink, and Dominic Yang.

I thank all the people who have shared their wartime experiences (or the experiences of their families) with me: Jerome Ch'en, Winnie Cheung, He Jibu, Samuel Ho, Hong Buren, Hsing Fu-ying, Jiang Jin, Lin Jing, Ju Zhifen, Fatima Lee, Bernard Luk, Vivienne Poy, Yang Tianshi, Ye Jiaying, and John Yu. Jerome Ch'en in particular taught me from early in my study of Chinese history how traumatic the war was and how much it changed Chinese society.

This project involved quite a lot of travel for research. For help and hospitality during my research travels, I want to thank the following people: in Beijing, Yang Tianshi, Bu Ping, Phil Calvert, Chantal Meagher, Ju Zhifen, Janet Lai, Qi Wenxin, Maggie and Andrew Watson, Endymion Wilkinson, and Zhuang Jianping; in Shanghai, Mary Boyd, James Mitchell, and Fei Lan; in Minnan, Li Minghuan, Wang Lianmao, and Ding Yulin; in Hong Kong, Hai Chi-yuet, David Jones, Gianni Mok, and Elzabeth Sinn; in Ottawa, Denise Chong and Roger Smith; and in Taibei, Chang Jui-te and Ch'en Yung-fa.

None of this travel would have been possible without a very generous research grant from the Social Sciences and Humanities Research Council of Canada. I have used the following libraries and archives: Second Historical Archives (Nanjing), Guoshiguan and Dangshihui (Taibei); National Archives (London); National Archives (Ottawa); Siemens Archiv (Munchen); and Xiamen University Library.

Finally, my deepest love and thanks for the joy they have brought me go to three small people who I hope will never experience war: Mabel, Jack, and Misha, my grandchildren.

Introduction: The Human Cost of War

残山剩水
A ravaged world

The Resistance War (*Banian kangRi zhanzheng*) (1937–45) was one of the greatest upheavals in Chinese history. It was a time of courage and sacrifice and a time of suffering and loss.[1] Virtually the entire country was engulfed by war. All of China's major cities were occupied, as were the eastern and northeastern regions and much of the southeast. The national government was forced to move inland. Almost every family and community was affected by war. Tens of millions of people took flight. Between 20 million and 30 million soldiers and civilians died during the war.

The war was the last of a long series of foreign invasions that started in the 1840s with the Opium Wars. The *leitmotif* of the 2008 Beijing Olympics was that the injuries and injustice of foreign invasion were finished, that China had come into her own after her long humiliation at the hands of the outside world and regained her rightful position in the world. China's encounter with imperialism started with Western aggression, but the Japanese invasion and occupation almost a century later were by far the greatest foreign assaults that China suffered in her modern history. The ultimate external assault on China came not from the West, but from an Asian country, part of the world that China had dominated so long herself.

In 1938, Mao Zedong made one of his most famous statements, in his essay 'Problems of War and Strategy', that 'political power comes out of the barrel of a gun [*qiangganzi limian chu zhengquan*].' This statement is generally associated with Mao's fight for the revolution, in the struggle between the Guomindang (GMD) and the Chinese Communist Party (CCP, Gongchandang), but at the time that Mao wrote these lines, the

---

[1] The Resistance War was incorporated into the larger conflict of World War II, which started in late 1939.

enemy was Japan, and the struggle was against foreign invasion. The CCP grew strong during the war and at its end was ready to challenge the GMD for power. The violence and turmoil of the war were the forces that propelled the CCP to power – by the end of the Civil War (1946–49), it was indeed the gun that brought the CCP to political power.

The scale of the human suffering brought on by the war was overwhelming – and almost indescribable. Wars are violent, destructive, and unpredictable. They are difficult to write about in a sober, analytical way because war is not controlled or rational. Wars promote violence and destruction, heroism and sacrifice, and passionate acts, not cerebral ones. Wars do not lend themselves to lucid analysis; they are times of chaos and confusion. Their outcomes are seldom predictable or conclusive. Many historians avoid looking at war and leave it to professional soldiers to write about. This avoidance has been a salient characteristic of the treatment of the Resistance War in Western historical works on modern China, which often pass over it and the Civil War that followed it, stop in 1937, or start in 1949.

In China, the momentousness of the Resistance War is now well accepted. The war is covered in great detail in history, novels, films, and memoirs. There are many interpretations but one common view: The war was a critical turning point in China's modern history. It was clearly a political turning point. The CCP and its armies learned to wage war in the battles against the Japanese armies and won the support of a society fundamentally changed and reduced almost to despair by warfare. The war also changed the face of Chinese society and made it ripe for revolution.

War and Society

Wars are the fracture lines of social history. We use the phrases 'pre-war', 'ante bellum', and 'post-war' in looking at European or American history as a recognition of the fundamental changes that wars produce in societies. Wars are often the death knell of an old social order, the grim handmaidens for the birth of new ones. This process does not happen in a planned or systematic way on a political or ideological blue print. The hallmark of war is chaos. War attacks the social fabric and brings loss of cohesion and fragmentation to systems and institutions that seemed solid and resistant to change in times of peace.

There are strong arguments in the opposite direction – that fundamental processes of social change may be interrupted but not changed in direction by war, that wars do not make fundamental changes in society, that the base is so strong that it cannot be changed by war. This view is held by those who believe in an essential China that never changes, from time immemorial. Another, very different version of the argument against wars as critical agents of change is that change is a long-term, gradual process. The distinguished historian of China, Prasanjit Duara, wrote that, in modern China, 'wars were, like natural disasters, utterly devastating but temporary'.[2]

I disagree. I find it difficult to accept these arguments for China or for any of the other countries that went through World War II and lived with total war for many years. These societies were changed fundamentally and often horribly during the war. Societies such as the United States or Canada that sent their soldiers to war but were not themselves invaded had a less disruptive experience but still a transformative one.

The Old Society

Before the war, parts of Chinese society were already going through rapid change. The collapse of the last dynasty, the Qing, the rise of the Republic (*Zhonghua minguo*), foreign incursions, industrial development, and the arrival of modern transport and communications had all begun to have major impacts on society, though at different speeds and levels in different parts of the country. Social change was rapid in the major eastern cities and the treaty ports and much slower elsewhere. A deep rural-urban divide was opening up. The traditional society was strongly entrenched in the countryside but in decline in the developed parts of China. There, the old social ideal of large families living together, four generations under one roof (*sishi tongtang*), was giving way to modern concepts of small families; in the countryside, where the vast majority of the population lived, social patterns – clan/lineage organisations, close connections to the ancestors, deference to elders, acceptance of arranged marriage and polygamy, and the subordinate status of women – had been only slightly touched by change. Deference to the gentry elite was dominant, though based now less on the traditional qualification of education than on economic power.

Did the beginnings of change mean that even in the rural areas the old society was doomed? There were enough assaults on the old order in the 1920s and 1930s from modern-minded intellectuals and political radicals to convince many people that this was so, that there was a systemic rural crisis that could be resolved only by a revolution that would end

---

[2] Prasanjit Duara, *Culture, Power and the State: Rural North China 1900–1942* (Palo Alto, CA: Stanford University Press, 1988), p. 249.

the old order. Revolutionaries believed that the old order was dying and were eager to speed it on its way. They were young people who themselves were breaking away from the oppression and paternalism of their own family elders. Their political revolution started with their revulsion for the old social order.

Some of these men went on to become the leaders of revolutionary China. In retrospect, it is easy to see a linear connection between their early activities and the CCP's rise to power in 1949. There was in fact no such smooth path. In the pre-war period, the CCP was in the deep wilderness, and its influence on the worlds they had abandoned was negligible. In the 1920s and 1930s, radical revolution failed. The CCP was driven out of its last bases in southern China and forced to flee on the Long March to a toehold in the Northwest. In 1937, the party's hope of ruling China was virtually nil.

Liberal reformers, within the GMD government and outside it, also failed to bring about radical social reform. The official blueprints for social change stayed as blueprints; few were ever implemented. The efforts of individual reformers, at places such as Ding xian (Hebei) and Zouping (Shandong), were worthy, but their success was local only. In the brief decade that the GMR ruled from Nanjing, there was not enough time or commitment to introduce real change.

China went into the war with Japan as a society still largely traditional, with signs of incipient change, few of them consolidated. The war forced change. The war brought fighting, bombing, and economic collapse and in the process turned the old society upside down and inside out. Some of the changes were sudden and extreme, so violent that they amounted to social deformation; others were more gradual but fundamental changes in basic social structures. The old order failed to provide answers to the Japanese invasion. It seemed ineffective and incompetent. As the war went on, there was a widespread revulsion against it, a sense of betrayal. Radical solutions began to seem possible, in a way could not have been imagined before the war.

Social Deformations

家破人亡

The family is destroyed, the people lost

One of the largest elements of social deformation was the loss of young men in combat. This loss inevitably led to a rise in the numbers of unmarried women and childless widows and soon to a reduced birth rate. This is a universal effect of war. It is often followed, once a war is over, by a compensatory baby boom; a period of many deaths is followed by a rise in the birth rate.

The death of soldiers also led to an enormous increase in the number of widows and orphans. In some parts of China, women came to out-number men. The widows had to learn to support themselves and to bring up their fatherless children on their own; the chances of a widow remarrying were low. A widow was only a marriage prospect for a very poor man; if she came with children and her husbands' parents, she was unmarriageable.

Many families and communities were deformed by another form of loss – the war-induced migration of many members. People were forced to flee away from fighting and bombing, and though many soon came home, others never did or did not return for decades after the war. When they did come back, it was to places and families they could scarcely recognise. In the meantime, they were lost to their families, in social, economic, and emotional ways.

The struggle to survive the upheavals of war changed the patterns of family relations and of the family economy. The grim demands of survival brought the intensification of the closest family bonds: parents and children. Parents struggled to keep their children alive, at the cost of ignoring less critical relatives – parents, grandparents, uncles, aunts, cousins, nephews, and nieces. The elderly and infirm might even have to be abandoned when a family fled. The shrinking of the family brought about the creation of de facto nuclear families. This new pattern led to a leaner definition of family ties, which now centred on the fierce love of parents for their children. This attachment was even more intense when a widow was bringing up her children alone; the sole focus of her life was her children.

These deformations of society helped to create a society that, in many parts of China, was scarcely recognisable from the pre-war one. It also was radically changed in structure.

Changes in Social Structure

The Resistance War is a black hole in systematic accounts of social change. The war was too chaotic, too fluid to allow for collection of data or for coherent analysis of what impact it was having on society. The war was followed by the Civil War and then a socialist revolution. It was impossible to do scientific survey work until after the end of the Mao era, from the 1980s on. However difficult it is to talk about a period of such chaos and confusion, some elements of change stand out very clearly.

The old elites suffered drastic losses in status. The inability of the old government and social elites to protect their nation or their localities could be put down to *force majeure* but also was seen as a sign of their incompetence and their lack of preparation for a conflict that in hindsight seemed inevitable. Their flight into the interior or their collaboration in the occupied areas undermined their legitimacy in the eyes of those they governed. After the war, there was no going back to their pre-war status.

Equally clear was the emergence of new social strata. The status of the military rose dramatically on both the GMD and the CCP sides. War demanded that the military be given the first call on human resources – and some of the brightest of young men went into the army. This process had been going on since the late Qing, with the end of the old examination system and the old path of elite recruitment; now it was intensified and permanently consolidated. The military, once despised, became the dominant political and social stratum. At the same time, the influence of intellectuals waned as the pace of war overtook the more leisurely world of ideas and as soldiers rather than men of education came to dominate the administrative elite. The old mandarinate, in which the civil and literary elite dominated, was gone.

War changed the gender balance in Chinese society. Many women had to learn to cope on their own and to step into roles that previously would have been performed by their fathers or husbands. Their forced independence started to change patterns of dependency and to give women opportunities to liberate themselves. At the same time, the huge numbers of men who went into the armies moved into an all-male world in which new standards of behaviour were inculcated – discipline, toughness, and sacrifice. Their lives changed completely, as did their futures. Soldiers who died might become heroes; the ones who survived had the consolations of medals, a permanent job, and the promise of veterans benefits, all at the cost, except for the officers, of loss of contact with their families.

In a time of great insecurity, the definition of wealth and prosperity changed from a preference for real property (i.e., houses, land, and vehicles) that was now insecure because it could be stolen or expropriated to small portable goods (i.e., gold and jewellery) and to invulnerable assets (i.e., foreign bank accounts and relatives abroad). The concepts of generating wealth and money making changed. The war-induced capacities to make do, to act swiftly, to see opportunities, and to haggle and bargain were more important than long-term financial planning or investment. Marginal people, previously despised when the society was stable, rose to the top of the economic pile and often stayed there. These people, who appeared like malign rats in wartime China, are universal beneficiaries of war. They go by a variety of names, none of them flattering – profiteers, spivs, wide-boys, carpet-baggers, scroungers.

The dubious people nourished by the war were one of the new types of people. Another, more important type, for the immediate future, was the dedicated revolutionary, willing to sacrifice his own family and community for the cause of socialism. Most of the CCP leaders had already done this. In the war, many younger people joined them, putting patriotism and the revolution ahead of their families. This was a fundamental change in society and a deeply threatening one: Young people were abandoning their families and lives of privilege for a cause; they were doing so in the context of a war that demanded resistance, which the CCP increasingly came to lead.

Grief

千辛万苦
Untold suffering

The greatest assault on a society in war is death and the grief that comes with it. The United States took decades, if not a century, to come to terms with the loss of 600,000 in its Civil War. After each world war, European countries were convulsed by grief. France after World War I was a nation in mourning, with over 4% of the population dead, mainly young men. The Soviet Union after World War II had to bear the loss of 26 million people.[3] The survivors wept for their dead, often for the rest of their lives. One of the most common and moving Soviet war memorials is of weeping women, widows, and mothers. The losses in China in the Resistance War, military and civilian, were on the same order as the Soviet Union's losses in World War II. China carried her own great burden of grief.

Grief had social and political implications. Personal loss and near despair detached people from their social moorings and precipitated some survivors into political radicalism – which meant, at the time, joining the CCP. Cao Richang, one of China's first psychologists, joined the party after his wife and two children were killed by the Japanese.[4]

---

[3] Drew Gilpin Faust, *The Republic of Suffering: Death and the American Civil War* (New York: Knopf, 2008); Stephane Audoin-Rouzeau and Annette Becker, *14–18, Understanding the Great War* (New York: Hill and Wang, 2000); and Catherine Merridale, *Ivan's War: the Red Army, 1939–45* (London: Faber and Faber, 2005).

[4] Cao Richang later studied at Cambridge, where he met and married Selma Voss, a Dutch Jew who had survived the war in hiding in Holland. She followed him to China,

He was only one of a great legion of people whose lives were shattered by the war – and saw the revolution as a replacement for their lost family.

Society and War

This book looks at the effects of the war on Chinese society – not at why the war happened or at how it was fought or who was to blame for it. The politics and the international relations of the war form only a backdrop here. This book sees the war through the eyes of the people who were on the receiving end of aggression, the Chinese in all their variety and their different circumstances, the people whose society was turned upside down. There are very few Japanese voices in the book. This is a deliberate omission. During the war, Chinese could only see Japanese as enemies. In the areas of China that were not occupied, their direct experience of Japan was as the recipient of bombs. In the occupied areas, the contacts often were experiences of fear or dread.

Organisation and Sources

This book is organised by period, the divisions determined by military and political events. The periods are of unequal length. The first covers the traumatic first six months of the war (1937), the second a year of defeat and retreat (1938), the third the years of stagnation until the start of the Pacific War (1939–41), the fourth two and a half difficult years (1942–44), the fifth the disastrous last year of the war (1944–45), the sixth the immediate aftermath of the war (1945–46). Within each period I discuss the major social themes of the period, though many themes continue from one period to the next.

During the war, China was divided into several parts. I have focussed on a few different regions to reflect these divisions. Besides talking about the GMD government capital Chongqing and the CCP headquarters in Yan'an, I have drawn examples from the early-occupied Shandong Peninsula, from partially occupied southern Fujian (Minnan), and from Guangxi, occupied only at the end of the war. The two worst disasters of the war occurred in Henan; I discuss both the breaching of the Yellow River dike in 1938 and the Henan famine.

I have used a wide range of sources. There is no single source for the social impact of the war in China, as, for example, the materials in the

and they lived happily there with their two children. They were amongst the first people I met when I worked in China in 1964. During the Cultural Revolution, Selma committed suicide, and Cao died of illness.

Mass Observation Archive in Britain, the source for Angus Calder's ground-breaking work, *The People's War*.[5] Very little social survey research was done during the war, although China's few sociologists wrote about the huge changes the war was bringing to society. There were no national newspapers or magazines during the war, although there were some good regional ones. I have used the invaluable collection of newspaper cuttings, *Moci jianbao*, held at Xiamen University. Government propaganda are a useful source. Other government records, Chinese and foreign, provide some data, although they are seldom concerned directly with social issues. The memoirs of people who lived through the war are rich; they have been coming out in streams in recent years, part of the huge revival in biography in China. The accounts of Western journalists, missionaries, and diplomats are important too. The *Materials on History and Literature* (*wenshi ziliao*) published for every region of China from the 1980s on contain invaluable accounts of the effect of the war in specific localities.

I have not used Japanese sources, which tend not to reflect the suffering of occupied populations. With some exceptions, notably the survey materials collected by the research unit of the South Manchurian Railway Company (Mantetsu), Japanese sources have little that is critical to say about the Chinese experiences of the war. Some sources even present the war as a happy time for China. In a recent volume, *Art in Wartime Japan*, the pictures set in China are triumphal; for instance, Kanakogi Takeshino, 'Triumphal Entry in to Nanjing', and Yukai Junkichi, 'Shadow: Flying above Suzhou', show happy Chinese welcoming Japan's armies.[6]

Beyond hard historical sources, I have used fiction and poetry to show the pain and sadness of the war. I share Michael Berry's conviction that 'inspired by pain and suffering, and built out of ruins and ashes, artistic representations of atrocity collectively write their own story, from which arises a new form of "historical narrative."'[7] Fiction and poetry provide the most moving descriptions of how people coped with their trials. I have included selections from contemporary fiction and from more recent fiction inspired by the war. The amount of fiction published in the war was limited. Publishing was difficult during the war. Censorships (GMD, CCP, and Japanese) and the shortage of paper made it hard for writers to get their works published. The restrictions of the Mao era continued the

---

[5] Angus Calder, *The Peoples' War* (New York: Pantheon, 1969).

[6] Hariu Ichiro, *Art in Wartime Japan, 1937–1945* (Tokyo: Kokusho Kankokai, 2007), pp. 21, 26.

[7] Michael Berry, *A History of Pain: Trauma in Modern Chinese Literature and Film* (New York: Columbia University Press, 2008), p. 3.

difficulty of publishing about the war, not then considered an acceptable topic. All this means that some of the most vivid stories of the war were not written or published until the last two decades, when writers finally could come to grips with the war. The same is true of film. In the last 20 years, major films about the war have been made, all providing vivid recreations of the wartime period. I list titles of some of the most important films. The work of artists, photographers, and cartoonists provides searing images of the war, and I have used contemporary illustrations, photographs, wood-block prints, cartoons, and paintings.

The voices of the great majority of the population are missing from written sources. Many of them were illiterate and have left no written records. Others lived under some degree or other of repression and were afraid to write things down. The oral memories of survivors of the war have been very important to me in writing this book. I was brought up in the shadow of World War II in a society where people talked constantly about the war, usually in glowing terms. Since I first went to China, I have heard many people talking about their experiences in the war with differing combinations of transcendence, loss, patriotism, and sadness. From these memories, I came to understand how much the war changed China. I have used oral interviews with people who lived through the period and with their children to give additional texture to the discussion of the war.

Throughout the text I have inserted *chengyu*, four-character phrases and quotations. Some of them come from classical literature and some from the oral tradition. They are very popular in Chinese and are used widely to sum up a situation or an attitude. They are sometimes called 'proverbs', but their use is so much more widespread and the repertoire is so much larger that I hesitate to use that translation. I have included Chinese characters for names and places. This is a return to the old practises of sinology made possible by modern word-processing capacities.

Theoretical Approaches

This book has been informed by the work of the French sociologist Pierre Bourdieu, who devised the concept of 'social suffering' as a way of understanding the lives of people caught up in catastrophes, natural or human-made, that attack the fabric of their society and make their lives hard, if not intolerable. They experience the *miseres du monde* – the 'misfortunes of the world'.[8] Bourdieu's work is engaged and compassionate; it is

---

[8] Pierre Bourdieu, *La misere du monde* (Paris: Editions de seuil, 1993); translated by Priscilla Ferguson as, *The Weight of the World: Social Suffering in Contemporary Society* (Palo Alto, CA: Stanford University Press, 1999).

without the remote chill that accompanies some academic research where the high value put on detachment makes empathy for one's subjects suspect. I try to show what happened to Chinese society during a war that brought social dislocation, disintegration, and collapse and to give my study some of Bourdieu's empathy and compassion for the lives of people in distress.

I have gained insight from trauma theory, normally applied in the study of literature but highly applicable to the history of periods of chaos and upheaval, where events were quite beyond the control of either governments or the people who lived through them. The chaos of war produced innumerable experiences of trauma, instability, and chronic anxiety. This has produced a morbid fear of chaos throughout Chinese society. In Chinese, chaos is *luan* the phenomenon most feared by Chinese leaders over most of Chinese history and the justification for continued authoritarianism.[9]

Outcomes of War

The pretext for war, the *casus belli*, may not be reflected in the outcome. Japan attacked China in the name of containing communism, preventing its export from the USSR into China. China never gave much credence to this justification for the invasion, not least because Japanese forces made only one aggressive move against the USSR, at Nomonhan in Mongolia in 1938. The result was disastrous. The Japanese did not attack the communist Soviet Union but anti-communist GMD-ruled China. By the end of the war, the pretext of attacking communism was not only threadbare but contradictory; by 1945, the CCP was far stronger than it had ever been and poised for success in the Civil War. The political beneficiary of the war was the CCP; it came to power in the aftermath of the war, hardened by the war and ready to take on the GMD government in the Civil War.

The outcome of the war was a devastated society. The regional variations were great, but this did not mean that any regions escaped the impact of the war.[10] This damage was the pre-condition the CCP needed to launch the new society, a 'poor and blank (*yiqiong erbai*)' society, a clean

[9] See Ban Wang, *Illuminations from the Past: Trauma, Memory and History in Modern China* (Palo Alto, CA: Stanford University Press, 2004); and David Derwei Wang, *The Monster that Is History: History, Violence and Fictional Writing in Twentieth Century China* (Berkeley: University of California Press, 2004).
[10] For a discussion of regional variations, see Stephen MacKinnon, Diana Lary, and Ezra Vogel (eds.), *China at War* (Palo Alto, CA: Stanford University Press, 2007).

slate on which to launch their visions of a new world. And the war also gave the CCP the tool it needed to get the people behind it – mass mobilisation. The first acts of political mobilisation in China had to do with resistance to Japan, in its earliest form in the May 4th Movement (1919) and in stronger forms after 1931 and the invasion of Manchuria. At the start of the war, the GMD and the CCP both took up mobilisation in the name of national resistance; by the end of the war, the CCP, operating mainly in occupied areas, where the need for mobilisation for resistance was greatest, had made its version of nationalism and socialism into a huge movement.[11]

The CCP adhered to an ideology brought into China from the West, Marxism/Leninism (with a later admixture of Mao Zedong thought). Under this banner it launched China after 1949 on a breakneck path to socialism, with the wounds of the war still not healed. The war and its miseries were the backdrop for the convulsive political movements of the 1950s and the disaster of the Cultural Revolution (1966–76). A huge question hangs unanswered: How to explain the awful savagery the country unleashed on itself. 'Like the European Holocaust of World War II, the Cultural Revolution was so horrific and irrational that people all over the globe wonder how it could have happened. So do we Chinese.'[12]

The Cultural Revolution is referred to as 'the ten lost years', often better passed over in silence. An obvious reason for the silence is that the party that launched the Cultural Revolution is still in power. A more fundamental reason, however, is that there is a deep sense of embarrassment and shame over the way in which a refined, carefully organised society, based on an ancient code of values, should be engulfed by a torrent of viciousness and mutual betrayal. The upending of all the traditional values had something in common with the Holocaust, but with a major difference: The Nazis turned on non-Aryan races; Chinese turned on each other.

There are many possible explanations for the horrors of the Cultural Revolution – a fundamental flaw in the fabric of Chinese society, distortions created by hysterical political campaigns, and the malignant influence of a megalomaniac leader, Mao Zedong. This book suggests another, historically based answer: The violence of the Cultural Revolution was an outcome of the eight years of upheaval of the Resistance War, which

---

[11] Chalmers Johnson, *Peasant Nationalism and the Communist Power: The Emergence of Revolutionary China* (Palo Alto, CA: Stanford University Press, 1962).

[12] Ji Chaozhu, *The Man on Mao's Right* (New York: Random House, 2008), p. 225. Ji was interpreter for Zhou Enlai and Mao Zedong.

came to an end only two decades before the Cultural Revolution started. The wartime violence and disruptions to Chinese society, followed by the upheavals of the 1950s, created a social dissolution and fragmentation in which people easily could turn on each other.

The Cultural Revolution and the Japanese invasion are tightly connected. The link is in the terrible damage done by the war to the fabric of Chinese society. The turbulence of the war lasted long after the war ended. The process of social unravelling and dissolution precipitated by the war and then exacerbated by the policies of the Mao era produced a society in which the communal ties of the old world were eroded. The process of erosion continued, and in the heat of class warfare in the early communist period, the attacks and horrors of the Cultural Revolution were possible – and they happened. The chaos of the war can be seen as a direct antecedent of the Cultural Revolution.

This was a tragic outcome and one in complete contradiction to the mood of national salvation (*jiuguo*) at the start of the war. The strange trajectory of the war is mirrored in one of the most famous anthems of the war, 'The March of the Volunteers (*Yiyongjun jinxing qu*)', and in the fates of the two men who wrote it. It was written as a protest against the occupation of Manchuria in 1931 and became almost a national anthem in the Resistance War. The words were written by Tian Han and the music by Nie Er. Both men met sad fates. Nie Er drowned while swimming in Japan in 1935 in what was probably an accident, although his death also has been interpreted as an assassination. Tian Han died in prison during the Cultural Revolution, labelled as a 'poisonous weed'. The song has survived; with different lyrics, it went on to become the national anthem of the People's Republic of China.

Reading

The March of the Volunteers (1934)

起来！不顾做奴隶的人们
把我们的血肉筑成我们新的长城
中华民族到了最危险的时候
每个人被迫着发出最后的吼声
起来起来起来
我们万众一心
冒着敌人的炮火前进
冒着敌人的炮火前进
前进 前进 进

Arise! All who refuse to be slaves!
Let our flesh and blood become our new Great Wall
As the Chinese nation faces its greatest peril,
All forcefully expend their last cries.
Arise! Arise! Arise!
Our million hearts beat as one,
Brave the enemy's fire, March on!
Brave the enemy's fire, March on!
March on! March on! On!

1   The High Tide of War: July–December 1937

The Prelude to War

In the late 1920s and early 1930s, China seemed to be entering a new era of unity and change. The Guomindang (GMD) established a new central government for China in 1928 and moved the national capital from Beijing (Northern Capital) to Nanjing (Southern Capital). Beijing was renamed Beiping (Northern Peace).

At its inception, the government controlled only a few provinces of central China; it grew stronger over the next few years, Chiang Kai-shek's (Jiang Jieshi) government gradually brought several of the major regional warlords (Feng Yuxiang, Yan Xishan, and the Guangxi Clique) under some degree of control. The Young Marshall of Manchuria, Zhang Xueliang, was critically weakened when Manchuria was occupied by Japan in 1931. In 1934, government forces evicted the Chinese Communist Party (CCP) from its remote base in Jiangxi and forced it to undertake the epic Long March. The march brought the party and its armies to a remote base in Yan'an (Shaanxi), where the communists could recuperate from the terrible hardships they had suffered along the way, sufferings that became the stuff of the CCP's vision of its triumph through adversity. In 1937, however, the CCP was still a tiny, battered rump of survivors, far from the centres of Chinese life.

In the great cities of eastern China, the early 1930s were a time of growth, and excitement in business, literature, education, music, and popular culture put together constituted the rapid arrival of modernity. Behind the growth, though, was a dark cloud – the threat from Japan. Japan had defeated China in 1895 and had taken the island of Taiwan. Ten years later, Japan defeated Russia and took the Liaodong Peninsula in the southern part of Manchuria.[1] In 1931, Japan took all of Manchuria. Over the following five years, there was further major encroachment in northern China. With one exception, the attempted Japanese occupation

---

[1] Manchuria, the three northeastern provinces of China (Liaoning, Jilin, and Heilongjiang), is usually referred to in Chinese as Dongbei (the Northeast).

of Shanghai in 1932, Chinese government forces did not actively resist the Japanese. They were focused on eliminating the regional forces and the CCP forces.

The failure to resist led to a stream of bitter protests against Japan and against the GMD government. These patriotic protests were centred in student and business groups, but the conviction that China was being humiliated by Japan and was suffering 'national shame (*guochi*)' was widespread. In late 1936, a dramatic episode changed the political situation. Chiang Kai-shek was kidnapped in Xian by armed forces under the Zhang Xueliang. As a condition of Chiang's release, he was forced to agree to a united front with the regional forces and with the CCP. China prepared to resist further Japanese incursions – and the Japanese, in turn, prepared to attack before China became too strong.

Events in 1937

还我河山
Give me back my rivers and hills

The Course of the War

On July 7, 1937, a nocturnal clash between Chinese and Japanese troops at Lugouqiao (Marco Polo Bridge), just outside Beiping, triggered an all-out war. In the late summer of 1937, the great cities of Beiping and Tianjin fell with sickening speed. The Chinese armies were no match for the Japanese in firepower, and against one of the world's great naval and air powers, China had only negligible air and sea protection. The Japanese expected to bring China to her knees quickly and to see her surrender.

Instead, China put up fierce resistance, fuelled by a crescendo of nationalist feeling that built on the existing nationalist movement. China was on fire with patriotism and with burning indignation that her sacred territory had been invaded. The clarion call was 'Return my rivers and hills', Yue Fei's cry in *Manjianghong* [Reading 1]. All over China, armies were mobilised; the regional forces rallied to the central government. The Japanese invasion produced something that Chinese politicians had not been able to achieve – a united nation. The united front declared at the beginning of the year became a political reality. On the military front, GMD and regional forces bore almost the whole load of the fighting in the first year of the war; CCP forces in the hills of the northwest were scarcely involved.

1.1. *Huan wo he shan.*

兵临城下
The enemy is at the gates

The GMD high command decided to take the war to the Japanese at the mouth of the Yangzi. The battles of the Shanghai/Nanjing campaign, which lasted until the end of the year, were fought in a blaze of publicity. The defence of Shanghai, with street-to-street and house-to-house fighting, ignited a patriotic storm in China. The saga of the Lost Battalion, the Eight Hundred Heroes, holed up in the Sihang warehouse across Suzhou Creek from the International Settlement, was covered hour by hour by Chinese and foreign journalists.[2]

---

[2] The Eight Hundred Heroes (in fact, only about half that number) eventually had to retreat in to the foreign concessions, where they were interned until all of Shanghai fell under Japanese control in 1942, and they became prisoners of war.

THE GREAT WALL OF CHINA

Chinese troops advancing to the attack in the cover of the Wall. For 2100 years the Great Wall has been the symbol of China's resistance to invaders. Frequently they have got in, but always in the end China and the Great Wall have triumphed over their enemies.

1.2. **Chinese troops on the Great Wall. (From O. M. Green,** *China's Struggle with Dictators***, London: Hutchinson, 1941, p. 144.)**

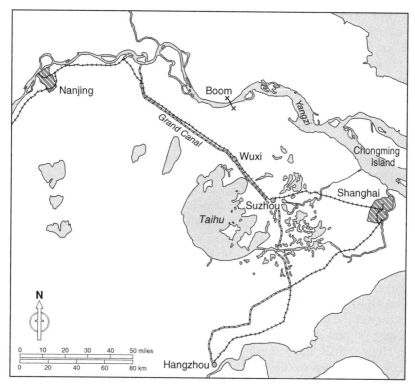

Map 1. **Lower Yangzi**

A second campaign, in Shanxi, ended with the retreat of one of the strongmen of northern China, Yan Xishan. The fighting in the south also ended in retreat. The Japanese armies turned the Chinese flank, with landings to the south of Shanghai in Hangzhou Bay.

In the late autumn, the Chinese armies fell back. The government left the capital Nanjing and moved inland to Wuhan; Nanjing was abandoned. At the end of the year, the key northern province of Shandong also was lost. Much of eastern China was now occupied; the Chinese phrase was 'inundated areas'. China's ability to resist seemed to have been destroyed. British intelligence reported from Shanghai at the end of December that 'the Chinese Army, as a modern and up-to-date force, has practically ceased to exist, and is of value in guerrilla operations only.'[3]

---

[3] General Staff, Shanghai, *Naval and Military Intelligence Summary*, December 28, 1937. National Archives of Canada, RG25/1753/8044/VII.

On December 13, Japanese troops entered Nanjing and embarked on six weeks of horrific killing, looting, and burning; it was what has become known as the 'Rape of Nanjing' or the 'Nanjing Massacre'.

The last six months of 1937 were amongst the most painful ever endured by China, and yet the devastation and destruction produced a new national unity and a sense of patriotism lacking before. The war also kick-started the transformation of Chinese society, building on the tentative steps taken in the previous decades to break out of what some young people had come to see as the prison or the straightjacket of the Confucian social order. The turmoil of war produced social levelling that had been inconceivable before, and the furious reaction to the invasion stimulated social mobilisation on a vast scale. The war was an earthquake that shook the old society to its foundations.

The events in China aroused little interest or sympathy in the wider world. All the major powers were preoccupied with their own concerns. The United States, just emerging from the ravages of the Depression, was firmly isolationist. Europe had pressing problems – the ascendancy of fascism and the rise of Hitler in Germany and Mussolini in Italy. In Spain, the civil war had just ended, with the victory of the pro-fascist side led by Franco. A major war between the fascist powers and other European countries seemed a real possibility. The USSR was suffering from the terrible damage done by the purges, not least to the Soviet military. Japan chose a time to invade China when there was almost no possibility of outside help for China. The only outside attention the invasion attracted was from the courageous band of Western journalists who covered the war with deep sympathy for the Chinese people.

Topics and Case Studies

Horror and Chaos

The prime creators of social upheaval were the terrible events of the early months of the war. In a matter of weeks, China was plunged in to an abyss of horror.

兵荒馬亂
Turmoil and chaos of war

Civilian Deaths   From the start of the war, the Japanese armies used terror as a weapon against the civilian population of China, part of which on the receiving end seemed to be a deliberate strategy to get the government to surrender. The Chinese had lived through turbulent times during the warlord period (1916–28), but nothing had prepared them for mass killing, whether from the air through bombing or on the ground through shelling and massacring. The Chinese found the onslaught of 1937 so hard to accept that they referred to the Japanese as 'devils', horrific visitations who could not be understood in human terms. There was a faint echo of the derisive term once used for Westerners, 'ocean devils', but the tone was quite different – stark terror rather than bemusement.

The largest and most awful mass killing of civilians came at Nanjing between the middle of December 1937 and late January 1938. There was a terrible symbolism to the avalanche of death that fell on the capital: The people of the capital were being annihilated, punished for their government's failure to surrender to Japan in the summer. The Japanese army claimed as a pretext for the killing the need to 'deal' with Chinese soldiers who had abandoned their uniforms, but by contemporary accounts, Chinese and foreign, the massacre took the form of an indiscriminate and vengeful blood-letting, in the process of which huge numbers of civilians – men, women, and children – were put to the sword.[4] The exact number of dead is not known and never will be. Many of the corpses were thrown in to the Yangzi, which bounds Nanjing on the north. The Japanese kept no records of their killing, as the Germans did of their killings in Europe. John Rabe, the man behind the establishment of the International Safety Zone (ISZ), estimated some time later that 50,000 civilians were killed in the massacre. He based his estimates on a pre-massacre population of 300,000 Chinese in the city. The ISZ saved about 250,000 civilians, leaving 50,000 unaccounted for and presumed dead.[5] These figures do not include the military dead. Rabe's figures are moderate, far lower than the 300,000 usually cited in Chinese sources and far higher than figure of less than a thousand dead according to some Japanese accounts. But even Rabe's moderate figures make the Nanjing Massacre one of the worst single atrocities in modern history.

---

[4] The best contemporary accounts of the massacre are Hsu Shu-hsi, *A Digest of Japanese War Conduct* (Shanghai: Kelly and Walsh, 1939), and Harold Timperley, *What War Means: The Japanese Terror in China, a Documentary Record* (London: Gollancz, 1938). The diaries of John Rabe have been published. Erwin Wickert (ed.), *The Good Man of Nanking: The Diaries of John Rabe* (New York, Knopf, 1998).

[5] *Siemens Archiv 9839;* John Rabe, *Notizen fur die 100-Jahre Feier* [*Notes for the Centenary*], 1943, p. 9.

血流成河
Blood flowing in rivers

The bitter disputes over the exact number of dead in the Nanjing Massacre have put a spotlight on the death toll in Nanjing and kept light away from the many other smaller massacres that occurred throughout the occupied areas, almost always in the immediate aftermath of the arrival of Japanese troops in a particular place. By focusing on Nanjing alone, we lose sight of the waves of horror that descended on cities and villages in north China and in the Yangzi Valley. In place after place, incoming Japanese troops killed civilians in numbers ranging from a few dozen to hundreds and even thousands.[6] The pretext was always the same – to round up soldiers who had melted into the civilian population. What followed was a period of indiscriminate killing of those people, civilians or wounded soldiers, who had not managed to flee.

杀人如麻
Killing people like flies

Added to the civilian casualties from massacres was the heavy toll of victims of bombing.

Bombing   China was the first country to be subjected to systematic bombing of civilian targets. The bombing of China started only a few months after the German bombing of Guernica in April 1937, an event that shocked the West. China had only a tiny air force and virtually no anti-aircraft installations; the Japanese air force could bomb at will. As soon as the invasion started, the skies above China were full of bombers. The terror raining down from the sky was for many cities and towns the first sign of war.

The first major bombing of Shanghai, by a horrible irony, was 'friendly'. On August 14, a Chinese pilot dropped four bombs on downtown Shanghai after a botched attack on the Japanese cruiser *Idzumo* anchored off the Bund. This is an eyewitness account of the carnage:[7]

Anti-aircraft fire from the ship not only drove the Chinese away, but hit the bomb racks on one of the planes. Four 250-pound demolition bombs were loosened. Unaware of the damage to his bomb racks, and apparently frightened, the

---

[6] Diana Lary, 'A ravaged place: the devastation of the Xuzhou region, 1938', in Diana Lary and Stephen MacKinnon (eds.), *The Scars of War* (Vancouver, Canada: University of British Columbia Press, 2001), pp. 98–177.

[7] Carroll Alcott, *My War with Japan* (New York: Henry Holt, 1943), pp. 238–239. Alcott was crossing Nanjing Road at Sichuan Road when the first bombs dropped.

pilot turned his plane at an altitude of fifteen hundred feet and flew over the International Settlement.

Two bombs, jarred completely loose from their fastenings, dropped on Nanking [Nanjing] Road. One hit the Palace Hotel, the other the street. Nanking Road was packed with thousands of Chinese refugees from the nearby hinterlands, and so unexpected was the bombing that none of them had time to scatter into the shelter of the nearby side-streets and buildings. When the smoke had cleared away, almost three thousand dead and wounded were piled in heaps on the pavement.

It was a bloody tangle of bodies that had been blown to bits. Heads, torsos, legs and arms were scattered about. ...

Less than a minute later, one mile away in front of the Great World Amusement Resort on Avenue Edward VII ... the other two bombs on the broken rack came loose and dropped. Approximately two thousand more dead and wounded were piled in the streets.

Later estimates of casualties were lower – 100 killed or injured on Nanking Road, 1,200 killed or injured at the Great World.[8] The first civilian bombing by a Chinese pilot was also the last. All other bombings were by Japanese planes, first in the Yangzi Valley and then in many parts of unoccupied China, unopposed, low-level bombing. Between August 15 and October 13, these cities and towns were bombed[9]:

Province	City/town
Shandong	Hanzhuang 韩庄, Caozhuang 曹庄, Yanzhou 兖州, Jining 济宁
Jiangsu	Nanjing 南京 Pukou 浦口 Shanghai 上海 Wuxi 无锡 Jiangyin 江阴, Xuzhou 徐州, Kunshan 昆山, Jiading 嘉定, Taicang 太仓 Songjiang 松江, Suzhou 苏州, Yangzhou 扬州, Nantong 南通, Haizhou 海州, Lianyun 连云, Huaiyin 淮阴, Nanxiang 南翔
Zhejiang	Hangzhou 杭州, Ningbo 宁波, Haining 海宁, Jianqiao 笕桥, Jiaxing 嘉兴, Zhuxi 朱溪, Jinhua 金华, Zhuxian, Shaoxing 绍兴
Fujian	Xiamen 厦门, Longhai 龙海, Jinmen 金门
Guangdong	Guangzhou 广州, Shilong 石龙, Humen 虎门, Yingde 英德, Guding 古丁, Lechang乐昌, Huiyang 惠口, Shantou 汕头, Huangpu 黄埔
Anhui	Wuhu 芜湖, Guangde 广德, Anqing 安庆, Zhuxiang 朱巷, Bengbu 蚌埠, Shucheng舒城清
Jiangxi	Nanchang 南昌, Shangrao 上饶, Yujiang 余江, Qinjiang 琴江, Jiujiang 九江
Hubei	Hankou 汉口, Wuchang 吴昌, Hanyang 汉阳, Xiaogan孝感
Hunan	Zhuzhou 洙洲

[8] Figures cited in 'Four Months of War', *North China Daily News*, Shanghai, November 1937, pp. 24–25.
[9] Timperley, *What War Means*, p. 120.

Most of these places were far from the actual fighting, and there was no obvious tactical objective for bombing them. The strategy behind the bombing has to be seen as an effort to reduce the civilian population to abject terror and submission, to get it to turn against the resistance policy of the Chinese government. Instead, the outcome of the bombing in China was a foretaste of the reaction to bombing in other countries later on – anger and defiance. Bombing as a means of getting a population to surrender was counter-productive. There are no figures for the total number of Chinese killed by bombs, but given that bombing went on until late in the war, the figure must be in the hundreds of thousands.

The damage to infrastructure from bombing was tremendous. Bridges, roads, and railways were obvious military targets, and many of them were bombed. But so was much of China's new educational system. In less than six months from July 1937, dozens of universities and colleges were bombed. The German sinologist Karl August Wittfogel described this destruction[10]:

A gale of devastation swept China's young cultural institutions, a gale which left in its wake the debris of looted dormitories, of smoking lecture halls, gymnasiums and laboratories, and the corpses of male and female students killed on the spot.

The most bombed city was Chongqing, the capital from the end of 1938. The story of the Chongqing bombing is told in Chapter 3.

Refugees and Evacuees The fighting and bombing in the second half of 1937 set off massive civilian evacuations and flights in to exile. The waves of refugees paralleled the spread of the fighting. More than 100,000 people fled into the foreign concessions in Shanghai in October and November as the Japanese attack on the Chinese parts of the city intensified.[11] All through the lower Yangzi, civilian populations fled in panic as the fighting came closer. Royal Leonard, a hard-boiled American pilot, flew low over Nanjing as the Japanese closed in on the city. He had seen other places before in the grips of panic evacuation[12]:

There was little difference. The minute expressions of the people who choked the roads with carts and wheelbarrows, cars and rickshaws, were the same: numbness,

---

[10] K. A. Wittfogel, '"Culture is war": is the bombing of Chinese universities caprice or policy?' in National Southwest Associated University Library, *Japan's Aggression and Public Opinion* (Kunming, 1938), p. 331.

[11] *Report of the Shanghai International Red Cross* (October 1937–March 31, 1939), p. 11.

[12] Royal Leonard, *I Flew for China* (New York: Doubleday, 1941), p. 188. Royal was personal pilot first to Zhang Xueliang and then to Chiang Kai-shek.

horror, despair. The sounds were there as they had been [elsewhere]: thunder and shaking and ruin. The sights were identical: fire, smoke, and dust.

The people Leonard saw were probably short-term refugees, escaping into the countryside while the fighting was going on. Poor people did not have the means to leave permanently. Money and the means to move were key factors in long-term flight.

When the central government retreated upriver from Nanjing in November, almost all senior officials and officers left, taking with them their dependents; every vessel on the Yangzi was commandeered to transport the government evacuees. Elsewhere members of local and regional governments fled from their posts ahead of the invaders. Provincial governments moved inland, the Shandong government, for example, from Jinan to Ningyang. In small towns and villages, many members of the local gentry and land-owning elites fled.

As the war moved south and west, so waves of people fled in advance of the fighting, with less panic than some of the earlier refugees but with greater sadness because many of them believed that they would be gone from home for a long while. Lin Yutang captured the stoicism of these refugees in his famous novel of the war, *Moment in Peking* [Reading 2].

Bombing was the trigger for much of the panic flight. The day after bombs fell on Fenyang (Shanxi), the patrician Ji family took to the roads, leaving a life of comfort and high status, heading for Wuhan. They entered a world they had not dreamt of before. Eight-year-old Ji Chaozhu made the long journey mostly on foot[13]:

We had to share sleeping *kangs* with smelly strangers, and eat our meals on the dirt floors of their tiny cottages, shooing away the dogs and chickens that pestered everyone for scraps. No one in our family had ever known anything less than privilege and prosperity. I could see in my parents' exhausted faces the toll this was taking, but they remained stoic through the inconveniences and discomfort.

Many people fled out of fear of what would happen to members of their families. Young girls were especially vulnerable to the incoming forces. Their parents would try to get them out of places about to fall to the Japanese, hearing rumours of what happened in many of the major cities that were occupied in late 1937. In Suzhou, more than 2,000 young girls were taken away as 'comfort women' – or sex slaves – after Japanese troops took the city in November.[14] The rumours about the

---

[13] Ji Chaozhu, *The Man on Mao's Right* (New York: Random House, 2008), p. 10. Ji was the younger brother of the celebrated economist Ji Chaoding.

[14] Xie Yongguang, *Rijun weianfu neimu* (Taibei: Lianya chubanshe, 1995), p. 76.

1.3. **Flight to the interior. (Wang Luzhi, _Guomin geming_**
dahuashi, Taibei, 1973, p. 220.)

danger posed to women were blood-curdling, enough to get families to
flee in panic.

Some of the people who fled from the areas occupied by Japanese
troops left not because they were panic-stricken but because they refused
to live under the enemy. Some of these people were students and other

young people leaving to fight for China. Older intellectuals fled because they knew they would be in trouble under the Japanese [Reading 3]. The remnant Chinese armies withdrawn from the north also intended to resist, as did the evacuees from Shanghai – merchants, factory owners, workers, journalists, and actors – who moved inland to defy the invaders.

Places in the front line saw the largest refugee movements. These are the proportion of the population that fled for three places in different parts of the country:

Anqing [on the Yangzi up-river from Nanjing, occupied early 1938]
By mid-December 1937 90% (of about 100,000) of the population had gone. Those left behind were wounded soldiers and private guards.[15]
Kaifeng district [on the Yellow River, eastern Henan, occupied spring 1938]
Before 1937 the population was 2.9 million. In 1945 only 50% was left. In the war 1,140,000 people fled to the interior, and over 300,000 died.[16]
Xiamen [Fujian coast, occupied late 1938]
Before 1938 the population was 260,000. By 1941 only 88,000 (including 10,000 in-comers from Taiwan) were left. The city was empty.[17]

Many of the refugees were gone only for short periods, during the worst of the fighting. They fled only as far as the countryside or the hills near their homes. Local flight sometimes involved moving to local safe havens, the compounds of foreign missionaries, or in larger cities, foreign consulates or concessions. By the end of 1937, in Shanghai there were over 300,000 refugees in almost 300 reception centres in the International Settlement and the French Concession.[18] Many more were denied access. The vast crowds trying to get into the French Concession at the height of the fighting were held at the borders of the concession by steel gates and guards.[19]

Long-range movements started in the first months of the war. There was a huge exodus from northern and eastern China, people moving west into the unoccupied parts of China. Most refugees had no definite destination; they were moving away from danger, not towards any particular place. Many moved repeatedly, never certain where they were or how long they would stay there. In the two years after the start of the

[15] *Chinese Recorder*, March 3, 1938, pp. 141–146.
[16] Xingzhengyuan shanhou jiuji congshu Luqing fenshu, *LuQing shanjiu xunkan*, 1946, July 10, p. 10.
[17] Hong Puren, interview in Xiamen, 12/05/05.
[18] Wei Hongyun, *KangRi zhanzheng yu Zhongguo shehui* (Shenyang: Liaoning renmin chubanshe, 1997), p. 166.
[19] 'Four Months of War', *North China Daily News*, p. 127.

war, the writer Ba Jin moved from Shanghai to Guangzhou, to Wuhan, to Guangzhou again, to Guilin, to Shanghai, to Kunming, to Chongqing, and finally to Chengdu. All these were appalling wartime journeys on crowded trains and ships or by any conveyance moving on the roads. Along the way he continued to edit a literary journal, wrote the three novels of the *Turbulent Stream* trilogy, and translated much of the anarchist Peter Kropotkin's writings.[20] Few people thought of themselves as long-term refugees; even those who fled long distances did not think they would be away permanently, only for the duration of the war.

The evacuations were never systematic. Most refugees had to rely on their own resources and ingenuity, which they did to an impressive, almost amazing degree. The vast movement of people did not become a chaotic rout but rather unrolled with a great deal of dignity and endurance, as if ordinary Chinese people were trying to tell Japan that they could be defeated but not destroyed.

The best means of long-range flight was by boat, by sea from north to south or by river from east to west up the Yangzi or up smaller rivers into the interior. In the north, railways seemed to offer a method of flight, but most lines were not operating; either the tracks had been destroyed in fighting or by retreating Chinese troops, or service was interrupted to give precedence to troop trains. Railways were dangerous places to be; railways lines, stations, and junctions were often bombed. For many people, the roads were the only routes to escape, and in much of China this meant a journey on foot or in carts; there were few cars or trucks in China and little fuel available outside major cities.

The total number of refugees produced by the war is difficult to calculate. Figures given after the war vary from 20 million to nearly 100 million, or almost a quarter of the population.[21] This figure undoubtedly includes people who fled more than once and people who fled only for brief periods. Even allowing for this, it was one of the greatest upheavals in Chinese history. It tore the fabric of society to ribbons.

The effect of the refugee flights was that the social and government hierarchy in much of the occupied areas was decapitated. The elite's decisions about whether to stay or flee undermined traditional elite dominance. The *ancien regime* ceased to exist. Those who fled ceased to

---

[20] Olga Lang, *Pa Chin and His Writings* (Cambridge, MA: Harvard University Press, 1967), p. 1960.

[21] Stephen MacKinnon, *Wuhan, 1938: War, Refugees and the Making of Modern China* (Berkeley: University of California Press, 2008), pp. 45–48; Wei Hongyun, *KangRi zhanzheng yu Zhongguo shehui* (Shenyang: Lianoning renmin chubanshe, 1997), p. 163; and Zhang Genfu, *Kangzhan shiqi de renkou qianyi* (Beiping: Chaoyang ribao, 2006), p. 39.

have local influence. Those who stayed were compromised. In the cities, towns, and rural areas, the members of the elite who stayed knew that they would have to work with the enemy or make some accommodation – or lead opposition. By the old ideal of elites based on merit and education, whose task was to care for the little people, those who left had betrayed their trust, as had those who stayed and worked with the enemy. By the communist view of the old elite as vicious and corrupt, the failure to flee confirmed their venality. Once the elite had either disappeared or gone over to the dark side, there were leadership vacuums throughout the occupied areas.

Relief The government had to confront the provision of relief for the refugees. Traditionally, the state stored grain for famine relief in huge granaries throughout the country. All other emergency needs were met locally through the family, the clan, and the community. The first port of call for those in need was always the family, but if a family could not help, local elites were expected to organise help for specific categories of needy: the elderly, orphans, unfortunate women, plague victims, beggars, the unemployed, those affected by disaster, refugees, and poor families. Temples and churches had often provided relief and refuge.

None of these social agencies could come close to alleviating the new needs; they were too vast. Private and religious charity continued, now augmented by government interventions and by appeals to all Chinese. Charity, aid to the victims of war, became a patriotic duty both for people in China and amongst Overseas Chinese.

The government came up with a plan for refugees, published in late 1937. The aim was to put responsibility for caring for refugees on to the localities. The government ordered that feeding stations be set up along the main routes of flight to provide some help to the refugees. Reception centres were established, often in temples and clan halls that were requisitioned to house refugees. These efforts could not come near to meeting the need. The number of functioning government agencies was small. In 1942, the Shehuibu (Ministry of Social Affairs) listed only 560 relief organisations in unoccupied China, most in Sichuan and Jiangxi.[22] Relief was restricted to areas under Chinese government control; there was no help at all for refugees in occupied China.

The government's inability to care for civilians was matched by its inability to look after the welfare of wounded soldiers. At the start of the war, plans were made to address the terrible shortage of doctors and

---

[22] Ke Xiangfeng, *Shehui jiuji* (Chongqing: Zhengzhong shuju, 1945), p. 85.

nurses at the front, but these plans were limited to dressing stations.[23] The treatment of wounded soldiers was horrible and continued to be so throughout the war; being wounded was usually a death sentence.

In areas on the front lines, missionaries provided sanctuary to local people as Japanese troops occupied cities and towns. Some missionaries saw 1937 and 1938 as the high point of their life in China, the most demanding but the most rewarding. Missionaries throughout the occupied areas made heroic efforts to save local people – and felt that they belonged to their communities. Their records, passionate, angry, and often searing, make a key record of the horrors of the initial occupation. Father Alphonse Dubé, a Quebec Jesuit missionary near Xuzhou (Jiangsu), wrote in May 1938[24]:

I have more than three hundred refugees ... women, children and men. All have their eyes fixed on me to determine their state of mind. If I laugh, their hearts expand. ... it means the situation isn't critical. If I don't laugh, their hearts contract, fear seizes them, the situation is critical. It is I who must be there thermometer. For the first time in my life I realize what responsibility is, and what it means to be the only person who can get us through. ... one false step and the boat is sinking (*la barque est a l'eau*).

All the local elite members had fled. Dubé became in effect the local chief, and he dealt directly with the Japanese on behalf of the local people:

I have become effectively the sub-prefect of the town.... it is I who has the right of life or death. ... if a fire breaks out, rapidly I send men to put it out. ... if something happens, it is up to me to resolve it. ... I hear that a woman and a young child are prisoners of soldiers in a house. ... I inform the chief who immediately rescues the women and brings them to me. ... someone finds an orphan whose father has just been killed by the Japs and sends the child to me. ... a little girl of three and her brother of fourteen whose father has been killed by the Japanese and whose mother has died of terror come and ask for refuge. ... a man is met on the way to be executed. ... I am asked to intercede and he is spared. ... one of the soldiers who has pity for the people tells me that there are at least two hundred people at the chief's who are waiting to hear their fate. ... if no one gets involved, there is a strong risk that they will be killed. ... I send twenty men to be guarantors for them. ...

Family Separations   For much of the Chinese population, the war meant separation, the flight of parts of families, and the departure of young men to join the armies and the guerrillas. The separations were

---

[23] Kong Jingzhou, *Kangzhan yu jiuhu gongzuo* (Changsha: Shangwu, 1938), pp. 3, 16.

[24] Cited in Diana Lary, 'Faith and war: Canadian Jesuits and the Japanese invasion of China', *Modern Asian Studies* 39(4):825–852, 2005.

sudden and random, with no term, unplanned, spontaneous. There were no financial preparations, no means of knowing where they were going. In the days before telephones, automatic teller machines (ATMs), and e-mail, those who left went off without any certainty that they would be heard from again.

The departure of single young people was simpler than the departure of several members of a family. This often meant making choices within a family – which members to take and which to leave behind. Those who went would be the fathers, older sons, and young women; those left behind would be the old, younger sons and daughters, some of the wives and concubines in a polygamous family, servants, and retainers. Li Zongren, commander of the 5th War Zone, sent his first wife and his son to Hong Kong and kept his second wife with him, protecting his child from the tough life in military headquarters. He Siyuan, head of the civil administration in Shandong, did something similar. He was married to a French woman. He sent her and their four children to the foreign concessions in Tianjin, while he went into the hills to lead a guerrilla operation.[25]

In flight, the refugees might have to abandon all or part of their family. The elderly often had to be left behind. Adult children knew that this might be a permanent separation; they would not be able to carry out the duties of filial piety to their parents and grandparents. Separation from family was a recurrent part of Chinese life, a standard part of education or making a career, but such separations were planned, and the handing off of responsibilities, usually to the extended family, was arranged in advance. The wartime separations were quite different. These separations caused deep pain and regret and often bitter resentment towards the invaders. Just before he left for Changsha, the new home of Peking University, President Jiang Menglin went home to visit his father in Hangzhou in August 1937[26]:

When I left him, I had the feeling that most probably I would not see my beloved father again, to whom I owe so much and had returned so little. When bombs visited the native city of my boyhood, he moved into the mountains and there enjoyed his trees, flowers and birds. After two years of war he got up early one morning as usual and felt dizzy. He went back to bed and there his spirit fled at the age of nearly eighty. He was but one of many indirect casualties of war. War is rather hard on old people.

[25] He Ziquan, *Yiwei chengshi aiguo de Shandong xuezhe* (Beiping: Beiping chubanshe, 1996), p. 33.
[26] Chiang Monlin (Jiang Menglin), *Tides from the West* (New Haven, CT: Yale University Press, 1947), pp. 211–212.

Some separations were accidental rather than deliberate. People who were away from home when the invasion came found that they were cut off from home. Hsing Fu-ying was away from home in 1937, at school in Tianjin, four hours by train from his home in Jinan. His school was evacuated to Sichuan. He joined the army after leaving school. He was sent to Taiwan at the end of the war and spent the rest of his life there. He never went home. The invasion brought a lifelong separation from his family.

Overseas Chinese endured similar unexpected separations. Those who were back in China on visits at the start of the war got stuck there and had to stay for the duration of the war, whereas the war prevented visits from those abroad to the families in the emigration districts (*qiaoxiang*). Barry Mar was taken to Guangdong from Canada by his parents in 1937 for a short stay. They were stranded in China and did not get back until 1947. When they got back to Moose Jaw (Saskatchewan), Barry had to relearn English.[27]

These family separations could hardly be described as atrocities, but they were painful and often long-term effects of the invasion. They cannot be portrayed statistically, but this does not make them less disruptive or even devastating. They marked, for many families, the end of the old home, the connections to a place where they would always belong.

Social Levelling

家徒四壁

A family with only four walls, all possessions gone

The Japanese invasion was a social leveller for China. The vagaries of war meant that people once cushioned by wealth were no more able to protect themselves than were the poor. There was a grim equality to suffering – to the destruction of property, the loss of income, and the death of family members. In the fight for survival, talent, money, and social status were often less important than fate (*yuanfen*), the mysterious force that many Chinese believed guided their lives. The war impoverished many of the previously wealthy. The great social gulfs of pre-war society started to disappear. The social spectrum was compacted as scholars, merchants, soldiers, and workers found themselves in much the same material situation (i.e., poor), joined together in a "fellowship of war and misfortune and hope."[28]

---

[27] *Globe and Mail*, 21/6/2007, p. L6.
[28] Edgar Snow, *Scorched Earth* (London: Gollancz, 1941), p. 235.

Affluent people in flight slid down the economic scale. Their sources of money dried up; once they left home, they could not collect rents, and they no longer had access to bank accounts. Their lives became tougher; they had to learn to manage without servants. This loss might seem trivial in a time of war, but Chinese with any degree of affluence had been pampered by servants all their lives. The household tasks performed by servants were arduous and time-consuming. Washing clothes could take all day, for one person; shopping for food and preparing it, occupied someone else's day. Caring for children was something that no well-born woman had ever contemplated. To their surprise, many of the exiled and dispossessed managed to learn how to fend for themselves. The architect Liang Sicheng learnt to cook and did all the cooking for his family in exile in Yunnan. His father, the great reformer Liang Qichao, would never have contemplated cooking, even at the lowest points of his career.[29]

In the occupied areas, social and economic problems were closely related. Many families lost the income of fathers who had fled with the GMD and could not send any money home. Others suffered from a loss of local jobs. In Beiping, the great centre of education, the loss of jobs related to the universities was enormous. Merchants suffered when Japanese and Koreans moved in and were given special treatments that threatened the survival of local merchants. The fear brought by occupation was accompanied by chronic economic anxiety, which could not be voiced. All that people could do was 'keep their heads down and work hard (*maitou kugan*)'.

Material Loss   The war brought material losses on a vast scale. These losses included actual, direct losses, as well as the loss of present and future income. Above all, it meant the loss of material security.

The simplest way to calculate material loss is to use statistics, to state losses in numerical terms that give them what seems like clarity. This approach does not work for wartime China. There was little systematic collection of data. Chinese agencies could no longer collect information from the occupied areas, and in the areas the government did control, producing accurate and meaningful figures was made difficult in the chaos of war. For the first years of the war, the Maritime Customs was one of the few impartial agencies in China. Japanese agencies collected data for the occupied areas and produced what are considered reliable statistics, but they cover only areas they controlled, not unoccupied

---

[29] J. K. Fairbank, *Chinabound* (New York: Harper and Row, 1982), p. 228.

China. And finally, as the war went on, inflation made any financial statistics meaningless.

The dearth of accurate figures should not give the impression that direct material losses were not enormous. The inability to apply monetary values to losses does not diminish the sense of loss derived from the destruction of objects whose worth was not monetary but emotional – family records, books, photographs, letters, and mementoes. With them the connection to the past was lost, the sense of family history, a loss not only of the present but also of the past.

The material losses from the war in China were not on the same scale as those in Eastern Europe and the Western Soviet Union, where vast tracts of land were laid waste and made uninhabitable; villages and towns were completely destroyed.[30] Nor were the losses to Chinese families and individuals as great as the losses that were to come, after 1949, in the Land Reform, the Great Leap Forward, and the Cultural Revolution. But they were significant, and they ate away at the social security of families and communities.

The most obvious material loss was the destruction of property in fighting or from bombing. This was the fate of many of the urban areas in the lower Yangzi Valley. Bombs destroyed civilian property, as did shelling. Neither side in the fighting showed any concern for civilian property.

Other forms of material loss came after the fighting was over. Looting goes hand in hand with war. Chinese cities were used to being looted during warlord conflicts, and people had well-developed techniques for hiding valuables. The rich protected them by sending them into the foreign concessions. What happened in late 1937 was a massive intensification. Looting spread like a plague throughout the lower Yangzi Valley. Retreating Chinese armies may not have been blameless (the tradition of departing armies taking what they could with them was firmly entrenched), but the in-comers were the prime perpetrators. This is a missionary report from Suzhou, one of the richest cities in China, written in November 1937[31]:

Between November 21st and December [11th] we went into Soochow [Suzhou] nearly every day. We saw that every bank and shop, every residence had been forced open. Japanese soldiers were passing in and out of them like ants loaded down with bales of silk, eiderdown quilts, shop goods and household effects of every description.

---

[30] Catherine Merridale, *Ivan's War: The Red Army, 1939–45* (London: Faber and Faber, 2005).
[31] Timperley, *What War Means*, p. 89.

A month later on the road from Songjiang to Shanghai, the missionary passed many groups of Japanese soldiers who had been out looting[32]:

... rickshas containing trunks and suitcases were hitched behind cavalry horses and Japanese soldiers were riding donkeys, cows, and even buffaloes, collected from the countryside. Live pigs were tied to artillery limbers.

A variant of looting was the forcible requisitioning of property, practiced both in the occupied areas and in unoccupied China. In the northern cities, great numbers of properties were requisitioned. The Japanese army took over the campus of Yanjing University in Beiping and turned it into an army hospital. Houses were taken over to house officers and government officials. In unoccupied China, large compounds, temples, clan halls, and family homes were taken over to house schools, government agencies, and refugees, usually without compensation.

A variant of loss was loss through abandonment. People who fled from the occupied areas had to leave their property behind, sometimes entrusted to the care of relatives or friends but often with no one to care for it. Much of this property could not be reclaimed after the war ended; it was gone for good.

All these material losses led to one outcome: the social levelling of poverty.

The sociologist Sun Benwen looked at the material losses of the war and saw the production of terrible social insecurity in the fighting and bombing as well as the plundering, theft, and destruction that flourished in war. The rich could try to protect their property by hiring guards, but even they could not protect their property from bombing. For many, the material loss was total – house, clothing, tools, animals, and food stores. Even the moderately well-off could be rapidly reduced to penury.[33]

Reactions to material loss are unpredictable. Some people see the loss of their possessions as a liberation, a way to rise above materialism; most religions teach that the abandonment of materialism is a key to fulfilment or enlightenment. China's long Buddhist and Daoist traditions that speak to the surrender of possessions, even to the extent of living as a hermit in the wilderness, helped some people to overcome their losses. Some people accept material loss as a challenge to their ability to survive and to their ingenuity. The 'make do and mend spirit', officially fostered by the government, was a dominant theme early in the war. Austerity was the official order of the day. Leaders made themselves examples, eating ostentatiously simple meals. After the government moved to Chongqing,

---

[32] *Ibid.*, p. 86.
[33] Sun Benwen, *Xiandai Zhongguo shehui wenti* (Chongqing: Shangwu, 1943), p. 204.

Chiang Kai-shek lived a simple life in a small bungalow perched on a mountaintop. The CCP adopted even more austere policies, partly out of necessity in the very poor region in which they lived. The leaders cultivated vegetable plots and wore clothes of homespun cotton. Mao Zedong grew tobacco, though probably not enough to provide his constant supply of cigarettes.

For all the positive reactions to material loss and the personal growth that might come with it, many people were badly affected by their losses; they became embittered, anxious, and confused. The loss of their material world left them feeling vulnerable and insecure. They developed intense feelings against profiteers, the people most likely to survive and do well in hard times.

Material losses are mitigated in the West by insurance and by government compensation in cases of disaster. In China in the 1930s, the insurance industry was in its infancy, and its scope scarcely reached beyond the treaty ports. People who suffered material losses relied on traditional systems of financial aid, revolving credit, and family support. These systems depended on three pillars: intact communities, a stable currency, and staggered calls for help. All these crumbled in wartime China. Communities were no longer intact; there were multiple, fluctuating currencies; and there was a tidal wave of need. This meant that most of the huge losses at every level of society could not be recouped in the short or long run.

Government and Mercantile Losses   One area of loss that *was* easy to calculate was the loss of government revenues. With many of the richest areas of China under occupation, the central government was impoverished. Tax income plummeted; the government lost 85% of customs receipts, 65% of the salt tax, and 90% of the consolidated tax. The only ways it could make up for this staggering loss was to cut expenditures (impossible in time of war), to levy new taxes (impossible given the loss of the tax base), to borrow (difficult given that there were few institutions ready to lend), or to print money. Printing money was the only feasible way to raise money – and it was the direct route to inflation.[34]

The losses in government income were related in part to the collapse of China's foreign trade. Between 1937 and 1938, customs revenues, a sign of trade activity, plummeted. International trade collapsed, a short while after it had started to rebound from the declines of the Depression. The river ports on the Yangzi were devastated by the fighting in the lower reaches and by the barrages put across the river by the

---

[34] Ji Chaoding, *Wartime Economic Development in China* (New York: Institute of Pacific Relations, 1939), p. 132.

government. Customs revenues on imports for 1938 were under 10% of 1937s (2,657,039 yuan as opposed to 30,905,107 yuan), while revenue on exports fell from 11,785,839 yuan (1937) to 626,980 yuan (1938).[35] This was an economic catastrophe.

Passenger traffic dwindled almost to nothing in the first months of the war. River traffic stopped after all available ships had moved upriver. International passenger traffic through Shanghai was almost halted. By the end of 1937, the Siemens representative in Shanghai reported that only French and Italian lines were still operating service from the port.[36]

Internal trade was completely disrupted in the first months of the war. Many of the major routes were cut. Government forces blew up railway bridges and blocked the Yangzi with a barrage, cutting most of the major routes. Meanwhile, the northern third of the Grand Canal was under enemy occupation. The transport routes that were not cut were vulnerable to bombing and to damage from fighting. The risks to goods in transit were so great that merchants would not ship them. As the war went on, merchants showed great ingenuity, and trade resumed, but in the early months, long-distance internal trade virtually collapsed. In the occupied areas, where there was less fear of direct damage, the main issues for merchants and traders were the loss of the hinterland and the Japanese authorities' policy of giving preferential treatment to Japanese and Korean businesses.

Local markets were a key element of the rural trading economy. The immediate effect of the war in the Yangzi Valley was to paralyse those parts of the economy that depended on buying and selling goods. In the 'land of fish and rice (yumi zhi xiang)', peasants produced crops for market, as well as for their own consumption. In the short run, farm incomes plummeted; the fighting made it impossible to market produce, and this in a very good crop year: '... owing to the disruption of communications, many farm products cannot find an outlet. For instance, prices of rice and cotton have struck the bottom in inland producing districts while a shortage of supply in other places has forced the prices to soar in to the sky.'[37] As the rural markets collapsed, so too did many of the other functions they performed, including financial services, medical treatment, and labour recruitment.

Employment was a key problem for workers and peasants. In the first months of the war, tens of thousands of manufacturing jobs in Shanghai and other industrialised areas were lost as some factories moved inland and others closed down. Employment in transport declined – unless men

[35] Ibid., pp. 612–613.
[36] Siemens Archiv 8104; G. A. Probst, report from Shanghai, 11/18/1937.
[37] China Year Book, 1939, p. 486.

were willing to go inland with the retreating government and armies. Along the coast, fishermen were no longer able to put to sea because the unoccupied areas of the coast were blockaded by Japanese naval vessels. Fishing incomes declined dramatically, often permanently.

The loss of jobs meant loss of income for families. For rural families that at least could feed themselves, the losses were less drastic than for urban families. But peasant families that depended on remittances from family members working in the cities, in Manchuria, or overseas were devastated. Loss of income put stress on families, stress that in the short run could not be relieved because there were no new employment possibilities. There were areas of job growth during the war – the military for one – but many more areas where jobs disappeared.

Social Mobilisation

Serve the country loyally[38]

The Japanese threat to China had been growing for so long that when it actually materialised, the invasion itself was not a shock. What was a shock was the scale of the attack, the fierceness of the fighting, and the devastation of the bombing. The onslaught produced a great wave of patriotism. The war was at the start a patriotic war, a war of resistance in which much of the population was involved.

The patriotic slogans came from the top, but they reflected mass feelings. The early months of fighting had a tremendously stimulating effect. For the first time, patriotism transcended regionalism, localism, and familism. The war was seen as a race war in which Chinese were being attacked as a people by aggressors who seemed to regard the Chinese as a lower order. A new national spirit (*guoqing*) blossomed. All the efforts of intellectuals and students to raise the spirit of nationalism, efforts that had been going on since the May 4th Movement in 1919, now came to fruition – and at a far higher pitch than anyone had imagined possible.

China cannot be lost

This was one of the great slogans of the early part of the war – shouted out, painted on walls, and chanted at rallies. The Japanese invasion made

---

[38] Yue Fei had these four characters on his back, tattooed by his mother before he first went off to war. Nine hundred years later they became one of the major wartime slogans.

most Chinese into nationalists; the old responsibilities to the family came second. Deng Yu, who died in August in the failed defence of Beiping, left a message to his mother before he went off to fight: 'I cannot fulfill filial piety and loyalty to the country at the same time. Please pardon me if death befalls me.'[39]

The national spirit and the unity forged at the level of the state bloomed at the same time that the bedrock of society, the family, was being broken down by the chaos of war. The upheaval and flight, the abandonment of home and possessions, and the sudden impoverishment and destitution created by the war were seen as sacrifices for the nation. In the uplifting propaganda accounts of the time, being forced into flight was a form of heroism that brought out the best in people and turned them into true patriots.

The patriotic spearhead was made up of young people. The first months of the war saw an extraordinary exodus of universities and schools from the occupied areas in the eastern and northern parts of the country into the interior and into the foreign concessions. The following table shows the scale of university relocation[40]:

	June 1937	%	June 1939	%
Occupied areas	92	82.9	4	4.4
Unoccupied China	13	11.7	59.2	65.4
Foreign concessions	6	5.4	27.5	30.2

Young students left their universities in groups, with their teachers, and set off on haphazard journeys by train, truck, boat, and on foot. The exodus was funded by the government, on the grounds that China had to make sure that she had an educated elite to run the country after the war was over. These young people were exempted from military service.

School children were also evacuated, especially ones attending the elite government-funded middle schools. Paul Ho was at middle school in Nanchang (Jiangxi), close to his home in Xinyu. When Nanchang was bombed at the end of 1937, the school took to the road and walked

[39] Quoted by Olga Lang, 'Foreign and Chinese Shanghai', *Amerasia* 1(9):419, November 1937.

[40] William Fenn, *The Effect of the Japanese Invasion on Higher Education in China* (Hong Kong: IPR, 1940), p. 12. The figures include universities, colleges, and technical schools.

inland 100 miles into the Jinggangshan. Paul had no chance to say good-bye to his mother or, for a while, even to tell her where he had gone. Letters took two to three month to cross about 80 miles. Paul's class was billeted in a village from which most of the boys and young men had gone off, willingly or not, on the Long March, and the parents whose sons had gone were glad to have other peoples' sons in their houses. Paul did not go home until the end of the war. When he walked into his house again, his mother was so overwhelmed that she could not speak, only weep uncontrollably.[41]

Paul's story was replicated among the hundreds of thousands of young people who were separated by the war from their families. For many of them, separation was a liberation from the restrictive coils of the old family system, but even those who were happy to be young and free still missed their families. They did not know then that many of the separations were permanent.

Conclusion

The first six months of the war brought a level of suffering and chaos that the Chinese could not have imagined possible. Even a revolution in 1911 and years of warlord wars had not prepared the country for the horror that came with the invasion. The shock was immense; the uncertainty and insecurity, even greater. No one knew how long the war would last, although many had their own guesses about how long it would be. These guesses were contradictory. Some people accepted that the Japanese were in China for good, that their victory was assured, and that the war would soon be over. They had to accommodate their lives to the 'new normal'. Many more felt that the war was not over at all and that it would last until the Japanese were thrown out; they decided to resist, to fight back. Even more people had no idea about what the future would bring; they were traumatised, driven by fear and anxiety without any clear path ahead.

The first stage of the war was a ghastly shock. The Chinese government and the Chinese people were horrified at the invasion but proud that they had resisted. Some people in the Japanese government and armies may have realised that they had fallen into what came to be known as the 'China Quagmire'; this dim realisation did not lead to a strategic withdrawal but rather to increased aggression [Reading 4].

---

[41] Interview with Paul Ho, Los Angeles, August 2006; Interview, Yongxin, March 2007.

Readings

Reading 1: 'The River Runs Red' (Manjianghong 满江红)

This poem connected the present struggle to one of the great national heroes, with the unspoken but well-understood rider that Yue Fei was betrayed and murdered.

怒髮衝冠，憑欄處，瀟瀟雨歇。
抬望眼，仰天長嘯，壯懷激烈。
三十功名塵與土，八千里路雲和月。
莫等閒 白了少年頭，空悲切.
靖康恥，猶未雨, 臣子恨，何時滅？
駕長車踏破 賀蘭山缺！
壯志飢餐胡虜肉，笑談渴飲匈奴血。
待從頭收拾舊山河，朝天闕。

My anger is so great that my hair lifts my hat. As I stand at the rail the fine rain eases
I raise my eyes to the sky and let out a long roar of rage
All that I have achieved, at thirty, has turned to dust, even though I have travelled eight thousand li.
Do not sit around in idleness, [wallowing] in empty sorrow, until your young heads grow white with age.
The humiliation of Jing Kang has not yet been washed away
Will the rage of his subjects ever be assuaged?
Let us drive our chariots through the Helan Pass,
There we shall feast and drink on barbarian flesh and blood.
We must start again, recover our ancient hills and rivers, and present them to the emperor.

Reading 2: Lin Yutang, Moment in Peking

This family saga ends with the flight of refugees from Hangzhou [Zhejiang] in January 1938. The heroine is named for the legendary woman warrior Hua Mulan[42]:

Below the temple tens of thousands of men, women and children were moving across the beautiful country on that glorious New Year's morning, shouting and cheering as the army trucks passed. The soldiers' song rose once again:

Never to come back
Until our hills and rivers are returned to us!

[42] Lin Yutang, *Moment in Peking* (New York: John Day, 1939), p. 814.

Mulan, drawing near them, was seized with a new and strange emotion. A sense of happiness, a sense of glory, she thought it was. She was stirred as she had never been before, as one can be stirred only when losing oneself in a great movement. … It was not only the soldiers, but this great moving column of which she was a part. She had a sense of her nation such as she had never had so vividly before, of a people united by a common loyalty, and, though fleeing from a common enemy, still a people whose patience and strength were like the ten-thousand *li* Great Wall, and as enduring. She had heard of the flight of whole populations in North and Middle China. And how forty millions of her brothers and sisters from the 'same womb' were marching westward in the greatest migration in the world's history, to build a new and modern state in the vast hinterland of China. She felt these forty million people moving in one fundamental rhythm. Amidst the stark privations and sufferings of the refugees, she had not heard one speak against the government for the policy of resistance to Japan. All these people, she saw, preferred war to slavery, like Mannia, even though it was a war that had destroyed their homes, killed their relatives, and left them nothing but the barest personal belongings, their rice bowls and their chopsticks. Such was the triumph of the human spirit. There was no catastrophe so great that the spirit could not rise above it and, out of its very magnitude, transform it in to something great and glorious

Reading 3: Lao She, 'A Personal Story' (Zishu) [43]

This story, written in 1941, four years after he fled from Jinan, recalls the sadness of parting from his family:

In the late autumn of the first year of the Resistance War [1937], I fled from Jinan to Wuhan with fifty dollars. … My wife was deeply aware of how critical it was. Normally, she is not very bold. But on the day I was to leave, when the shops were all closed, and the air was full of the sounds of planes, and people were utterly terrified, she held her tears inside her and calmly packed my things. She knew she had to let me go, and so there was nothing more to say. … The children were small, and did not understand the bitterness of parting. Little Yi helped Mummy to get Daddy's things together, and managed to get in her way. I snapped at him, and he bit his lip, not daring to cry. I still feel bad towards him. Over the past four years, whenever I have some spare time, I think of my wife's calmness when I was leaving Jinan, and at Little Yi wanting to cry when he was snapped at, and then my own tears come. But in wartime it seems that you must keep your own sorrows to yourself, and you mustn't appear with a tear-stained face. So I dare not cry in public. But I don't seem to be able to keep busy all the time, to have no spare moments, and so not to have time to feel sad.

---

[43] First published in *Dagongbao*, 1941. Republished in *Lao She wenji* (Beijing: Renmin wenxue chubanshe, 1989), XIV, p. 180.

Reading 4: Murakami Haruki, The Wind-up Bird Chronicle

Two soldiers in the Japanese army in Manchuria talk about what happened during the invasion of China. Murakami captures Japanese doubts about the invasion, and the common rationalisations for army behaviour.[44]

Ordinarily a fresh young officer like me would be laughed at by a seasoned non-commissioned officer like Sergeant Hamano, but our case was different. He respected the education I had received in a non-military college, and I took care to acknowledge his combat experience and practical judgement without letting rank get in the way. We also found it easy to talk to each other because he was from Yamaguchi and I was from an area of Hiroshima close to Yamaguchi. He told me about the war in China. He was a soldier all the way, with only grammar school behind him, but he had his own reservations about this messy war on the continent, which looked as if it would never end, and he expressed these feelings honestly to me. 'I don't mind the fighting,' he said. 'I'm a soldier. And I don't mind dying in battle for my country, because that is my job. But this war we're fighting now, Lieutenant – well it's just not right. It's not a real war with a battle line where you face the enemy and fight to the finish. We advance and the enemy runs away without fighting. Then the Chinese soldiers take off their uniforms and mix with the civilian population and we don't even know who the enemy is. So then we kill a lot of innocent people in the name of flushing out "renegades" or "remnant troops", and we have to commandeer provisions. We have to steal their food because the line moves forward so fast our supplies can't catch up with us. And we have to kill our prisoners because we don't have any place to keep them or and food to feed them. We did some terrible things in Nanking. My own unit did.'

Films

City of Life and Death 南京南京. Director Lu Chuan, 2009.
Diary of John Rabe 拉贝日记. Director Florian Gallenberger, 2009.

---

[44] Haruki Murakami, translated by Jay Rubin, *The Wind-up Bird Chronicle* (New York: Bantam, 1998), p. 143.

2   Defeat and Retreat: 1938

Events

越挫越勇

The more one is defeated, the more courageous one is

In the first two months of 1938, China drew its breath and tried to come to terms with the horror of the losses of late 1937. There was a widespread expectation amongst foreign observers that the government finally would surrender to Japan and that Chiang Kai-shek, the man most closely associated with the defeat, would be forced to resign. Neither thing happened. The Japanese had united China. "The propaganda of her bombs, and even more the domineering attitude of her soldiers, has been far more effective in instilling a hatred of all thing Japanese into all classes from the illiterate coolie upwards."[1] United China needed a leader, and the only one available was Chiang; he held onto his position, although his autocratic style was severely curtailed. The political culture that flowered in Wuhan was unfettered and creative, possibly the freest that China had ever known.[2]

Early in 1938, the Chinese armies prepared a counter-attack. It came in March in Jiangsu, to the north of the Yangzi. For the first time, Chinese troops defeated the Japanese at the battle of Taierzhuang. The counter-attack did not hold; by May, Chinese troops were falling back again, but China's will to resist had been established, and surrender was no longer an option. A sign of how far China was prepared to go to resist was the desperate scorched-earth policy, the first example of which was

[1] Roger Hollis, 'The Conflict in China', in *Japanese Aggression and Public Opinion* (Kunming, 1938), p. 129. Hollis was in China working for British American Tobacco; given his later role as head of MI5, he may already have been involved in intelligence work for the British.

[2] Stephen MacKinnon, *War, Refugees, and the Making of Modern China* (Berkeley: University of California Press, 2008).

"CHIANG KAI-SHEK MEDITATES ON A MOUNTAIN
TOP ABOVE TENTS OF WAR," BY CHANG KWANG-YU

2.1. **Chiang Kai-shek on a mountain top.** (Jack Chen, *Asia*,
May 1938.)

the breach of the Yellow River dike in June; it unleashed a flood that
killed hundreds of thousands of peasants.

The flood saved the new capital at Wuhan from a Japanese attack
coming south from north China but exposed it instead to a massive
assault by Japanese forces up the Yangzi. Through the torrid heat of
the summer, Chinese troops waged a fierce but unsuccessful resistance. One place after another fell to the enemy. Guangzhou was

captured. Wuhan turned out to be a temporary capital; in October it had to be abandoned. The government moved further west, up the Yangzi Gorges to Chongqing, into virtual isolation from the rest of the world, with access only from Burma, India, and Central Asia by land and from Hong Kong by air. The positional war of big battles was over, and the second phase, guerrilla warfare, was just starting. By the end of 1938, it was clear that the Japanese attack into China had not resulted in outright victory. The Japanese, though technically in control of all of northern and eastern China, actually controlled only the major urban centres and the railway lines between them. Guerrillas operated freely beyond these lines, even in the hills just outside Beiping.

In 1938, the huge refugee movements that had started the year before continued as tens of millions people continued to flee before the advancing Japanese. One of the largest movements was caused by the breach of the Yellow River dike; another came in advance of the burning of Changsha (Hunan), when it was erroneously thought to be in danger of falling to Japanese forces.

Those who did not flee from the occupied areas had to find ways to live with the occupiers for an indefinite period. People could go only on flimsy guesses as to how long the war would last. Some thought that it would go on forever; others hoped that the Japanese would soon disappear. In the meantime, they had to survive.

For a few people, living with the enemy meant active collaboration; for many more, it meant accommodation, finding a *modus vivendi*, an unhappy form of survival. The level of direct fraternising with the enemy (*tongdi*) was low. The number of people who had direct dealings with the Japanese was small, most of them members of the old elite. For others, direct contact was either with the many Koreans and Taiwanese (at the time Japanese citizens) who came to work for the Japanese or with Chinese collaborators.

Many of the Japanese armed forces behaved with awful brutality, behaviour that guaranteed the hostility of the bulk of the population in a country too vast to be completely controlled by force. Establishing effective civil government was a problem that the Japanese could not resolve. The ferocity of the war made it inevitable that Chinese who took major roles in civil government would be seen as traitors. This meant that few were willing to do so. The calibre of the members of the Reformed Government in Nanjing (*Weixin zhengfu*) and other new administrations in north China was low; all were beholden to the Japanese military [Reading 1]. Chinese use of the term 'puppet

PITIFUL PILGRIMAGE : some of the millions of
homeless Chinese refugees who fled into the
deep interior from the advancing Japanese

2.2. Refugees. (Rhodes Farmer, *Shanghai Harvest*, 1945, p. 144.)

(*kuilei*)' to describe these people and the administrations in which they worked was accurate. Japan did not bring over any really senior Chinese figures. Efforts to recruit the former warlord Wu Peifu were rebuffed; Wu retreated and died in 1939 of blood poisoning caused by a decaying tooth. Then in late 1938 came a major defection, of Wang Jingwei.

2.3. **Beijing Provisional Government. (Andrew Caniff, *Asia*, March 1938.)**

Wang Jingwei

Wang Jingwei was the head of the pro-Japanese government in Nanjing from 1940 until his death in 1944. As a young man, Wang was a patriotic hero; he tried to assassinate a Manchu prince just before the 1911 Revolution. He was one of Sun Yat-sen's closest followers, an intelligent, capable man. His lack of military connections meant, however, that he never achieved the top position he felt he deserved. He was an attractive figure, handsome and charming. In May 1938, when an English translation of his poetry appeared, a reviewer said: 'In this poet I discover a fervent reformer, yet fond of long conversations with a friend, fond of wine, a lover, a husband, and one who delights in little children and in that perpetual innocence of sea, sky and land.'[3]

The assessment was wrong. Wang was more complex. In late 1938, on the second anniversary of Chiang Kai-shek's kidnapping in Xian, he slipped away from Chongqing, appeared briefly in Hanoi, and then moved to Nanjing. Wang's defection was one of the worst shocks of the early stages of the war. Once the shock wore off, he was bitterly denounced. In the Chinese press, an avalanche of abuse called him a traitor (*ni, pantu*), a puppet (*kuilei*), a man conspiring to sell his country (*maiguo yinmou*). A more sober account had this to say[4]:

[3] *China Critic*, XXI, 5 (May 5, 1938), p. 59.
[4] *China Critic*, XXIV, 2 (January 12, 1939), p. 19.

Wang has committed political suicide, and, at a single stroke, has wiped out the record of forty years' service to the nation, has alienated the sympathy of his former friends and supporters and has earned the hatred and contempt of his fellow countrymen, branding himself forever as a traitor to his country.

Wang died before the end of the war, in 1944. He was never called to account for his actions, although several of his close colleagues were executed. He did claim to have been driven almost to despair by the Chinese government's scorched-earth policy. But how this despair led to acting as head of a collaborationist government is not clear.[5] He has never been forgiven for his willingness to act as a puppet for the Japanese.

Topics and Case Studies

The first eighteen months of the war saw the beginning of a spontaneous and impromptu social revolution that had no specific ideology, no programme, and no blueprint. In the intense crisis of the invasion, the old, 'normal' society disappeared. Much of the population was suddenly caught up in the chaos and confusion of war. The new reality was survival – survival through the agonies of bombing, fighting, and flight.

Survival

The dominant concern for the civilian population was the most fundamental – survival. Survival itself was a mystery, with many interpretations. For some, it seemed a matter of fate or luck. These fortunate survivors (*xingcun zhe*) felt that they owed their survival to good luck, and the proof was that the unlucky were dead. The more self-satisfied survivors attributed their survival to their own efforts, talents, wealth, or social status. Some survivors even exulted in their own survival, even though what they had survived had brought disaster to others. Their attitude echoed the ancient phrase, from the *Zuozhuan*, China's earliest work of history: 'It is better that bad things happen to others, not oneself (*xinghui legu*)', an antique version of the German *Schadenfreude*, pleasure in the misfortune of others.

Some people put their survival down to religious faith, proof that a deity was on their side, whether Buddhist or Christian. The wartime records of Christian missionaries are full of testimony to the power of

---

[5] Lo Jiu-jung, 'Survival as justification for collaboration', in David Barrett and Lary Shyu (eds.), *Chinese Collaboration with Japan, 1932–1945: The Limits of Accommodation* (Palo Alto, CA: Stanford University Press, 2001), p. 121.

prayer: 'One of our members, Mr. P'eng, was kneeling, praying at the railway station during the raid. When he got up he saw eleven people dead at his side. He was full of joy after such a deliverance.'[6] Jesuit missionaries in the Xuzhou region put their courage and energy into saving thousands of refugees from the Japanese onslaught down to the fact that the occupation of their district took place in Mary's month, May; Mary was present in the region to protect those who called on her.[7]

Survival could be a hell of its own. In the abandoned capital, the desolation was total. A professor at Jinling University in Nanjing, L. S. C. Smythe, carried out a sample survey of the surviving population between March and April 1938. The survey was conducted in an atmosphere of terror and makes only discreet allusions to the massacre that had just occurred. The results showed the civilian population reduced by over 80%, and of those remaining, 43% were living as refugees in their own city, dependent on foreign aid and protection in the International Control Zone or just outside it. 'Normal' families, with husbands and wives and children, had declined dramatically, replaced by 'broken families' headed by women whose husbands had died or been 'taken away' and almost certainly killed.[8] The people remaining were destitute; 78% of the people surveyed reported no income; another 16% had inadequate income. Only 6% of the population had adequate income. Most of those surveyed had small businesses or had worked in manufacturing. They had stayed to protect their only capital or because they were too poor to flee. Now, only 36% of those who had formerly worked were doing so.[9]

The material fabric of Nanjing had fared no better than the people. Nanjing was not fired by the retreating government, but it had already suffered tremendous damage from bombing before the Japanese arrived and then from looting. About 89% of the buildings had been destroyed or damaged, the majority (63%) by looting. In monetary terms, the greatest losses were from fire, most the result of bombing (67%). Some property had been taken away by those who fled, but most had been lost during the occupation. What was not looted by Japanese troops was taken from abandoned houses and shops by local thieves. Most of those left in the

[6] *China's Millions*, LXIV, 3 (March 1938), p. 37 (report from Mrs. Weller, Xuancheng, Anhui).

[7] Diana Lary, 'Faith and war: Canadian Jesuits and the Japanese invasion of China', *Modern Asian Studies*, XXXIX, 4 (2005), pp. 825–852.

[8] L. S. C. Smythe, 'Nanking's population in wartime', *China Critic*, XXII, 7 (August 16, 1938), pp. 115–118. The survey was a one-in-fifty survey of 4,423 people. Comparisons are based on earlier studies of the Nanjing population.

[9] L. S. C. Smythe, 'The plight of Nanking's wartime population', *China Critic*, XXII, 8 (August 25, 1938), pp. 121–122.

city had no possessions at all, not even bedding.[10] Their survival must have seemed cruel – living in a ruined city surrounded by the ghosts of the dead. The people of Nanjing were so traumatised that they were not able to show any gratitude or joy at their survival.

Whatever the interpretation of survival, survivors were changed by their experiences. They had been violently uprooted from their old world and were living a new reality, often in new places. Those of the modern elites who fled into the interior discovered a China they had not known before, less advanced than the east, much more traditional, less comfortable. Their accounts speak of the jarring loss of material comfort and an unpleasant acquaintance with rats, bed bugs, cockroaches, and dirt. They had to live in new languages. Most were unable to understand the heavy western dialects; they felt that they had come to a different world.

In the early stages of the war, the need and the ability to cope with these difficulties were treated as ennobling, a willingness to suffer for the nation, to abandon comfort and prosperity for the national cause. Early in the war, almost all the people who fled into the interior prided themselves on not complaining. Later in the war, this changed; coping well with hardship came to be more associated with the Communist Party in Yan'an.

The Spirit of Defiance

The mood that gripped China during much of 1938 was defiant, a rebounding from the despair and shock that fell over the country at the end of 1937. The resurgence of the Chinese armies, and particularly the victory at Taierzhuang, produced a powerful shift in the public mood towards a spirit of defiance. This mood was fostered by skilful propaganda campaigns in Wuhan and Chongqing and in the unoccupied parts of Shanghai. Financial help and encouragement poured in to China from overseas communities and from foreign aid organisations.

The mood was upbeat and inspirational. 'For the country, for the race, for democracy, for freedom, for oneself, for one's family, for one's descendents (*wei guojia, wei minzu, wei minzhu, wei ziyou, wei jiaxiang, wei zisun*)'; this early wartime slogan captured the mood of patriotism, self-sacrifice, and endurance.

The spirit of 'we can take it' was a precursor of the spirit of the Blitz that emerged in London two years later. With it came resilience and

---

[10] L. S. C. Smythe. 'Nanking's building losses', *China Critic*, XXII, 9 (September 1, 1938), pp. 138–140.

a determination to continue normal life, however hard things got. Guangzhou (Canton) was bombed repeatedly in the early summer of 1938. After two weeks of bombing, the city was unbowed[11]:

Canton today is a city of sharp contrasts. Normal life goes on in many districts with the attendant hustle and bustle familiar in a big, noisy city. Yet, desolation and destruction much the same as that of Chapei [part of Shanghai] during hostilities may be found but a few paces away. Such conditions have come into being after intense Japanese air raids on the city. Where missiles left their marks of death and destruction, and where continued stay is considered to be extremely perilous, few living souls may be found. Shutters have been put up and doors barred. Craters, some being 30 feet in diameter, charred ruins of buildings, piles of bricks and masonry, and shattered windows give grim evidence of horrors from the sky.

An entirely different picture of the city is provided almost side by side with these areas. Motor cars, rickshaws and other kinds of vehicles jostle the thoroughfares with large numbers of pedestrians moving about on the pavements. Shops and restaurants open their doors fully for business. Hawkers yelling at the top of their voices sell fruits or other goods.

The spirit of defiance included a deep appreciation for the defenders of China's sacred soil – her soldiers.

The Popularity of the Military   In the elite tradition, the military was despised. The popular love of martial arts and knights errant did not penetrate into the upper echelons of society. The New Army that emerged in the late Qing and did much to bring the dynasty down degenerated in the 1920s into warlordism, and the Guomindang (GMD), itself strongly militarist, did not manage to do much to raise the standing of the military in the early 1930s. The war did. China's soldiers became popular, even beloved, heroic men fighting to save China. They ceased to belong to their regional units, as they had during the warlord period, and became soldiers of the nation.

The epitome of the heroic military was the Lost Battalion, the unit that had held a warehouse in Shanghai in late October 1937. In 1938 these men became the new national heroes, promoted in a barrage of propaganda. A film about the battalion was released in mid-1938 (one of the few films made in Wuhan), and a song in praise of their courage became almost a national anthem. The military's image rose and rose [Reading 2]. The words of the old saying about soldiers were reversed. The saying 'Good iron does not make nails, good men do not make soldiers (*hao tie bu dang ding, hao ren bu dang bing*)' became

---

[11] Hsu Shu-hsi, *Guangzhou Kangri ji* (Hong Kong: Kelley and Walsh, 1939), pp. 25–26.

IN SACRED NANYO : Soldiers marching from
their billets in the great Nanyo Temples
pass under a typical Chinese war poster

2.4. Soldiers at Nanyue. (Farmer, p. 193.)

'Good iron must make nails, good men must make soldiers (*hao nan yao dang bing, hao tie yao dang bing*)', as displayed on a poster in Wuhan.[12]

The Chinese armies paid a huge price in 1938 for their new role, in lives and in injuries – and for many soldiers a wound was a delayed death sentence. The English journalist Violet Cressy-Marks described

---

[12] MacKinnon, p. 81.

the scene in March 1938 just west of the battlefield at Taierzhuang as a trainload of casualties was unloaded[13]:

The doors swung open slowly, and inside was Hell! On the iron-bottomed trucks they lay; the blood had congealed and they were stuck to the bottom. It was bitterly cold and there was not even straw for them to lie on. Quickly the doctor pointed out those that were dead, and they were removed and piled in a little heap. Next he pointed to those that were dying; they were put into another little heap. Those too serious to have quick attention also came out, and the others were brought out, and given what attention was possible, to try to save their limbs and life. In the middle of this another train drew up behind this one. I took a lamp and walked along to it. The same conditions existed.

The wounded were extolled for their courage and stoicism, and special hospitals were set up in the rear. But the praise and the care could not heal them in a society where medical care was very limited. Dr. Norman Bethune, the Canadian surgeon who worked with communist forces in Shaanxi, brought unknown skills to the care of the wounded and was singled out after his death in 1939 by Mao Zedong as an example of internationalism and service.

Wounded soldiers who did survive were destined to destitution; there was no long-term medical care, no pensions for the wounded. Their plight became the focus of bitter criticism of the government, as did the fate of conscripts who were brought in as the war went on to fill the armies. Soldiers' lives were hard and often sad. They were separated from their families indefinitely. Their families suffered in parallel, from isolation and poverty – and on both sides anxiety [Reading 3].

Praise for the military was a major theme in another new wartime phenomenon – choral singing.

A Singing World   One unexpected and hugely popular innovation of the war was a surge in mass singing. Choral singing was something new to China. Traditionally, the only forms of singing were opera arias, almost always solos, work songs, and folk songs. The first popular song was 'The March of the Volunteers (*Yiyongjun jinxing ju*)'.

As soon as the war started, China was engulfed in a wave of singing. New songs appeared by the day; in one collection alone there are over 1,500 titles.[14] There were martial songs, songs of homesickness, songs to support soldiers, songs to recruit soldiers, songs of freedom, and songs of anger. Immediately after every major event, new songs appeared.

---

[13] Violet Cressy-Marks, *Journey into China* (London: Hodder and Stoughton, 1940), p. 247.

[14] Xingzhhengyuan wenhua jianshe weyuanhui, *Kangzhan gequ xuanji* (Taibei, 1997).

2.5. **Songs of Resistance**

They could be sung by a few voices or by many and required no musical accompaniment; they became the most popular and immediate form of wartime culture.[15]

Some of the librettists were predictable. Tian Han and the poet Ai Qing both wrote streams of librettos, as did the writer Lao She and the poet Wen Yiduo. Hu Shi, a major intellectual and later ambassador to the United States, wrote the words for 'Up into the Mountains (*Shang shan*)', set to music by the linguist Zhao Yuanren. The polymath Guo Moruo wrote several songs, among them 'The Song of Chinese Women Resisting the Enemy (*Zhongguo fu Kangdi ge*)'. Other song writers were members of the political and military elite. In China, officials and generals had always written poetry. Now they turned to song. It would be hard to imagine a senior British or American politician writing popular songs, let alone Montgomery or Patton. The GMD politician Chen Guofu wrote the words for 'The Song of Youth (*Qingnian ge*)', 'Esteem the Military (*Shang wu ge*)', and 'The National Flag (*Guoqi ge*)'. His brother Chen Lifu wrote 'Resist (*Dikang*)'. Song writing crossed party lines. He Xiangning, widow of the early revolutionary Liao Zhongkai wrote 'Send Winter Clothes to the Soldiers at the Front (*Zeng hanyi yuqianfang jiangshi*)'. General Bai Chongxi wrote a song to encourage young men to enlist, 'Hard-Working Men Join the Army (*Jinfu congjun*)'.

---

[15] Lin Yutang, 'Singing patriots of China', *Asia* (February 1941), pp. 70–72.

The music for the new songs came from different sources. Some tunes were adaptations of folk songs (*minge*), Chinese and European, a few were traditional tunes (*gudian*). The music of foreign composers was popular, adaptations of classical and contemporary tunes. Mendelsohn's 'Larchengesang' was put to the words 'The New Air Force (*Xin kongjun*)'. Tunes by Gounod provided the music for 'Song of the Advancing Army (*Jinjun ge*)' and 'Long, Long Live the Republic of China (*Zhonghua minguo wan wan nian*)'. 'Down with Japan (*Da Riben*)' was set to one Bach air, while 'Advance for the Well-Being of the Motherland (*Wei Zuguo xingfu xiangqianjin*)' was set to another. 'Crossing the Pacific (*Guo Taipingyang*)' was set to a Verdi tune. Beethoven wrote the music for the song 'In Memory of the Soldiers of SongHu (*SongHu chenwang jiang-shi*)'. Schumann, Hayden, and Faure also provided music. The music for the 'Marseillaise' accompanied a song in praise of Sun Yat-sen. Hymn tunes were also borrowed.

There was new music, composed by men who had studied Western music. The most prolific was Xian Xinghai, a Cantonese composer who had trained at the Conservatoire in Paris. He went to Yan'an at the start of the war. He wrote the 'Yellow River Cantata' (*Huang He dahechang*) in 1939, using the symbolism of the Yellow River to express his conviction that China eventually would triumph. He also wrote songs incorporating elements of folk music. Another great song to come out of Yan'an was 'Beautiful Nanniwan (*Meili de Nanniwan*)', a hauntingly lovely song in praise of land reclamation. (This song resurfaced in a rock version in 1991 sung by Cui Jian, the king of Chinese rock and roll.)

These songs continued to be sung for decades, both by people who had lived through the war and by later generations.[16] However much they lifted the mood of unoccupied China, they could not in the end alleviate the sadness that was settling over China as people realised how much they had lost. Beyond deaths and material loss, the pain of separation from family and friends began to sink in during the second year of the war.

Family Separation

流离失所

Forced to leave home and wander aimlessly

A widespread and devastating effect of the war, one that often lasted far beyond the war, was family separation. The war drove families apart, suddenly, without warning. Sometimes the departure was voluntary,

---

[16] Information from Jerome Ch'en, June 2009.

more often involuntary; soldiers, civil servants, and employees were ordered to leave by their superiors. Fear was the major driver, followed by patriotism, or a combination of the two. 'Millions of people have been separated from their relatives and even their parents, some by army conscription, some in the course of escaping from death, but thousands by voluntary desertion of their family for the country.'[17]

Flight usually meant leaving neighbours, friends, and possessions, as well as members of the extended family. When a 'whole' family fled, it was likely to be only two generations, parents and their children – that is, the large family was divided. Family divisions sometimes meant literally that families had been destroyed when homes were destroyed by bombing or by fire. The same character *jia* is used for family and for home. The Japanese tactic of destroying villages where there was resistance started early in the war. In April 1938, a Japanese truck was ambushed near Songjiang, just outside Shanghai. The same day, a large Japanese force razed all the villages along ten kilometres of road.[18] With their homes and livelihoods gone, the only solution was for the whole family to flee or for the young to go and search for some way to support the rest of the family. In the process, families were broken up.

Flight, destruction, and the requisitioning of property meant erosion of the large family unit, the demise of the traditional extended family of dozens of people living together in one compound. The ideal was 'four generations under one roof'. One part of a family, usually the older members, might stay; other members, usually younger ones, would leave.

Family separations were political as well as physical. Family members often disagreed with each other about how to respond to the invasion. This might mean some members turning against another member of a family who was actively collaborating, as the daughter of the head of the puppet Beiping government, Wang Kemin, did. She despised her father and fled from Beiping. There were many less dramatic examples, all of which had the same outcome – division of the family on political grounds, a foretaste of what was to come in the Mao era.

Family separations were haphazard. The family of General Jiang Guangnai moved to their house in Hong Kong when Guangzhou was attacked, and then, in late 1941 when Hong Kong fell, they fled to the interior of Guangdong and settled near the Fujian border. Even though General Jiang was stationed in the same province, he and his family were separated for the duration of the war.[19]

---

[17] Edgar Snow, *Scorched Earth*, Vol. 2 (London: Gollancz, 1941), p. 233.
[18] *China Critic*, XXI, 2 (April 14, 1938), p. 21.
[19] Interview with Jiang Jin, Vancouver, March 30, 2009.

The decision as to whether to put family first and to stay or to flee and abandon the family was almost impossible. These three stories of men who made different decisions show how sudden the decisions often had to be, how often the decision was wrong, and how unpredictable the outcomes were.

Feng Zikai   Feng Zikai was China's most famous cartoonist, a witty commentator on Chinese life as it changed in the 1920s and 1930s. He introduced to China an art that he had learned in Japan, *manga* (in Chinese *manhua*), translated into English as 'cartoon' but ranging beyond the limited English usage of funnies and political commentary. In late 1937, when Feng was at the height of his career, he was forced to abandon his home and studio in Shimenwan, on the Grand Canal in Zhejiang. A bombing raid on the village was blamed on Feng's two-storey house; the tower stood out over the mass of single-story buildings and caught the eye of a Japanese pilot. Thirty-two people were killed in the raid.[20]

Feng left Shimenwan at once, taking with him sixteen people – his mother-in-law, his pregnant wife, his sister, six children, other relatives, and servants. The group travelled by boat, heading inland. They eventually reached Guilin, where Feng and many other artists spent the war. Eight years later, when he finally went home, he discovered that his house and all his collected work had been destroyed. He held his family together, but at a huge cost in terms of his own artistic career.

Guo Moruo   Guo Moruo was a brilliant Sichuanese intellectual. He was a student in Japan and lived there except for a short period during the Northern Expedition (1926–28). He married a Japanese woman and had five children with her. In 1937 he came under suspicion as a spy for China and fled from Japan, leaving his family behind. In China, his rise in the cultural world was meteoric; he was immensely successful as an ardent propagandist for resistance. In Wuhan and then in Chongqing, he was an intellectual star, famous for his work on ancient history, for his poetry, and for his cultural administration. His family in Japan meanwhile was abandoned. Guo may have felt some pangs of guilt, but within a short time he had acquired a new wife, who gave him another five children. He blamed the complexity of his personal life not

---

[20] Geremie Barme, *An Artistic Exile: The life of Feng Zikai* (Berkeley: University of California Press, 2002), p. 238.

on himself but on the war: 'It was the Japanese militarists who caused all this.'[21]

His first wife, Anna, paid a heavy price. By marrying a foreigner, she lost her Japanese citizenship. She and her children lived through the war on the verge of destitution. She found her husband again after the war, but there was no question of reconciliation. The best that could be arranged for her was that she should take up Chinese citizenship. She moved to Dalian (Liaoning) and taught Japanese there. Despite what she had endured, she lived to the age of 99.[22]

Zhou Zuoren   Guo Moruo abandoned his Japanese wife and their children. Zhou Zuoren, whose wife was also Japanese, took the opposite path and refused to leave Beiping and his family.

Zhou was an accomplished writer, a polymath, a translator from Greek, English, and Japanese, an enthusiast for psychology (especially the sexology of Havelock Ellis), and an eloquent spokesman for many causes. He was, in the 1930s, more famous that his brother, Lu Xun (Zhou Shuren), later recognised as China's greatest modern writer.

In 1937, Zhou was living in Beiping with his wife and children and teaching at Peking University. In the summer, most of his colleagues fled before the incoming Japanese. He decided not to leave the city; he thought that resistance was futile, that the Japanese were bound to win. He continued his work, including appearing at events sponsored by the occupiers. His collaboration, as seen by other intellectuals, caused shock and disgust on a scale similar to that levelled at Louis-Ferdinand Celine in France. Zhou was not proud of what he did and claimed to have kept his collaboration to a minimum, but the damage was done. His colleagues did not forgive such a celebrated scholar for allowing his name and prestige to be used by the occupiers [Reading 4].

At the end of the war, he was indicted for collaboration with the enemy and was sent to prison. He was released in 1949 and worked on memoirs of his brother's childhood and youth. He was killed by Red Guards in 1967.[23]

These three sad stories of family separation and division happened to people who left personal records and who have attracted the attention of biographers. This is not the case with the victims of the terrible acts of scorched earth, almost of all of whom died without public notice or were driven from their homes into exile.

[21] Lu Yan, *Re-understanding Japan* (Hawaii, 2004), pp. 96–97.
[22] *Ibid.*, pp. 244–245.
[23] *Ibid.*

Scorched-Earth Policies

破釜沉舟
Smash the cauldrons, scuttle the boats[24]

Some of the greatest casualties of the war came not from Japanese actions but from the scorched-earth policy. The two most devastating actions were the opening of the Yellow River dike at Huayuankou and the firing of Changsha.

Scorched earth was framed as a policy of national sacrifice. The premise was that China could use her size and her vast population to trade space and place for time without any apparent concern for human losses. From the Japanese takeover of Manchuria in 1931 on, there was much, often histrionic talk in the press and in military circles that China would have to defend herself against Japan with one of the weapons of a weak country, scorched-earth actions. The Chinese army would fight to the last drop of Chinese blood, the land would be turned into a great swathe of scorched earth, and the people who lived on it would vanish.

In the early phases of the invasion, the Chinese armies destroyed many assets that could be used by the enemy; bridges were blown up, roads cut, railway track lifted, and buildings fired. In Shandong, Jinan, the provincial capital and commercial centre was fired just before Japanese troops entered the city in December 1937. Japanese-owned cotton mills in Qingdao were torched at the same time. These were acts of pre-emptive destruction to deny the enemy strategic resources. They were small in scale compared with the later scorched-earth policies.

Scorched-earth tactics were seen as a promise that China would ultimately defeat the Japanese. The GMD military promoted scorched earth as their most successful policy. General Xue Yue reported after the Japanese had been thrown back from Changsha[25]:

We have won the war in China, or rather we have prevented the Japanese from assuming complete political control over China, and we have done this simply by employing the scorched earth policy. This has been our major strategy. We have destroyed China – removed every stone, burnt down every farm, torn up every railway track upon which we could lay our hands and we have done this so successfully that the Japanese have already repented of their invasion. They are tired and weary of their invasion.

---

[24] Attributed to Xiang Yu, the prince of Chu, as his troops were about to be defeated by Han forces, during the war at the end of the Qin.

[25] Quoted in Robert Payne, *Forever China* (New York: Dodd, Mead, 1945), p. 77.

Xue did not mention that willingness to sacrifice land and resources also meant willingness to sacrifice people, the inevitable concomitant. His attitude could be seen as the callousness of officialdom, the unstated assumption that, in a huge population, huge losses would not be noticed. But they were. Every person was a member of a family, and most families kept detailed records of their members and remembered their dead. In any case, callousness is an inadequate explanation for the two most infamous scorched-earth events; upper-level panic is a better one. The unfolding of the actions suggests that they were less the product of a calculated strategy than of panic and confusion. What they unleashed was not damage to the enemy but a catastrophe for Chinese people; the purported military objective was negated by the magnitude of the suffering.

Huayuankou   Huayuankou is a tiny place on the southern dike of the Yellow River in Henan Province. It is where one of the greatest disasters of all time started, when the dike was deliberately breached in June 1938 and the waters of the river allowed to flow through the breach. The flood unleashed drowned hundreds of thousands of people, one of the first mass killings in what became World War II and one of the largest of the whole war. The breaching of the dike followed from the Chinese high command's decision to 'use water as a substitute for soldiers (*yi shui dai bing*)', to turn the Yellow River into a strategic weapon to stop the enemy advancing westward along the LongHai Railway and at the same time ensure the escape of the huge Chinese army (about 200,000 men) that had fought in the Xuzhou campaign.[26]

The Yellow River's water gushed out over the North China Plain. The breach became the head of a vast fan that spread out to the south and east. The flood waters flowed southeast across the pancake-flat plain towards the Huai River, the Grand Canal, and the Yangzi. Eventually, 70,000 square kilometres were flooded.

The impact on the flooded areas (*huangfan qu*) was almost beyond imagining. The local authorities had no means to warn the dense rural population in villages and small towns strung out across the plain that the flood was coming. In any case, warnings would have made little difference in helping people to escape the flood. There were no refuges out on the plain, no hills, not even any high buildings, in an area where most houses were single-storey adobe buildings. The only structures that rose above the plain were the dikes of the river and the walls of county towns.

---

[26] Diana Lary, 'The waters covered the earth: China's war-induced natural disasters', in Mark Selden and Alvin So (eds.), *War and State Terrorism* (Rowman and Littlefield: Lanhma MD, 2004), pp. 143–170.

The flood waters were shallow – seldom more than two or three feet deep – but they were implacable. With nowhere to escape to and no rescue in sight, hundreds of thousand of peasants died, either swiftly by drowning in the flood or by hunger or illness over the next weeks and months. The official death toll was over 800,000. Millions of people on the western edge of the flood became refugees, fleeing into West Henan and Shaanxi provinces. In 1945, there were six million refugees from the flood zone still in the places they had originally fled to, some resettled, others completely destitute. No one fled to the east, into the Japanese-occupied areas; the fear of the enemy was greater than the fear of the water.

The disaster unfolded in silence. Huayuankou was barely covered in the media in the weeks and months after the breach, either in China or abroad. The military action had shifted south, to the Yangzi – which itself was in flood after abnormally heavy rainfall. It is incredible that such an enormous catastrophe should escape public attention, but it did, as did the inferno at Changsha.

Changsha: City of Fire (Huo cheng)   Changsha was a wartime symbol of heroism and resistance, as Leningrad was for the USSR. The city came under attack four times (1938, twice in 1942, and 1944) but fell only on the last occasion. The heroic image masks the story of the tragedy of 1938.

Before 1938, Changsha was a wealthy provincial capital with a long cultural tradition. The city dominated the trade that flowed along the river, north from Guangdong and south from Wuhan. It was one of the major rice markets in the country and one of the most important centres of education and learning in south China. Changsha produced generations of cultivated mandarins and intellectuals. The young Mao Zedong studied there. Changsha played a major role in modern political movements. The Hunanese were famous as anti-foreign activists and as political radicals; the province's most celebrated martyr was Tan Sitong, executed in 1898 for promoting political reform. In the 1920s, Hunan took up federalism and promulgated its own provincial constitution.

In late 1937 and early 1938, Changsha became the refuge for many people fleeing from the coast and the north. The population swelled to half a million. The city was the new intellectual hub of China. Three northern universities (Peking University, Qinghua University, and Nankai University) and many Shanghai publishing houses moved to the city; much of the resistance propaganda from the early stages of the war was produced there. Then came disaster. Wuhan fell to the Japanese in late October, and Hunan was threatened. Changsha seemed doomed to fall. The city was already being bombed, and it was difficult to defend; there were no natural barriers between it and the Japanese.

On November 9, Chiang Kai-shek convened a high-level military meeting in Changsha. In a dramatic speech he raised the example of the Russian burning of Moscow to prevent Napoleon from taking the city; he proposed that all Changsha's public and private buildings be torched when (and if) the Japanese armies seemed about to take the city. Zhang Zhizhong, governor of Hunan, was ordered to make preparations to do so; stores of gasoline were placed at points throughout the city. The provincial government moved out, as did many of the refugees. On November 12, a rumour started that the Japanese were very close, sparked by the confusion of two place names, one a long way away and the other close by. At 2 a.m. on the morning of November 13, fires were set all over the city.[27] The city burned for three days, leaving a wasteland of blackened ruins and ashes. Only a third of the city's structures survived.[28]

	Original stock	Destroyed	Half-destroyed
Total buildings	31,884 *jian*	20,838	299
Stores		10,336	85
Residences		10,198	169
Schools		55	16
Government Offices		62	13
Banks		11	2
Hospitals		13	
Temples		108	4
Factories		10	3
Foreign property		55	7

Along with the domestic and commercial buildings, almost all the city's ancient monuments, temples, and mansions of the wealthy were destroyed. The rice warehouses, filled with 1.9 million *shi* of grain, were burned.[29]

---

[27] Ren Guangchun, *Huocheng Changsha* (Beiping: Tuanjie chubanshe, 1955), p. 39; Liang Xiaojing, Chen Xianshu, *1938: '11.13' Changsha dahuo* (Wuhan: Hebei renmin chubanshe, 2005) pp. 79, 81; LuoYuming, *KangRi zhanzheng shiqi de Hunan zhanchang* (Shanghai: Xuelin dushu, 2002), p. 106.

[28] *Hunan sheng zhengfu chenbao Changsha dahuo zaiqing*, 1512–3. The losses of buildings are expressed in *jian*, the space between roof beams. A similar list of destruction is given in Luo, p. 109.

[29] Liang Xiaojing and Chen Xianshu, *1938: '11.13' Changsha dahuo* (Wuhan: Hebei renmin chubanshe, 2005), pp. 11–13.

Much of the local population escaped, as did many of the refugees, but the casualties still were huge, including almost all the wounded soldiers, who could not be moved. Two members of teams sent in to clean up the ruins recorded that their units buried about 20,000 corpses in the country outside the city. Two hundred thousand people were homeless.[30]

The disaster was so immense and the miscalculation so gross that someone had to be held responsible. The government turned on the men who had carried out the orders to burn the city. Chiang Kai-shek came to Changsha the day after the fire started and stayed for several days. Three senior commanders were arrested, tried by a military court, and executed.[31] The summary justice did not resolve the damage or prevent the spread of rumours that the fire was a plot led by Wang Jingwei, who was about to defect to the Japanese, to undermine the will to resist in China.[32]

The life of the city was annihilated. An Englishman who arrived in Changsha soon after the fire was appalled[33]:

When I arrived five weeks later the city was still dead. A few of the very poor had crept back to build themselves hovels of matting between the remaining walls, and in outlying areas a few shops, still intact, were beginning to open their shutters, but the main streets were not only destroyed, they were obliterated without trace in the indistinguishable acres of rubble and ash.

Changsha was the first major world city to suffer the total destruction that was later to become commonplace in World War II. It was the only city, until the burning of Guilin in 1944, to be destroyed by fire set by the 'defenders' rather than by incendiary bombs dropped by the enemy. It was a sacrifice to a combination grandiloquent patriotism at the top and incompetence on the ground.

These two scorched-earth disasters happened in areas still under Chinese control. There were no such disasters in the occupied areas. The damage there was less in physical scale but greater in terms of psychological pain.

Social Reconfiguration – Occupied China

The people who were left behind in the occupied areas were affected in quite different ways by the war than were those who left for uncertain

---

[30] Tang Xun, Mao Ling, 'Yi Changsha dahuo de shanhou gongzuo', in Bing Xin (ed.), *Kangzhan jishi* (Beiping: Youyi chubanshe, 1984), p. 125.

[31] Ren 40; Luo 112. The version that the local commanders alone were to blame was repeated for many years; see Wu Yixin, p. 7, 1948.

[32] Haldore Hanson, 'Firebrands and Chinese politics', *Amerasia*, III, 2 (April 1939), pp. 78–82.

[33] Richard Dobson, *China Cycle* (London: Macmillan, 1946), p. 135.

futures in unoccupied China. They were thrown in to a chronic state of uncertainty and insecurity that gradually distorted their lives. The social order was upset. The pre-war social and political hierarchy had been decapitated as government leaders and many members of the local elite fled into the interior. In the short run, there was no real elite placement.

The Japanese military and its civilian cohorts were poor occupiers. They made almost no attempt to acculturate to the world they had taken over. Instead, there was an insistence on humiliating and punishing local populations. Chinese were compelled to bow when they met a Japanese on the street, to perform an obeisance, an act that in Japan would be part of normal courtesy but was not in China. For all the official Japanese insistence that Chinese were happy with their new rulers, the reverse was true.

In the cities, the occupation severely restricted ordinary life. The activities of the Kempeitai, the Japanese secret police, and the Korean and Taiwanese agents of the occupiers created a climate of fear and mistrust that fostered insecurity and turned society in on itself. The civilian world was dominated by a fearful, anxious attitude towards life that drained much of the pleasure and spontaneity out of the lives of civilians. This description from an English missionary, Winifred Galbraith, who had gone for a brief visit to Beiping from her post in Hunan, contrasts the nature of fear in the two Chinas[34]:

In 'Unoccupied China' men fear air raids and the approach of the enemy; they fear greatly poverty and bandits and death. But fear of air raids is an exhilarating, if unsettling preoccupation; anything may happen at any time; one cannot possibly prepare for it, so take the short view and leave the future [to itself]. In the north that fear is removed, but the deadlier canker of caution inhibits action, and angers, all the more terrifying because they are unknown, lurk round every corner and at every chance meeting with a friend or acquaintance. Men fear to be noticed, walk carefully with a backward glance over their shoulder, suspect everyone, even members of their own family, only dreading that they may one day disappear and no one will ever know what has happened to them.

In the rural areas, remaining gentry members had already made the choice of staying and being willing to at least cooperate with the occupiers. The wisdom of their choice was soon undermined because in many of the rural areas the Japanese presence was fleeting and that of guerillas much longer term.

Japanese propaganda promoted a return to the old order, to Confucianism. In many places, the human remains of the old order

---

[34] Winifred Galbraith, *In China Now* (New York: William Morrow, 1941), p. 255.

2.6. **A Japanese cartoon.** (*Asia*, **November 1938.**)

re-emerged in the form of elderly survivors from the *ancien regime,* out of power since the 1911 revolution, who came out from the shadows and took on roles in the puppet governments. The dominance of youth that had come into being in the 1920s, with the emergence of young men in positions of military and political power, was reversed; the young had left, and the old had a second chance. With the re-emergence of the old men came the old outfits, taken out from the trunks in which they had been stored, the smell of camphor on them still. Zhongshan suits and leather shoes gave way to silk gowns, padded jackets, and cloth shoes.

A JAPANESE PROPAGANDA POSTER

The Japanese are doing all they can, by posters, to win over the Chinese. The wording on this poster says : " Come back to your homes ; Food will be given you ; Trust the Japanese Army." But the Chinese peasants are not convinced.

2.7. **A Japanese propaganda poster. (O. M. Green, 1941, p. 129.)**

In the 1920s and 1930s, the first tentative steps had been taken towards the emancipation of women. In the occupied areas, the war stopped that process in its tracks. The gender balance in the occupied areas was distorted. More men than women had departed into the army or as refugees. This distortion occurred at a time when women were especially vulnerable to an occupying army that showed little respect for women. Rape and the fear of rape kept women in constant anxiety, often virtual prisoners in their homes. Some courageous women did manage to continue lives outside the home, but many more retreated behind the walls of their homes.

People left in the occupied areas had an urgent problem in 1938 – to work out how they would live with the Japanese, how they would reframe their lives.

Living with the Enemy   The English word 'collaboration' covers a wide range of meaning from positive to deeply negative. The concept of 'collaboration with the enemy' is almost impossible to translate into Chinese. In Chinese, there are several terms to cover the negative end of the spectrum. The most heinous, *hanjian*, means 'traitor to the Chinese people'. No less evil but more derisory is *kuilei*, 'puppet'. Two less emotion-laden terms are *tongdi*, 'consorting with the enemy', and *qinRi*, 'being close to the Japanese'; both carry a strong overtone of opprobrium. The neutral translation of collaboration, *hezuo*, 'cooperation', had no meaning in the wartime context, but there *was* a term that expressed an understanding of what it meant to live under occupation: *huozhe*, meaning 'to live, to stay alive'.[35] The number of people who could be labelled with the first four terms, that is, those working actively with or for the Japanese, was quite limited. There were far more in the last category, people who simply tried to survive – regarded by the population of unoccupied China with varying degrees of pity and condemnation as 'slaves in a lost nation (*wang guo nu*)'.

There were regional variations in how people reacted to the Japanese. Taiwan and Manchuria were already under permanent Japanese control in 1937. Taiwan was the 'model colony', and Manchuria had been recast an 'autonomous' state, Manzhouguo. Taiwan prospered, with a well-developed infrastructure, efficient government, and a population that seemed to accept Japanese domination, although the Taiwanese were second-class subjects of the Japanese emperor.[36] Manzhouguo

---

[35] This is the title of a wonderful novel by Yu Hua and of the film based on it. Both describe the struggle for survival of a couple through three decades of modern history; their travail started in the war.

[36] Shao Minghuang, 'Taiwan in wartime', in Stephen MacKinnon and Diana Lary (eds.), *China at War* (Palo Alto, CA: Stanford University Press, 2007), pp. 91–109.

was denounced by China as a 'false (*wei*)' or 'puppet' state. Despite the trappings of statehood and installation of the former emperor Puyi as emperor, the reality was that the Japanese army was in charge. In both places, tough Japanese control made living with the enemy the only possible strategy. Resistance in Taiwan was out of the question – and in Manchuria, only in remote areas of mountain and forest was it possible for anti-Japanese guerrillas, the Manchurian Volunteers, to operate.

In the great northern cities, there was little overt resistance, but this lack of resistance could not be read as welcoming the in-comers. Those who did not or could not leave the cities at the start of the war accepted the Japanese occupation with resignation, without protest. But the city had a long tradition of living with occupiers, and the population had much recent experience of living with new rulers, given the frequency with which the government changed during the warlord period; there were eleven presidents between 1912 and 1928, some not exercising control much beyond the city. There was little support in Beiping for the GMD, which had moved the capital to Nanjing in 1928 and brought economic gloom to the old capital. Lin Yutang described the reactions of the Beiping population in the summer of 1937[37]:

Most of the people of the ancient capital, the true natives, gossiped imperturbably and even good-humouredly in their homes and teahouses about the coming of war and speculated about its outcome, but they went about their business as usual.

They disliked an invader, but they had seen other invaders before. There was a wild assortment of people living in Peking [Beiping], old, retired Manchu officials and young patriotic students, chicken-hearted officers and bland, cynical politicians, honest tradesmen and the poorest riffraff working as Japanese spies. But the average man was too civilized to like violence and war, and little inclined to terrorism and riots such as there were in Shanghai. He was mild, reserved, peace-loving, and indomitably patient.

The people of Beiping carried on a discreet resistance to their new rulers. One daily practice had to do with time. The Japanese put the time in occupied China forward by one hour, to Tokyo time – a sign of China's incorporation into a world governed by Tokyo. Wolfgang Franke, the German sinologist who lived in Beiping throughout the war, noted that local people continued to make their appointments by 'old time (*jiubiao*)', a tacit, daily reminder that their city was occupied.[38] He also witnessed a surprising act of patriotism: A teahouse girl he had brought home kissed

[37] Lin Yutang, *Moment in Peking* (New York: John Day, 1939), p. 742.
[38] Wolfgang Franke, *Im Banne Chinas* (Dortmund: Edition Cathay, 1997), p. 130. Uighurs in Xinjiang use a similar technique today, arranging their own lives by local time, which is three hours behind the official (Beijing) time.

a picture of Chiang Kai-shek in a German magazine that happened to be lying on his desk.[39]

The most famous depiction of life in occupied Beiping was the novel *Four Generations under One Roof* (*Sishi tongtang*), by Lao She. He fled to the interior at the start of the war, but his family lived through the occupation in Beiping.[40] He became the chronicler of the damage that the war was doing to Chinese people. In *The Traitor* [Reading 1], he also discussed the self-serving pretexts used for working with an incoming conqueror, something that the Chinese bureaucratic tradition had allowed for, and in the process conquering the conquerors.

Functionaries One of the obvious problems of the Japanese occupation was the low calibre of the leaders chosen to run the puppet governments. Some were men who had once had high reputations, such as Wang Jingwei and Wang Kemin, but Pu Yi, the emperor of Manzhouguo, was an unprepossessing young man said to be addicted to opium. Some of the men who served in occupation governments were even less attractive. A devastating critique of the members of the Beiping provisional government, sent to the Secretary of State for External Affairs in Ottawa, spoke in a stern Presbyterian voice[41]:

1. They are all old. They represent the 'old regime' which existed before the rise of the Kuomintang [Guomindang] Party to national power in 1927–28, and have been out of office in most cases since 1924 or earlier.
2. Their record and tradition is replete with treachery, intrigue, dishonesty and treason.
3. Almost without exception their personal lives have been loathsome and degraded.

Some of the collaborators in the business world were more impressive. Fu Xiaoan, who became the mayor of greater Shanghai, was a formidable financial brain – and a long-time opponent of the GMD. He returned from thirteen years in exile in Japanese-controlled Dalian to run Shanghai. His intention, like that of other business people, simply was to keep business going – unlike the patriotic capitalists who had moved their businesses to the interior. As Parks Coble has shown, the latter group was only a small proportion of the Shanghai business world.[42]

---

[39] *Ibid.*, p. 91.
[40] Lao She's *Sishi tongtang* was published in instalments between 1946 and 1950. An abridged translation, *The Yellow Storm* (translated by Ida Pruitt), came out in 1951 (New York; Harcourt Brace).
[41] National Archives of Canada, RG25/1753/804/VII. Report date 15/12/1937.
[42] Parks Coble, *Chinese Capitalists in Japan's New Order* (Berkeley: University of California Press, 2002).

Local Traitors   The low calibre of occupation functionaries was even more evident in county administrations, where opportunists came to the top, along with the dregs of society. This was particularly true in places where chaos was the norm for much of the war.

In some of the most contested areas, it was often difficult to tell who was in charge – or for how long. In Penglai, on the northeast coast of Shandong, the local government changed hands with sickening frequency. Penglai was a historic town, the jumping-off point for the mythical Islands of the Immortals, and a prosperous port, heavily involved with trade to Manchuria. The GMD garrison and the magistrate fled at the end of 1937. After that, the county was divided and re-divided between GMD supporters, Chinese Communist Party (CCP) supporters, active collaborators, and local gentry. In the county gazetteer, the changes in magistrate and township leaders over the next eight years cover six pages of dense print; the previous twenty-four years covered only one and a half pages.[43]

One of the few men to stay in power for the duration of the war was a local brawler, Hao Mingzhuan, who rose rapidly in 1938 after departure of the magistrate and local garrison, thanks to his own militia of several hundred men, recruited from friends and family and armed with weapons he manufactured in the old arsenal. He held power only in the county town and the area immediately around it. Magistrates came and went, but Hao stayed on top until the end of the war. He had a Japanese advisor, but Japanese troops scarcely came to the town. Hao maintained his own intelligence unit, whose job was to hunt down and assassinate anyone who threatened him; the pretext was always that the victim was a communist. One of his preferred methods of execution was burial alive.[44] Hao was in the mould of the former governor of Shandong, Han Fuju, a tough, crude, uneducated man. His role as top man in a county that had a long reputation for culture and prosperity was a sign of the degradation that the war had brought to the town.

There was a fundamental contradiction to the role of collaborators. Very rarely were they trusted by the Japanese, for the simple reason that they were traitors to their own people. In the areas under direct Japanese control, the collaborators were little more than window dressing; in areas such as Penglai, where there was no direct control, they were allowed a degree of independence – so long as they did nothing that might upset the Japanese, in which case retribution would have been swift.

---

[43] *Penglai xianzhi* (Jinan: JiLu sushe, 1995), pp. 11–17.

[44] Gong Zhugan, 'Wo suo zhidao de Hao Mingzhuan', *Penglai xianzhi* 1 (1985), pp. 23–o.

Conclusion

The second year of the war was as traumatic as the first for much of the population of China. Continuing military losses wiped out the brief elation of the spring counter-attack, the refugee movements were even greater than the year before, and the tragedies of Huayuankou and Changsha brought suffering on a scale close to the Nanjing Massacre. In the midst of all this chaos, however, the Chinese people showed stoicism and resilience – above all, China had not surrendered.

Readings

Reading 1: Lao She, The Traitor[45]

This story, written by Lao She in 1938, shows the cynicism that led some people to collaborate – or, put in more neutral terms, the realism that had always made men in certain positions work with and for whoever was in power:

Everything that a twentieth century Chinese can possibly enjoy and possess, Pao Shan-chin [Bao Shanqin] has been enjoying and possessing. He has money, a western-style house, an American motor car, children, concubines, curios, and books which serve as decoration; he also has reputation, position, and an impressive chain of official titles which can be printed on his visiting card and eventually included in his obituary notice; he has friends, all kinds of friends, and he has already enjoyed a fair share of longevity and health in a body fortified by varieties of tonics and stimulants.

If only he would allow himself to take things a little easier, to be a bit retiring-minded, he could rest wrapped in comforts. With his children and concubines to attend to his wants, life would be one effortless existence. Should he die at this moment, his wealth would more than provide for the comforts and pleasures of one or two generations of his children, and in the customary biographical sketch written for distribution after his death there would be enough poetic eulogies and lamentations to glorify his name. His coffin would be made of such expensive wood as to stand against erosion for scores of years. And he would, of course, have sixty-four coffin-bearers and be properly paraded through the main thoroughfares.

But Pao Shan-chin would not think of giving up what he and most people in China call 'a political career'. His political career does not involve any policy, or political ideal. He has only one determination, that is, not to be idle. He could not stand seeing other people in power and in the swim of

45 Wang Chi-chen (ed.), *Stories of China at War* (New York: Columbia, 1947), pp. 107–109.

things. He somehow feels that whatever he has no part in will eventually work against him; he must do all he can to frustrate it or crush it altogether. On the contrary, he misses no chance of getting into something. Like a fisherman, he always makes full use of the wind with his sail in order to reach the exact spot where he is sure to make the biggest catch. It matters little whether the direction of the wind would work havoc to others; so long as its sets his own sail flying he likes it.

That he has been able to sense which way the wind is blowing and to set his own sail to it accounts for the success of his political career. Once the sail is set right and has the full support of the wind, he will reap with the least effort what a politician in China rightfully expects.

Pao Shan-chin has no wish to retire. It would be doing himself injustice, to say the least, to let such foresight and genius as his go to waste. As he grows older, he becomes all the more conscious of the accuracy of his political fore-sight and the immaturity of others; to deny such gifts of expression would be absurd. He is only just past sixty and is confident that as long as he lives and his facilities remain what they are, there will be political activity wherever he breathes.

He hates those who have newly sprung into political prominence; even recent events seem distasteful to him. The older he grows, the more he feels that his old familiar friends are the best. For the good of his old friends, he would seize every opportunity that comes his way. He seems to have a natural aversion to things new: new terms, new systems, new theories; and that makes him cling to his old ways all the more tenaciously. He is ready to cooperate with anyone, foreign or Chinese, so long as his 'abilities' are recognized; for the same reason those who deny him power at once become his enemies. He admits that his 'political views' are extraordinarily tolerant; and that in deal-ing with people he is at times unscrupulous, and not entirely unoccupied from jealousy and prejudice. But why shouldn't he be so? All statesmen, he thinks, have been more or less like him. He is proud of the fact that he understands himself so thoroughly and that he is no hypocrite. Before those he can afford to challenge, he is capable of a kind of defiant showdown, expressed in a smile on his plum face which seems to say: 'Be my friend, or be my enemy; take your choice now!'

He has just celebrated his sixtieth birthday, and his photograph appears again in all the newspapers in the occupied territories. This time it bears the cap-tion: Mr. Pao Shan-chin, newly appointed head of the Commission on National Reconstruction. Glancing a few times at his photograph in the paper, he nods to himself complacently as if to say: 'The old guard, they can't do without me!' He thinks of his past political career and the experiences he has gone through, all of which seem to lend weight and prestige to his present new title, which in turn will give him still more experience, more prestige, paving the way for even higher titles to come. For what the future may yet hold in store for him, he can't help feeling expansively ambitious. For over two years, his picture has not appeared widely in the papers. To him, it is evidence enough that he is still going strong. New men may crop up from time to time, but he, old Pao Shan-chin, is like the firs and cypresses, which grow greener, firmer, and more luxuriant with age. For him, the consistent formula has always been to have and to hold. There is no other way to get along in this world, and for the *kuanliao* [officials] in China, this has always been and still is the golden rule to success.

Reading 2: 'The Eight Hundred Heroes'

This song, written in 1939, commemorates the battalion that fought on in Shanghai against certain defeat.

中國不會亡,中國不會亡,
你看民族英雄謝團長。
中國不會亡,中國不會亡,
你看那八百壯士孤軍奮鬥守戰場,
四方都是砲火,四方都是豺狼,
寧願死不退讓,寧願死不投降。
我們的國旗在重圍中飄蕩飄蕩,飄蕩飄蕩,飄蕩。
八百壯士一條心,十萬強敵不能擋,
我們的行動偉烈,我們的氣節豪壯,
同胞們起來!同胞們起來!
快快趕上戰場,拿八百壯士做榜樣。
中國不會亡,中國不會亡,
中國不會亡,中國不會亡!
不會亡!不會亡!不會亡!

China must not be lost, China must not be lost
See our peoples' hero Colonel Xie.
China must not be lost, China must not be lost
See the eight hundred heroes, cut off, holding the line
With shell fire all around, with savage beats all around
They choose to die rather than retreat, die rather than surrender
Surrounded by the enemy, our flag flies, flies high, flies high,
A hundred thousand enemy soldiers cannot defeat eight hundred united heroes
We are brave in action, heroic in spirit.
Rise up, fellow Chinese! Rise up fellow Chinese!
Rush to the battlefield, with the eight hundred heroes as our model
China must not be lost, China must not be lost
China must not be lost, China must not be lost
Must not be lost, must not be lost, must not be lost.

Reading 3: 'Open Letter to Zhou Zuoren'[46]

This bitter denunciation appeared in *Kangzhan wenyi* on May 14, 1938. It was signed by 18 major intellectuals, including Mao Dun, Yu Dafu, Hu Feng, Hu Qiuyuan, Zhang Tianyi, and Ding Ling. The elegance and erudition of the language make the denunciation all the more scathing.

Mr. Zuoren:

Last autumn when Beiping and Tianjin fell, and the members of the literary world came south, we learned that you had stayed in the old capital. Every time we heard about how the violent enemy was trampling on culture, and persecuting young students, we were concerned for your safety. Friends even telegraphed you to find out what was going on, and found out from your reply that you had decided to hang on in Beiping. We understood the difficulties that had prevented you from leaving. We hoped you were carrying on the fight on the literary front. But to our shock we have found out from the enemy's recent publications that you have taken part in meetings for the revival of Chinese culture organised in Beiping by the enemy bandits. The photographs and the text prove it; this is not a fabrication. Your behaviour is a betrayal of your people; you have grovelled before the enemy. In the literary world there is not one of us who does not feel regret at what you have done, not one who does not feel it is shameful. You have been one of the pillars of our literary world, you have been a professor in a national university, you have been honoured by the state and by society. But now you fly in the face of public opinion, you bequeath to the literary world the disgrace of betraying your country, and toadying to the enemy. Although we care deeply for you, we cannot, on this great moral issue, go against our conscience because we care for you.

Unless what you did was accidental, we feel that the basic reason for your making friends of the enemy must lie in your long-standing disdain for the Chinese people and your pessimism about them. Someone who buries their head in books, and cuts themselves off from the world may easily develop what amounts to an illness of abnormal psychology. Your may have been pleased with your self-satisfied detachment, and your mastery of indifference, but to young people who loved reading what you wrote you have done immeasurable damage. If you are willing to take even a brief look at the present reality, you will understand our people's heroic battle over the last ten months, which showed the spirit of a great people, who could be killed but never disgraced. At the same time the wicked killing and destruction that the enemy has inflicted in so many places just shows how shallow and brittle the civilisation of the island country [Japan] is.

[46] First published in *Zhanshi wenyi*, 7/6/1938; reprinted in Zhang Juxiang et al., *Zhou Zuoren nianpu* (Tianjin: Tianjin renmin chubanshe, 2000), pp. 550–552.

continued

When civilisation and savagery are so far apart, then what you normally like or dislike is irrelevant. At this moment when the nation lies between life and death, it is impossible not to ask whether an individual deserves honour or disgrace. After close examination, we must accuse you.

For one last time we give you our sincere advice, and hope that you will realise the wrong that you have done, repent and leave Beiping as soon as possible, and come south and take part in the work of resisting the enemy and building up the nation. Because of your past contributions to the literary world, if you can show your repentance, it will not be difficult to restore our esteem. Failing that [course of action], there can only be denunciation, and a public declaration that you are a great national criminal, and a traitor to the literary world. A wrong decision taken in a moment of weakness will lead to [the kind of choice between] loyalty and evil behaviour that fortunately occurs only once in a thousand years!

Reading 4: 'Soldiers' Wives'

This is a song sung by a group of soldiers to ward off anxieties about what their wives might be doing by convincing themselves of how much their wives were missing them.[47]

> In the night's first watch, the moonlight shines on the paper pane
> Why does my husband not come back?
> When a soldier leaves he is three years gone
> How can I bear those three years long?
> In the second watch the moon shines full on the paper pane
> I'm sorry I married a soldier!
> A soldier lad is like a river on its long way to the sea,
> Always leaving ... leaving ... never coming back to me
> In the third watch the moon shines bright as can be,
> The Spinning Girl waits on one bank of the wide, wide Milky Way
> While the herd boy stands alone on the other.
> But they are gods who have a least one day a year together.
> But the soldier and his wife will not meet in a thousand autumns ...

[47] T'ien Chun (Xiao Jun), *Village in August* (London: Collins, 1942), pp. 41–42.

In the fourth watch the moon is waning now,
Will not the soldier and his wife meet even in their dreams?
A baby's empty rice bowl drove you away from home.
Two who loved one another are as far away from each other
As the East from the West
When the fifth watch comes the moon hangs in the western heavens:
In all the world are there any who know the hardships of the soldier?
Winning, he must only go farther away,
Losing his bones will rot on the field, his bones will rot on the field

Film

To Live (Huozhe). Director Zhang Yimou, 1994.

水深火熱
The water is deep, the fire hot

Events

In 1939, the war entered a new phase. The end of the first phase of the war left China severely bloodied but not defeated. 'Eighteen months of war had left her stronger rather than weaker. The first terrifying shock had been met and absorbed. Both the people and the army knew what to expect now. They were binding their wounds and setting their teeth with grim determination.'[1] The next three years were a period of prolonged stalemate that ended only after the war expanded at the end of 1941 into the Pacific War. The government put a positive twist to the gloomy picture of stalemate; the Japanese advance had been halted[2]:

	Days	Total Japanese advance	Advance per day
1937	177	3085 km	17.4 km
1938	365	2765 km	7.6 km
1939	365	415 km	1.1 km
1940	365	215 km	0.6 km

The lines held largely because they were real topographic lines; the Japanese armies could not fight mechanised war in the ranges of mountains and hills that form a barrier from the north to the south of China.

---

[1] Evans Carlson, *Twin Stars of China* (New York: Dodd, Mead, 1940), p. 295. Carlson was a brilliant young American army officer who travelled widely in China in 1938, in both occupied and unoccupied China.

[2] Lin Yutang, 'The four-year war in review', *Asia*, July 1941, p. 335.

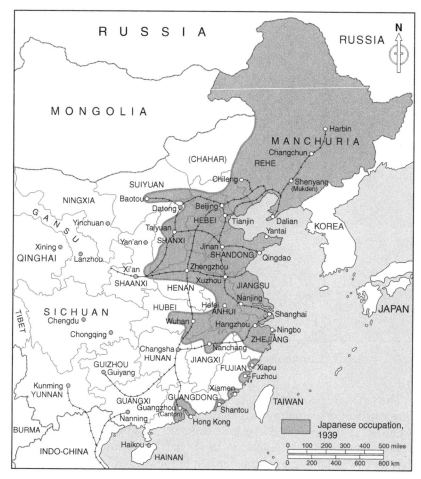

Map 2. **Japanese Occupation, 1939**

The major battles were now over, but there was active guerrilla resistance in Shandong, Zhejiang, Jiangxi, Fujian, Guangdong, Hubei, and Shanxi, some launched by Guomindang (GMD) troops, some by Chinese Communist Party (CCP) forces, and some by local militias. There were also independent fighters, known simply as *minbing*, 'soldiers from among the people', who might be bandits, outlaws, or armed peasants. The guerrillas were not well coordinated, many were poorly armed, and they lived off the local population, but their sporadic attacks on railway lines, roads, convoys, and military outposts made the Japanese insecure outside the major urban centres in the vast area they technically occupied.

Map 3. **Chongqing-centred China**

The Japanese occupation of north China was an administrative failure. One reason for the failure was the false assumption on the part of the occupiers that there would be little difficulty in administering a people whose language was so similar to their own. The similarity was deceptive; it allowed for some comprehension of the written language, through common characters, but none at all of the spoken language. Another, much more important reason was the Yamato nationalism that inspired most Japanese soldiers and civilians at the time and made them feel racially superior to the Chinese. The Japanese in China did not establish closeness with the people whose land they occupied, not even with the people who worked for them. They could not go beyond being occupiers who dealt out harsh treatment to anyone who resisted them; resistance meant the arrest or execution of individuals and reprisals against communities [Reading 1].

Forced out of eastern China, the GMD government consolidated its hold over western China, something it had not managed to do before the war. The west was less isolated than it had been. The war demanded the opening of the back doors to unoccupied China. The first were in the southwest, through Yunnan, along the single-track railway to Haiphong and along the Burma Road, built in 1938 through precipitous mountains. The second was in the northwest, through Xinjiang along the ancient Silk Road; major road-building projects were started, notably a 2,500-kilometre stretch from Xi'an to Urumqi. The use of these back doors was not reliable; geopolitics got in the way. The Nazi-Soviet Pact (August 1939) made the Xinjiang connection almost useless. Chongqing still had air connections to Hong Kong and increasingly to India over the stupendous mountains referred to ironically as the '*Hump*' but these limited connections could not diminish the feeling in Chongqing that China was alone, that her allies were impotent or otherwise engaged.

An obscure event in the summer of 1939 changed the direction of the war. Soviet troops defeated Japanese troops who had moved across the Manchurian border into Mongolia. The crushing defeat at Nomonhan convinced the Japanese high command that there was no possibility of defeating the USSR; their attention turned permanently away from the north and northwest towards the south and southwest. Equally threatening to the southwest was the formal establishment of the Germany-Italy-Japan Axis in September 1940. The Vichy government in France gave Japan the right to station troops in Indochina, cutting off China's access by rail from the sea.

The long period of military stalemate saw a steady growth in the strength of the CCP. Mao Zedong appeared to have consolidated his hold on the leadership of the party. In the rural areas of north China, the CCP began to have some success in exerting control over existing guerrillas and in mobilising rural populations. Communist cadres began to fill the gap left in local affairs by the departure or collaboration of the local elite, although in many areas guerrilla actions were still locally organised. Guerrilla actions were dangerous to local populations. The reprisals after guerrilla actions were terrible. If, as Mao said, 'the guerrillas were fish who swam in the water of the people', the Japanese army responded to guerrilla actions by 'draining the water' – launching campaigns of terror against villages throughout north China.

A blood feud

In the political arena, the united front between the GMD and the CCP turned sour. The long-running hostility between the two had not been resolved. The growing military strength of the CCP was demonstrated in late 1940 in the Hundred Regiments Offensive, although the Japanese counter-offensive was so powerful that the CCP did not mount any further positional campaigns. The New Fourth Army Incident, an armed clash between GMD and CCP forces in Anhui, was the last straw. By early 1941, it was clear that the united front had broken down and that neither side was interested in repairing it. Their mutual antipathy handed Japan an unexpected advantage.

The first half of 1941 was one of the lowest points of the war. Then came a cascade of international events that changed the course of the war. In June, Germany launched Operation Barbarossa, an invasion of the USSR. The war in Europe shifted into a new gear, with the USSR now one of the Allies – and the major focus of German attacks. At the end of the year, the Japanese attack on Pearl Harbor catapulted the United States into the war in Asia and in Europe. American fury at Japan brought new energy and material support into the China's war.

The Reach of Government

The war brought a seismic shift in Chinese political power. With all the old seats of power in enemy hands, the locus of power shifted to the interior, carried by the migrations of the government, the armies, and much of the academic and creative talent of the nation.[3]

Future historians of the Sino-Japanese War will emphasize, to the China National Government's credit, a feat that is obvious but little realized in its full magnitude. This feat was the successful transfer in the midst of a desperate war of the National Government's complete administrative apparatus from those parts of China which it dominated formerly to those where prior to the war Nanking enjoyed only nominal authority.

West China was opening up. Where in the past 'superior' people had gone there only when sent as a form of punishment, now they were settled there for the duration, in patriotic flight. Provincial towns, once regarded by sophisticates in the east as hopelessly backward, were transformed, Chongqing as the capital, Guilin as the hub of culture, and Kunming as the university centre. The movement west meant the rapid growth of interior cities. Between 1937 and 1942, the population of Chongqing went from just over 450,000 to over 760,000, Guilin from 81,000 to 275,000, Guiyang from 121,000 to nearly 200,000 people, and Kunming from 151,000 to over 200,000.[4] Smaller towns in the interior went through similar booms.

---

[3] *China Weekly Review*, October 18, 1940, p. 223.

[4] Zhang Genfu, *Kangzhan shiqi de renkou qianyi* (Beijing: Chaoyang ribao chubanshe, 2006), p. 51.

With the move west of so many people came a simultaneous social levelling. Part of the levelling was financial. Many of the newcomers were now poor, without the resources they had enjoyed before the war. The host communities, by contrast, were booming, both the urban areas and the rural areas beyond them. The demand for labour increased rapidly, as did the prices of primary products. A by-product of the bombing was an acute housing shortage. Many of the refugees from the east went to live in villages and actually lived in peasant homes, something unthinkable before the war. The locals and the in-comers influenced each other in unexpected ways. The sociologist Fei Xiaotong described the impact of his family on the household they shared with a peasant family near Kunming[5]:

My landlady is able to learn from my wife the way of bringing up children. And, owing to my constant interference, the beating of his wife by my landlord has become less frequent in our house than before.

The war was creating a wave of social change in unoccupied China on a scale and at pace that even the most ambitious social reformers (including Fei himself) would ever have imagined possible before the war.

Topics and Case Studies

Endurance

吃苦耐劳
Eat bitterness and endure hardship

At this stage of the war, the uplifting ideal of transcendence through suffering dominated public predictions of how the war would go. The concept of endurance was based on the belief that China was inured to suffering and could transcend it, as she had done so often in the past. China's greatest strength was the ability to 'eat bitterness and endure hardship'. W. H. Donald, an advisor to Chiang Kai-shek, made an analogy between man-made disasters and natural ones. 'Natural calamities, which have had a habit through the centuries of wiping out thousands and thousands, sometimes millions, of people in one fell swoop, have bred in the blood and the bone of the Chinese race the powers of survival

---

[5] Fei Xiaotong, 'Some social problems of unoccupied China', in H. F. MacNair (ed.), *Voices from Unoccupied China* (Chicago: The University of Chicago Press, 1944), pp. 54–55.

that enable them quickly to subdue and overcome the effects of appalling catastrophes.'[6]

Owen Lattimore, the pre-eminent expert on China and Inner Asia, had a variation of the theme. China had the capacity, because of its vastness in land and people, to overcome hideous adversity: 'China's greatest power of resistance has lain in its ancient resources – an amorphous, decentralized territory and a multitudinous people capable of spontaneous unity.'[7]

There was real force to the belief in endurance. F. M. Edwards, a British psychologist working in China with the International Red Cross, was impressed by the Chinese ability to cope and by their 'realistic attitude' towards the war. 'There was no minimizing of the horrors, the privations and the miseries, nor yet a stoical endurance of them; but one saw an acceptance of them as an essential part of things as they are.' People just got on with it.[8]

The constant reiteration of a theme so ancient and so atavistic had a compelling impact; it turned people's minds away from the victories of the Japanese and the terrible humiliation they had brought to China. The stress was on survival, on keeping going, enduring – in the words of novelist Pearl Buck in November 1939, 'He who lives, wins.'[9] It also made the war seem quintessentially Chinese because the reference was not to humanity in general, to any country under attack, but to their own ancient culture. It linked endurance to nationalism and to national unity. By enduring hardship, every Chinese could contribute to the war effort.

To underline the message, the government mounted propaganda campaigns to mobilise the population. Those who tried to stay aloof from the war effort were vilified in speeches, writings, and cartoons. The New Life Movement, started in the mid-1930s, was intensified. It laid down simplicity, an almost ascetic approach to life. Clothing changed to match the new mood. In Chongqing, men now wore military uniforms or sombre Zhongshan suits; women wore simple cotton gowns. In Guangxi, a provincial uniform was promoted. 'To brand the shirker publicly and shame him into usefulness, the Kwangsi [Guangxi] Provincial Government had provided every war-worker, male and female, with a Sun Yat-sen suit – a highly practical semi-military uniform with flap pockets and buttoned

[6] W. H. Donald, Letter to Harold Timperley, December 30, 1938, p. 55. National Archives of Canada, RG25/1755/XIV.

[7] Owen Lattimore, Letter, November 11, 1938. National Archives of Canada RG25/1754/XII.

[8] F. R. Edwards, 'Impressions of China under war conditions', in *Individual Psychology Medical Pamphlets*, Vol. 22 (London: C. W. Daniel, 1940), p. 43.

[9] Pearl Buck, 'He who lives, wins', *Asia*, November 1939, pp. 635–636.

up to the neck so that collars are unnecessary. Badges worn on the left breast denoted the organisation to which the person belonged.'[10] The movement also attacked personal behaviours in sometimes petty ways, such as forcing labourers to wear shirts to cover their naked chests. This was mocked by many journalists and intellectuals, who saw it as superficial and silly, but one campaign was universally appreciated – the one to stop men peeing and crapping wherever they felt like.

By mid-1941, the spirit of endurance was wearing thin. However great the willingness to support the national cause, many people who had fled to unoccupied China were worn down by the constant shortages and discomforts of their lives. They were aware that the people they had left behind, the people living in the occupied cities, were living much better than they were. The reasons for the sacrifices they had made were hard to keep fresh. The war had already dragged on for four years. Madame Chiang Kai-shek (Song Meiling) was a forceful critic of what she saw as the moral weaknesses of the people around her [Reading 2].

Movements of People

The great flight migrations that started in 1937 and continued in 1938 were still going on in 1939 and 1940. People and institutions moved further and further inland. The flood of humanity moved into poorer and poorer provinces – Guangxi, Yunnan, and Guizhou. These places were remote enough to be safe from Japanese attack – and also remote enough that they had seldom received 'outside province (*waisheng*)' people before. The outsiders moved into places whose dialects they did not understand, and they ate foods they had never seen before. Some of them complained bitterly and constantly, others adapted, but few of them felt at home. They were in limbo, not in a new home.

Separation and Reunion   The huge refugee movement had produced innumerable family separations and divisions. Now the reality of the separations was settling in, and with it came the fear that the separations might be permanent. A veteran journalist described the pain of separation[11]:

In both the Chinese and Japanese-occupied areas there are hundreds of thousands of homeless people who have lost all contact with their families. Husbands

[10] Rhodes Farmer, *Shanghai Harvest* (London: Museum, 1945), p. 200. The Zhongshan suit was later adopted virtually as a uniform in the Mao era and hence is often known in the west as a Mao suit.
[11] Hallet Abend, *Chaos in China* (London: Bodley Head, 1940), p. 138.

do not know whether their wives and children are living or dead. Aged parents cannot contact sons or daughters, and may never hear from or see any of them again. These personal griefs and uncertainties collectively constitute a mighty and unrecorded drama of sorrow.

There were reunions as well as separations. Some refugees found themselves in places with which they had ancestral connections; they could move in with relatives whom they had never met. In 1939, the young writer Han Suyin and her new husband arrived at her uncle's house in Chongqing; it was their first meeting[12]:

But this is not real! It is a dream and a memory out of a past that is gone, with all its graces and amenities. The clean-swept courtyards, the spacious *keh-tang* [*ketang*], with its softly shaded lights, its deep-piled rugs, its chairs and sofas spread with tiger skins and golden monkey furs, the gleam of lacquer and gilding, the tall blue vase with its great branches of *lah-mei* [*lamei*, wintersweet], translucent gold flowers with the scent of spring – all of this luxury and comfort are of another world. With the dust of our abominable journey [Wuhan-Changsha-Guilin-Guizhou-Chongqing] still upon us, we lean back in huge, soft arm-chairs and sip tea from cups of thin porcelain

It *was* unreal – the house was destroyed in a bombing raid soon afterwards, and the young couple was once again homeless. Their refuge was in the city that came to be one of the most heavily bombed in the world.

Chongqing   Chongqing was transformed in late 1938 and early 1939 from a remote provincial city into the capital of China. The population ballooned. The central government, the military high command, universities, schools, and several hundred factories moved up through the Yangzi Gorges from Shanghai, Nanjing, and Wuhan to the 'temporary' capital (*peidu*).

Behind the Yangzi Gorges, Chongqing was safe from invasion. This security was one of its few assets. As a place to live, it left much to be desired. The city is built on the cliffs at the juncture of the Jialing and Yangzi Rivers. In the late 1930s, there were few roads, steep flights of steps crawled up the cliffs, and on the top the streets that ran along the peninsula were narrow and congested. The city teemed with humanity. There was an acute housing shortage, and even the government leaders lived in cramped conditions. Most of the in-comers did not have houses but lived in any kind of temporary shelter or crowded into tiny apartments.

---

[12] Han Suyin, *Destination Chungking* (London: Jonathan Cape, 1942), p. 167.

Chongqing had a hideous climate – chill cold in winter, torrid heat in summer.[13] It was frequently blanketed in fog. Humidity levels were so high that walls were permanently covered in black mould and green slime. Human beings shared the city with rats, cockroaches, and voracious mosquitoes. The humidity bred diseases, especially tuberculosis and dysentery. The smell of disease was in the air, in the 'damp, urinous smell which hangs over Szechwan like a cloud.'[14]

For all its disadvantages, the city functioned well for the first years of the war. The population was energised by strident and sometimes effective propaganda campaigns and put to work in organised volunteer work. The greatest contribution to the war spirit in Chongqing, however, came from the enemy and its relentless bombing.

Chongqing was the first world capital to be systematically bombed. Between February 1938 and August 1943 the city was bombed over 200 times, on virtually every day that the skies were clear. The city was an easy target, a fairly short flight from Wuhan, where Japanese bomber bases were installed after the city was captured. Japanese pilots simply had to fly west along the Yangzi, with no fear of encountering resistance. There was virtually no anti-aircraft cover; the city's only protection was bad weather. Thirty thousand people were killed and injured in the raids.[15] In the single most ferocious raid, on May 4, 1939 (the twentieth anniversary of the start of the nationalist May 4th demonstrations against Japanese territorial ambitions in China), 4,400 people were killed and 3,100 injured. An American standing in the garden of the US embassy on the river bank opposite the city observed the May 4 raids[16]:

... the city of Chungking [Chongqing] boiled in a sudden upheaval of flying wreckage and black dust, while, with the terrific of bursting bombs which seemed to explode simultaneously, there came a fierce blast of air that bent the trees around us. The black shroud billowed over the whole rock of Chungking, and for some minutes it seemed as though the whole city had gone. As the dust settled the smoke rose above it, and in that cloud which was Chungking's sunset to a cloudless day strange red flares half a mile above the city showed the location of the fires that raged below. By nightfall the entire horizon was red with fires.

---

[13] Chongqing is one of the three furnaces of the Yangzi Valley, with Wuhan and Nanjing. Summer temperatures over 40°C are common.

[14] J. K. Fairbank, *Chinabound* (New York: Harper & Row, 1982), p. 228.

[15] Zhang Ruide, 'In the shadow of the bombs: Psychological responses to air raids on Chongqing during the Anti-Japanese War', pp. 1, 2. This article was based on interviews with 40 survivors of the Chongqing bombing conducted in 2004.

[16] Robert Ekvall, 'The bombing of Chungking', *Asia*, August 1939, p. 472. May 4 is a symbolic day celebrated in China as the anniversary of the start of the nationalist movement in 1919.

Chongqing fought back. The city authorities developed an efficient system of air raid alarms that gave people time to reach the air raid shelters dug into the sides of the cliffs. The population learned how to react[17]:

Late in the evening there was an air-alarm; the red triangles were hoisted on the mast above the Meifang Bank, and the Street of the Seven Stars was in swirling flood – people were rushing in every direction, small carts piled with luggage, rickshas weighed down with six or seven packing cases, even bicycles were loaded with the family property. The shutters went down with a bang. Motor cars went screaming out into the countryside. There is something merciless in this great river of people rushing down the streets in the dust and smoke of the evening, something terrifying, resembling the Yangtse [Yangzi] in full flood. They run not because they are afraid, but because the sound of the sirens and the great triangles on the high buildings remind them of the past; and instinctively they race towards the shelters. Even if they took no thought of running, their limbs would carry them away.

Thanks to the shelters, the loss of life was less than it might have been, though still high amongst fire wardens and the police [Reading 3]. The physical damage was enormous. Many of the bombs were incendiaries, and much of the city, built of wood and bamboo, was destroyed. Occasionally, a worthy target was hit. Chongqing people experienced a high degree of *Schadenfreude* when the German embassy was destroyed (without casualties), coincidentally on the same day that Buckingham Palace in London was hit by German bombs – September 13, 1940, of course a Friday.[18]

Bombing of civilian targets was a new form of warfare for combatants as well as civilians. There was a complete detachment between the pilots inflicting the damage and their unseen victims below. The detachment amounted to indifference and callousness, captured in the account of a Japanese observer flying with a bomber formation in 1941 over the city[19]:

... there, a bit ahead, spread out the half-ruined city of Chungking. It seemed familiar enough – the block of buildings on a sandstone bluff between two rivers – for I had seen many air views of Chiang's capital. From that height and distance its honey-combed ruins looked like the excavated remains of a very ancient civilization. Was it pure fantasy or was it a prophecy?

... Now we were striking across the sky directly above the blotchy city. No fighting planes rose to challenge the attack. Then bomb after bomb could be

[17] Robert Payne, *Chungking Diary* (London: Heinemann, 1945), p. 274.
[18] *China Critic*, XXX, 12 (September 14, 1940), p. 68.
[19] Kinji Sudo, 'How we bombed Chungking', *Asia*, October 1941, p. 585.

seen bursting and throwing up myriads of freakish cloud formations, movie-slow motionwise, like so many brown roses bursting in to bloom.

Chongqing was bombed more than any other city in China, but almost every city and town in unoccupied China was bombed at some point during the war. The Japanese air force had complete control of the air and could bomb at will. The main aim seems to have been to spread terror amongst the civilian population.

Wartime bombing of China[20]

	Raids	Bombs	Deaths	Injured	Buildings (jian)
1937	1,076	10,240	3,532	5,252	5,364
1938	2,528	50,252	19,885	30,060	75,834
1939	2,603	60,174	28,463	31,546	13,8171
1940	2,069	50,118	18,829	21,830	107,760
1941	1,858	43,308	14,121	16,902	97,714
1942	828	12,435	6,718	3,853	17,609
1943	664	13,642	2,333	3,406	14,161
1944	917	11,266	557	766	1,173
1945	9	3,718	84	91	151
Total	12,592	255,153	94,522	114,506	457,927

The terror induced by the sound of sirens and the intense fear never went away; many of the people who experienced the bombing were haunted by nightmares for the rest of their lives and could never hear a siren without jumping out of their skin.[21] The bombing had a positive side effect: It created an atmosphere of discipline and order. When the alarm signals went up, people hurried into the shelters in an orderly way, helped those who were less speedy, and looked after each other once inside the damp, gloomy shelters. The bombing created a collective consciousness and a sense of community that went beyond the propaganda efforts of the government.

Xinan Lianda[22]   The students who fled from the northern universities went first to Changsha and Wuhan. In late 1938, they had to move again. Some went to Chengdu, the provincial capital of Sichuan. Others went to Guiyang and Zunyi, two small cities in Guizhou. Most

[20] Guoshiguan, *Riben zai Hua baoxinglu* (Taibei: Guoshiguan, 1985), p. 755.
[21] Zhang, pp. 3–5.
[22] For a detailed study of the university, see John Israel, *Lianda: A Chinese University in War and Revolution* (Palo Alto, CA: Stanford University Press, 1998).

went to Kunming, the capital of Yunnan, a beautiful lakeside city, with one of the best climates in the world: 'four seasons all spring (*siji ru chun*)'. They made the journey by road, in buses and trucks, and on foot. A large contingent of Qinghua students marched for two months across the mountains from Changsha to Kunming, following almost the same route that the Long March had taken four years before. One of their leaders was the frail poet Wen Yiduo.

In Kunming, one of the world's greatest universities came in to being, Xinan Lianda, the South West United University, made up of faculty and students from Peking, Qinghua, and Nankai Universities. Students found themselves at a university at which many of China's foremost academics were teaching. Zhu Ziqing, Wen Yiduo, Qian Duansheng, Chen Da, Wu Han, Pan Guangdan, Fei Xiaotong, Feng Youlan, Qian Mu, and Liang Shuming were members of the brilliant transitional generation of Chinese intellectuals, educated as children in the classical tradition and then at one of China's new universities. Most of them had done graduate studies abroad, and most spoke fluent English.

The official attitude towards students and war was different from that in Western countries, where young men were expected to put their education on hold and 'do their bit'. In China, students were not expected to go into the armed forces; they made their contribution by studying, preparing for the return of peace, and the resumption of government by men (and a few women) of talent and training. They did not pay fees or residence charges, and they were given modest government grants for food and books – never a large amount and, as inflation took hold, quite inadequate, so students were usually near destitution. Whatever their privations, the distinction of having studied at Lianda put the students into a select intellectual elite, made even more distinguished when two of its former students, Yang Zhenning and Li Zhengdao, shared the Nobel prize for Physics in 1957.

As the war went on, the students' mood changed, from excitement to disenchantment and eventually anger with the GMD government, which they labelled increasingly as 'reactionary'. They were not communists; they wanted a liberal, Western-style of politics that the GMD had come to abhor. The hostility between government and intellectuals crystallised shortly after the war in the assassination, on the streets of Kunming, of two of the leading liberal academics, Wen Yiduo and Li Gongpu.

Rural resettlement   The universities' stay in the southwest was assumed to be temporary. Other wartime relocations were not. The assumption at the start of the war was that refugee movements all would be temporary, but soon it became clear that many refugees were not going home. Something had to be done with them. This conclusion meshed with a traditional predilection of Chinese governments to settle Han Chinese populations in the south and west, turbulent areas that they periodically tried to control. One means was the forced settlement of people whom governments considered undesirable – criminals, dissidents, soldiers, and the poor. The chief target area for wartime resettlement was the west, the vast region that accounts for almost half of China's land area; it has very low population densities, rich resources – but very little water. The western regions had been visited by periodic waves of Han resettlement since the first dynasty, the Qin. The process was never easy. Some form of coercion was needed; convicts and dissidents were branded on their foreheads to make sure that they could never return. The war presented a chance for the GMD government.

At the end of 1938, the government announced plans to resettle five million refugees.[23] The scheme was driven not only by the need to resettle refugees but also by the need to open land for grain cultivation because the eastern grain baskets were occupied.

These ambitious plans were not implemented in full, but the government did develop some settlement projects for refugees. The largest was the Huanglongshan Project in Shaanxi, where over 50,000 people from Henan were settled. These were some of the refugees who fled into Shaanxi during the war, increasing the province's population by 35%, from just under 10 million to almost 14 million. Of these, 900,000 were refugees from the Yellow River flood.[24]

The government encouraged local authorities in all parts of unoccupied China to resettle refugees, but the needs were so great that government intervention alone could not solve the problems. Voluntary organisations got involved. In Gansu, the China Industrial Cooperatives (INDUSCO), led by the energetic New Zealander Rewi Alley, set up workshops to provide work for refugees and local people.[25] George Hogg, a young English teacher, described a village outside Lanzhou where 200 refugees from the bombing of Lanzhou made blankets – 13,000 of them – out of wool purchased from local peasants.[26] The wool spun in Gansu had once been sent to Tianjin, where it was woven into 'Tientsin' carpets for export to the West. The war had broken this

[23] *China Critic*, XXIII, 10, p. 158, 1938.

[24] Li Lixia, Wang Jianjun, '*Kangzhan shiqi ruShaan yimin chunti de renkou fenxi*', *Xibei renkou*, 3.3 (2006), p. 5.

[25] The short form of INDUSCO was *gonghe*; it entered the English language in its old romanisation – Gung Ho.

[26] George Hogg, 'The new countryside', *China Journal*, XXXIV, 3 (March 1941), pp. 138–142.

network and left the local producers with nowhere to sell their wool. The cooperatives filled the gap.

The CCP was also involved in the resettlement of peasant refugees. Its most famous Shaanxi resettlement project was at Nanniwan, developed by the 8th Route Army. There was spontaneous resettlement of refugees throughout the communist-held areas. In one of the largest, the Shanganning Base (*Shanganning genjudi*), there were over a quarter of a million refugees, 20% of the population.[27] Refugees also settled in previously uninhabitable areas. When the Yellow River changed course in 1938, after the dike was breached, the old bed of the river dried up. The river bottom was covered in rich soil. Tens of thousands of displaced peasants settled there, in several hundred new villages. This solution was not as neat as it seemed. The inhabitants of the new villages were still dispossessed. New villages are looked at askance in China; they have no history and are assumed to be made up of rootless people, probably of dubious morality; the term 'mixed surname village (*zaxingcun*)' is one of contempt. In their sad condition, these people turned out to be excellent recruits for the CCP, which was becoming expert at providing leadership and some hope to the distressed and dispossessed. They were offered a new society to replace the old.

All these means of resettling refugees could not resolve the problems of uprooted people. Some found that they could not take the hardships of involuntary migration and trickled home; others wandered from place to place, hoping to find a new home. They were victims of upheaval. They experienced very little of the transformative aspects of upheaval that official promotion of endurance promised.

While the government planned to resettle refugee peasants on the land, some local peasants were going in the opposite direction. In the unoccupied areas, there were new opportunities for labour in the army, in construction, and in industry. This was particularly true for those at the bottom of the rural economy, the day labourers, once at the mercy of landowners and now able to find work outside their villages.

Refugee resettlement divided peasants from the wider family, the cousins, uncles, and aunts, all of whom are defined very precisely in Chinese; some matter more than others, but to have none at all was desolate. Saddest of all was the loss of formally unrecognised family connections, those of a woman with her natal family (*niangjia*), connections that might have remained close and warm after marriage if only she had stayed close to her own home but now were broken. Refugee women lost

---

[27] Zhang Genfu, pp. 199–200.

contact with their own families, and refugee families lost touch with their married daughters.

One thing that was clear was that the war had produced permanent social damage and that in many areas no return to normal life was possible; too much of the physical basis of society had been destroyed. An American missionary who had been a refugee in the summer resort of Guling when he finally came down from the mountain to be evacuated from the Yangzi port of Jiujiang reported[28]:

Our journey to Kiukiang [Jiujiang] took us through an area which had been totally devastated by the war. The countryside was entirely denuded of its inhabitants. The only people we passed on this lonely road were scattered groups of those collies who had helped carry our baggage down the mountain, who were returning on foot to Kiukiang. The houses and farmsteads on either side of the road were in ruins. The usually well-cared for farm lands of this area were untilled and untended. When we entered the city of Kiukiang itself we found the same dreary desolation on every hand. Apart from that area which had formerly been the British Concession the city was in ruins and deserted.

This region was only one of the areas of China that were ravaged by the war. All along the rivers, main roads, and railways, especially in Jiangsu, Zhejiang, Jiangxi, and Hunan, the destruction was so total that revival seemed impossible.

Social Transformations, Growth, and Liberation

Warfare always brings great disruption to a society; young men are killed or injured, buildings are destroyed, women are raped, and property looted. China has a long record of the ravages of war, going back to the blood-thirsty first emperor, Qin Shihuang, and to the brutal Shang Dynasty. Pre-modern disasters seldom affected the whole society, even when the greatest of upheavals, a dynastic change, was in progress. Before the advent of total war, the effects of war were limited to the areas where fighting actually took place. In the Resistance War, the effects of warfare went far beyond what had ever occurred before, involving civilians within and beyond the zones of actual fighting. Vast numbers of families were disrupted and dislocated in the mass refugee movements that accompanied the start of the war, in the bombings that continued throughout the war, and in the economic turmoil that came with the fighting. This was total war, and it had 'more profoundly shaken the Chinese family-clan system that any previous catastrophe'.[29]

---

[28] F. W. James, *Changing China* (Kilmarnock: Ritchie, 1946), p. 176.
[29] Edgar Snow, *Scorched Earth*, Vol. II (London: Gollancz, 1941), p. 232.

The family system   The old family system was designed to care for its members. Now that role was threatened, often unable to cope with the needs of its members; the stress on the system was too great, and the numbers of people in need was too great for their own families to help them[30]:

China is sometimes called the land of disasters. During an ordinary flood along the Yangze [Yangzi], the surplus waters are carried off by the lakes, tributaries and swamps along its course, and this results in no serious damage to the fields. The same is true with the social structure of the country. For a calamity of ordinary dimensions. The social system in China is able to absorb the resultant shock with little strain. But in an unprecedented disaster such as now confronting China, as a result of the Japanese invasion and the extension of hostilities over no less than ten provinces, the system has neared breaking point.

There was little guidance in how to deal with the new social breakdown and fluidity and live through it. Confucianism offered little help. It had already been under attack for three decades. And Confucianism was now deeply compromised by its new sponsor in China, Japan. The New Peoples Society (*Xinminhui*) was a network of deeply conservative organisations that talked of obedience to authority. The GMD recognised the scale of change but was equivocal about fostering further social change, unwilling to sponsor a new vision of society that might be considered too radical – that is, socialist. The CCP *was* revolutionary but avoided promoting radical social revolution in the early 1940s. Its growing success depended on appearing to be moderate.

The breakdown of the old social order aroused different reactions amongst those who went through it. For some, especially the young and the radical, this was a great opportunity, which carried with it the promise of creating a new society. As millions of relatively youthful bureaucrats, intellectuals, businessmen, and soldiers moved inland, they left behind a society that many were glad to leave; they did not attempt to replicate it in the interior. The old, stultifying, and restrictive society had been so shaken that it seemed to have been shattered – and they had no regret. Fei Xiaotong, then in his early thirties, spoke of an 'age of cultural metamorphosis that has been initiated by the long and wide struggle for national existence' and saw 'the gradual breakdown of the traditional system under our eyes'.[31]

The young sociologist Frances Hsu (Xu Liangguang) was one of those who was optimistic about the outcomes of social turbulence[32]

---

[30] *China at War*, Vol. II (January 1939), pp. 52–53.
[31] Fei Xiaotong, p. 52.
[32] Francis Hsu, 'China's new social spirit', *Asia*, September 1942, pp. 506–509.

[Reading 4]. He saw it as the breaking of the bonds of traditional familism that focussed on family, land holding, and success through intellectual achievement. Now these ideas were dead, and nationalism was replacing familism. Young people, separated from their families, were able to live their own lives and make their own decisions. Filial piety was dying a quiet death. Habits of deference to the elders and obedience to their commands were destroyed without a struggle – in the absence of the elders, it was impossible to receive their orders, let alone obey them. The intense intra-family fights and struggles described in Ba Jin's famous novel, *The Family*, published in 1933, were a thing of the past.[33] They were a casualty of the disruption of war, which caused the large family to melt away. Very few families now had the preconditions to maintain a multi-generational family – the presence of a large number of members in one place, ample leisure to spend with each other, money to keep the outfit afloat, and the absence of other pressing problems.

Sun Benwen took a more sober view of the effects of the social upheaval. He asked what would happen to the family system during the period of emergency. He saw the effects of warfare on the family not as the destruction of a moribund old world but rather as the deformation of the key building block of society, the family that looked after the economic and social needs of its members; that cared for the young, the old, and the weak; and that was the repository of most material property. Without a strong family, the whole society was built on shifting sand.[34] Sun was deeply troubled, feeling that Chinese society had been reduced to chaos and that only bad could come of it. His conservative view, so different from that of Francis Hsu, was a reflection of his age. The two analyses of the social impact of the war were two ends of the spectrum of interpretation of the social impact of war. For the young, the restless, and the talented, the war meant opportunity, excitement, and – at first – a fairly cheerful separation from their families. For the old and the conservative, the social upheaval of the war brought something close to despair, the end of the only world they knew, and the promise of the bleakest possible future.

The old family system was not, of course, as dead as some people hoped it might be. Chinese still had to depend on their families for support in illness, old age, and need. There were no systems of pensions, unemployment insurance, medical insurance – the impersonal systems that make families less critical in the structure of society in the modern

---

[33] Ba Jin, *The Family* (New York: Garden City, 1972).
[34] Sun Benwen, *Xiandai Zhongguo shehui wenti* (Chongqing: Shangwu, 1943), pp. 202–204.

West. But the short-term decline of many of the family's roles was leading to fundamental social rearrangement.

Rearrangement of the social hierarchy   The old social hierarchy was dominated by men of learning. Next came peasants, then merchants, and finally soldiers. The hierarchy was now virtually reversed. The men who had been at the bottom of society, the soldiers, were now at the top. In a time of war, the military was always dominant, but where once the 'generals' were officials practising warfare only in an emergency, such as the commander who put down the Taipings in the 1860s, Zeng Guofan, now the generals were real soldiers. The GMD government was led by the Generalissimo, Chiang Kai-shek. The military had first call on all resources and was admired or at least respected by civilians. The war had put the military at the top of the social order.

The merchant stratum was another beneficiary of the social upheaval. Entrepreneurs flourished in the economic instability created by the war. The social status of the once-despised merchant had already risen in the early Republic and climbed rapidly. A new entrepreneurial class emerged, thanks largely to war-induced shortages. The opportunities for anyone involved in production, at however small a scale, were enormous; they could set up their own small businesses to produce goods to substitute for items not otherwise obtainable. Items as simple but as indispensable as ink, pens, and writing brushes were hard to find. A family that set up a little workshop at home to make ink from soot was on the way to wealth.

Inflation helped entrepreneurs in a particularly unpopular way – hoarding. The government had to finance the war through printing money. Inflation gradually took hold in the early years of the war and provided opportunities for hoarders, who only had to have a small initial stake, which they could use to buy products. Then they could sit back, watch the price go up, and sell when they felt they had made enough money. People in the service sector could make money by an indirect form of hoarding. They took money up-front for services they had not yet rendered and then used the money paid to them to buy goods for their businesses and for speculation.[35] Entrepreneurial success in hoarding was double-edged. Hoarding might look like successful entrepreneurship to those who did it. To those who did not, it meant war profiteering.

---

[35] As a young student in Kunming, on a government stipend, Jerome Ch'en barely managed to afford to eat. At the start of each month he took his whole monthly stipend and bought a place at a local restaurant that guaranteed him one meal every day for the rest of the month.

New women   The war brought a revolution in the status of many women – the possibility and often the necessity of emancipation from the domestic prisons in which many had existed before the war. Women in huge numbers had to join the workforce, both in the occupied areas and in unoccupied China. Some were women who responded to the patriotic call to do their part for the war, but others were women separated from their husbands who now had to earn a living to support themselves and their children. The demands of survival forced them to work. In western China, the war brought demands for female labour in factories and the possibility for local peasant girls to leave their villages and go to work in the towns, a choice that many took. With the move came a de facto emancipation from the influence of their parents.

The war lifted some of the age-old pressures against women being involved outside the home, and capable women, particularly young ones, saw their opportunity. In the communist-run areas in rural north China, female emancipation was a part of formal socialist policy. Women started to get involved in political activity in village governments, some of them elected, some appointed.[36] The CCP's policies of female emancipation tended to be practised more at low levels than in the top leadership. Jiang Qing, Mao Zedong's fourth wife, was forced by the disapproving wives of other leaders to keep out of public life, a slight that she resented bitterly, with dreadful consequences twenty years later in the Cultural Revolution, when as the leader of the Gang of Four she turned on the people who had humiliated her in Yan'an.

The war gave a large category of women, so-called unfortunate women, the possibility for escape from their miserable situations by getting jobs: These were 'girl students of poor families, forsaken girls, unloved wives, refugee women, slave girls, fugitive prostitutes, sing-song girls, rear wives, wives-on-hire, oppressed concubines and all-sorts of miserable women. The fact that women could now work meant that these unhappy women now had a way out, a possibility of survival.'[37] This sad sisterhood was offered the chance of redemption through work, the possibility of putting their dubious pasts behind them.

Government propaganda extolled the virtues of the new women. Official publications carried glowing stories about China's new 'career girls': Zhang Dengfeng, age twenty, was supporting her widowed mother

---

[36] Dagfinn Gatu, *Village China at War* (Vancouver, British Columbia, Canada: UBC Press, 2008), pp. 232–233.

[37] Hsu Meng-hsiung, 'The unoccupied women of unoccupied China', *Asia*, March 1941, p. 123. The characters for their names are not given in the article. No characters were printed.

and her younger brother on her wages as a clerk in the Ministry of Finance. Peng Zifang was the star girl reporter with the major newspaper, the *Dagongbao*, one of ten female reporters in Chongqing. 'She goes out to visit various offices and individuals, rushes back to her home to supervise the work of her cook and to see if her one-year old baby is well.' Li Shuping was a thirty-two -year-old judge in the district court in Meishan, near Chongqing, and the mother of seven children. Her husband was the magistrate in a neighbouring county. Mary Fei, widow of a pilot, combined mothering her two children with being a violin teacher at the Sichuan Academy of Fine Arts.[38]

Single women who had moved west with their schools or workplaces were beneficiaries of the new freedoms for women, especially freedom from arranged marriage. They could now contemplate finding their own husbands; there were no parents around to find them one. This freedom promised the fulfilment of the dream of romantic love, the blissful thought that Chinese women could escape the hell of an arranged marriage and find the love they had read about in the translations of the romantic novels of Tolstoi, Zola, and Dumas.

Finding a husband had its dangers. There was the strong possibility that the husband-to-be was already a husband, with a wife at home with his parents. The checks usually made by a go-between could not be done at long distance, and there was no way of finding out about the man beyond how he described himself.

Another danger was that a woman might not find a husband at all. In 1941, this plaintive tale was published[39]:

I am already thirty years old, still have no house to keep, no husband to argue with and no son to be proud of. It is rather an unfortunate thing to happen to a Chinese girl, for being an old maid in China is still an embarrassment to the social order and a shame to the family.

The question of motherhood was a thorny one. The most prominent women in China, Song Meiling and her older sister, Song Qingling, the widow of Sun Yat-sen, had no children. The nearest Song Meiling came to being a mother was in her virtual adoption of her niece Jeanette Kung (Kong Lingwei), a strange, androgynous person who lived with her aunt.[40] The most prominent woman on the communist side, Deng Yingchao, the wife of Zhou Enlai, had no children, although she and her husband did adopt several 'revolutionary orphans', including the infant

---

[38] *China Newsweek*, 114 (November 23, 1944), pp. 7–10.

[39] Chai Chi-chen, 'Being an old maid in China', *Asia*, September 1941, pp. 492–494.

[40] Some people have suggested that Jeanette actually may have been Song Meiling's child, brought up by her older sister, Song Ailing, who was the wife of Kong Xiangxi.

Li Peng.[41] Adoption of orphans, especially the children of martyrs, became a standard practice in Yan'an.

Song Meiling was the leading exemplar of modern womanhood – talented, beautiful, educated, bilingual, and increasingly as the war went on an international celebrity.[42] At the same time, traditional female heroines were brought back into the limelight; leading the way was Hua Mulan, the legendary girl who dressed as a man and joined the army in place of her father. In 1939, a film of Mulan's exploits came out, *Mulan Follows the Army* (*Mulan cong jun*). There were plays and cartoons about the heroine, now recast as a woman willing to do battle against the Japanese. The ancient poem 'Song of Mulan (*Mulan shi*)' swept back into popularity.

The changes in the status of some women were threatening to their families, if they were conservative or traditional. Fei Xiaotong observed in his village near Kunming that parents were unhappy that their daughters had gone off to work in factories[43]:

Factory work is much lighter and more interesting than toiling in the mud. Attracted by high wages and urban life, girls rush to the city with or without the permission of their parents. They come back with bare legs, on high heels – and with permanent waves! Betrothals previously arranged by their families are broken, and romantic dreams bewilder their outlook.

In many societies wartime improvements in the status of women were reversed when the boys came home. This did not happen in China; the changes were often permanent; women did not go back to servitude. The Civil War and the CCP triumph meant that it was impossible to go back to the traditional lowly status of women. Part of this was due to the communist insistence on equality between men and women, even more to the need for almost all women to work. The days of total dependence on their husbands and fathers had gone.

Women Victims   The changes in the status of women referred mainly to women in unoccupied China, who were not direct victims of war and occupation. In occupied China, many women were victims. One of the issues that still causes great bitterness between China and Japan is the treatment of women kidnapped by Japanese forces and made to

---

[41] Li Peng was premier of China in 1989, at the time of the June 4 Massacre, and has been widely held responsible for it.

[42] Diana Lary, '*Chuangzao yige lingxiu jianneiju de jiaose: duiRi kangzhan shiqi de Jiang Furen* (Creating the role of the leader's consort: Madame Chiang Kai-shek in the Anti-Japanese War)', in *Jiang Furen nushi Song Meiling yu jindai Zhongguo xueshu taolun ji* (Taipei: Zhongzheng wenjiao jijinhui, 2000), pp. 558–565.

[43] Fei Xiaotong, p. 58.

work as 'comfort women (*weianfu*)' in military brothels. The tragic stories of these women have been coming out over the past decade or so as survivors take their cases to courts in Japan in a search of apologies and compensation. They appear along with much larger numbers of Korean, Philippine, and other Southeast Asian women, all victims of the brutal system of forced prostitution run by the Japanese military. The total number of 'comfort women' in Asia is disputed but is generally accepted to be about 200,000 – the doubters being some Japanese, including former Prime Minister Shinto Abe, who insist on claiming that the 'comfort women' were prostitutes.

The details of what happened to these women are deeply painful. Many who survived their ordeals chose never to talk about the years of abuse and degradation. Their pain was often too deep to recall. Beyond this was the unspoken recognition that their return to their families was predicated on them *not* talking about what they had been through.

The tragic fate of the women who were captured led directly to a kind of imprisonment for a vast number of women in the occupied areas; they lived in fear of being taken as 'comfort women' or of being raped. The nascent movement towards women's emancipation was nipped in the bud by the need for women to be sequestered in their homes – for fear of what might happen if they went out on their own.

Children   The war distorted the childhoods of many children. Childhood had been anything but uniform before the start of the war. The nature of childhood depended on family circumstances, gender, family rank, and many other factors. The war brought an unwanted sameness to childhood: In whatever part of China they lived in, children's lives were dominated for the duration of the war by insecurity. There was no political or economic security so long as the country was at war and divided.

Insecurity was the common denominator. After that, childhood was interrupted or lost altogether in different ways. Children who fled with their refugee parents lost their extended family, including their grandparents; they might miss the opportunity to go to school, to get an education; they lived in poverty. Li Meifeng grew up on the road, fleeing repeatedly with her parents from Guangzhou to Hong Kong and back again, driven by the tides of war. Her parents were impoverished by the war, her two older sisters were sold to keep the rest of the family alive, and she herself was sent to work as a child maid.[44] Vivienne Poy's

---

[44] Lee Mei-fung, *Childhood Lost* (Burnaby, British Columbia, Canada: Bauhinia Press, 2004).

wealthy family did not suffer real poverty, but it too had to flee repeatedly, from Hong Kong inland, then to Guangxi, Guizhou, and finally, Chongqing. The extended family was broken up, dispersed throughout southern China. The life they had once lived in a huge family compound in Happy Valley was gone forever.[45]

Children who came to the end of the war with their own parents still alive and their families intact were better off than the great number of children who were orphaned during the war.

Orphans

无家可归

No home to return to

Traditional Chinese society had no concept of anonymous orphans. Adoption was common – but always within the extended family; the idea of stranger adoption or of foundlings was unknown. Couples without a son often would adopt a nephew to make sure that they were not alone in their old age. Children who lost their parents would be taken in by relatives; the extended family operated as a welfare institution. The child still belonged to a family and did not suffer the psychological pain of abandonment. The sense of belonging was real and essential; without it, it was almost impossible for a person to exist in a society that had no formal registration beyond entry in a family genealogy.

The war produced a vast new need: Tens of thousands of children, probably far more, were completely separated from their families. Painter Liu Guosong was such an orphan [Reading 5]. Most orphans did not know if their parents or extended family members were still alive, and some of the younger ones did not even know their own names. To meet the needs of this new kind of orphan, the Child Protection Agency (*Ertong bayou hui*) was set up in March 1938. Song Meiling was its chair and Li Dequan, wife of Feng Yuxiang, her deputy. By the end of the year, there were twenty-eight orphanages in Sichuan, Guizhou, Guangxi, Fujian, Jiangxi, Guangdong, Hong Kong, Zhejiang, and Shan/Gan; the number later grew to sixty-one.[46] The orphanages were run on strict lines, rather like the missionary boarding schools that had appeared in China in the decades before the war. The children were kept clean, well fed, and well dressed. They were endlessly appealing, and their photographs (usually

[45] Vivienne Poy, *Profit, Victory and Sharpness: The Lees of Hong Kong* (Toronto: York Centre for Asian Research, 2006), pp. 120–129.

[46] Lin Jiahua, 'Zhanshi ertong baoyuhui de jianli yu zuzhi yunzuo', *Shihui*, X (September 2006), pp. 269–320.

taken with prominent GMD figures) provided vivid publicity for China's war effort. They stimulated an outpouring of generosity in Overseas Chinese communities and in North America.

Other groups of orphans were rescued by foreigners and taken to safety from war zones. Their epic journeys have been captured in films. In 1940, the tiny, indomitable Gladys Aylward led a group of orphans through the hills of Shanxi, away from the advancing Japanese. The film, *Inn of Sixth Happiness* shot in Wales, with Chinese children from Liverpool as the orphans, turned the spinster Aylward into a glamorous figure, played by Ingrid Bergman, and added a major love interest. George Hogg took another group on a much longer journey from Shaanxi to Gansu in 1944. A version of this journey appears in the 2008 film *Children of Huangshi*, starring Jonathan Rhys-Myers.

Orphanages might save the lives of children, but they did not guarantee them a happy future. Not knowing who their birth parents were or what family they belonged to meant that the rest of their lives would be complicated by not having a family, to use the dismal Chinese saying 'having no home to return to'. They were examples of why family membership was still fundamental. The official treatment of orphans seemed to mean that the nation could become the new family, but this was a faint hope, and the idea that the nation could trump the family was no consolation to those who had no family.

Revolutionary and Guerrilla Society   Much of rural China in the occupied areas was not controlled permanently or effectively by the Japanese. In these areas, new social forms evolved. The model of the new society emerged in the communist capital Yan'an. In this small, dusty remote town in a valley in the poverty-stricken loess lands of Shaanxi, the tiny band of survivors of the Long March was joined in 1936 and 1937 by young revolutionaries from northern China and Shanghai.

Yan'an life was simple and spartan, the inhabitants united in an equality of poverty. They lived in cave houses, rooms carved into the soft loess soil with a wooden front door and windows. Each person did some manual labour, from the top leaders down. They wore simple, rumpled clothes. There were no servants, only orderlies and 'little devils'; there were no banquets, only communal sing-songs and folk dances.

To the few outside observers who managed to get to Yan'an, the life there seemed to be true socialism, complete commitment to a common cause. The Yan'an communists became the darlings of left-leaning Western reporters. Journalists such as Edgar Snow, Nym Wales, and Anna Louise Strong were impressed with the clean-living and dedicated lifestyle of the communist leaders – a contrast to what these observers had

THE
AUTHOR
AND MAO
TSE-TUNG
(P. 163)

3.1. Mao Zedong with Violet Cressy-Marks. (Violet Cressy-Marks, *Journey into China,* **1940, p. 157.)**

come to see as the self-indulgence of some of the GMD leaders. They were struck by the apparent unity of the party and by its charismatic leader, Mao Zedong. They saw what they wanted to see, a new world in birth – and one presented to them with the high level of propaganda skill that was becoming the hallmark of the CCP.

The Yan'an base area was the headquarters of the CCP. In other guerrilla areas in north China, which were less well organised and the attachment to CCP policies less absolute, if not absent, other new social forms evolved. These might involve recreating traditional social forms based on the vivid worlds portrayed in novels such as *Shuihu zhuan*. The leading figures were romantic characters, such a bandits and smugglers, who existed in worlds that were governed by physical prowess, cleverness in strategy and scheming, and loyalty to each other rather than to an established social hierarchy. This was an exciting but terribly insecure life.

Nationalism Versus Personal Ties   In the occupied areas, loyalty to the nation was not dead. The old society underwent a different transformation in which some people put their love of country ahead of personal attachments to family and employers. In the middle years of the war, acts of resistance, including murders and assassinations, undermined old concepts of personal loyalty. People whose loyalty was assumed started to turn against the Japanese and their agents in ways that defied traditional, personal loyalties.

In September 1940, Beiping was rocked by the news of a string of arrests and executions of 'Chongqing agents'. The 'agents' turned out to be 70 young students, aged between thirteen and twenty. They were arrested for membership in the underground 'Resist Japan Save China Association'. Thirty of the students were executed; the forty others were jailed. What made the story especially poignant was that the young people were children of men who were working for the occupation authorities.[47] Their fathers cannot have imagined that after they had decided against patriotism, their children would take up the cause and die for it.

In Shanghai, Mayor Fu Xiaoan was murdered in his bed as he slept heavily after a party. Fu's throat was slit, apparently by his own servant of ten years, who sauntered through the Japanese guard on Fu's house after he had done the deed.[48] The murders, assassinations, and mysterious deaths in the occupied areas were usually blamed on communists or criminals, but many were carried out by agents of the GMD's enforcers, Du Yuesheng and Dai Li and the Juntong.[49] The fear of assassination and the inability to trust other people made life for active collaborators nerve racking, especially when they could not trust even the people closest to them.

Personal Contacts

Post Office   After four years of war, China was firmly divided. One of the few nationwide institutions that managed to keep going in the divided country was the post office. The China Post operated, as it had for more than fifty years, with an extraordinary level of efficiency, much of it down to the devotion to duty of its staff. The number of 'green clothes men' (for the colour of their uniforms) actually increased during the war, from 28,800 to 31,800; the service even started to hire women.[50] Letters were the only means that separated families had of keeping in touch with each other, and even though the service slowed down from time to time, it was still there.

There was danger and many difficulties in using the post. The danger was that the secret police on either side (the Japanese Kempeitai, the GMD Juntong, or the CCP surveillance system run by Kang Sheng)

---

[47] *China Weekly Review*, September 7, 1940, p. 2.

[48] *China Weekly Review*, October 19, 1940, p. 228.

[49] The atmosphere is captured in Zhang Yimou's 1995 film *Shanghai Triad*. The Juntong (Office of Military Statistics) was the GMD's intelligence unit.

[50] *China Newsweek*, 134 (April 26, 1945), pp. 5–7.

3.2. Letter writer. (Violet Cressy-Marks, *Journey into China*, 1940, p. 109.)

would open letters and might take action against recipients of whom they were suspicious. The difficulties were the length of time that letters took and the inability to locate many of the refugees, given how impermanent their new addresses were.

It might be thought that literacy would be a requirement of letter writing and reading. It was not. China had a long tradition of employing professional letter writers. This is a description of letter writers in Xian in 1938[51]:

> Outside the busy Post Office, under a balcony, sat dozens of letter writers. They mostly were old and wore glasses. Illiterate clients arrived and either dictated their letters and the writer would write them or he would listen to their troubles and acting as adviser or lawyer, write what he thought fit to 'let the punishment fit the crime'.

Lack of Contact   Many parents whose children left the occupied areas had no idea of what had happened to them. They sat at home and worried themselves sick over their children – whether they were alive or dead. The debilitating worry was a mixture of respect for their children's political stance, anger that they had abandoned their parents, and the

---

[51] Violet Cressy-Marks, *Journey into China* (London: Hodder and Stoughton, 1940), p. 111.

daily disappointment when the post brought no letter. In her short story 'North China (*Bei Zhongguo*)', Manchurian writer Xiao Hong described the gradual decline of two wealthy Manchurian parents after their son left home rather than live under the Japanese. They received only two letters from him. His mother wept constantly. 'She cried at the drop of a hat – at weddings, when she saw someone holding a grandchild, and even when she heard that so-and-so had announced his engagement.' The boy's father reacted differently: '[H]e assiduously steered clear of any mention of his son, so his family avoided that subject like poison. He had the door to his son's room sealed, and from then on the room was deathly silent and soon covered with a layer of dust.' The family gradually disintegrated; the departure of the young master had taken the life out of it.[52]

These are universal parental reactions to the disappearance of a child. The fact that their son had gone to fight in a patriotic cause did not make it easier. The worst was that they had no idea where he was or what had happened to him. Their loss was replicated innumerable times in the families left behind in occupied China.

Children themselves might be the victims of separation. Ye Jiaying's family lived in Beiping, a long-established Manchu family. When the war started, her father was working in the Aeronautical Administration in Shanghai. He withdrew with the government, first to Wuhan and then to Chongqing. He had no contact at all with his family in Beiping for the eight years of the war. Four years into the war, Ye Jiaying's mother died, leaving her to be cared for by her uncle. Both her parents were gone and with them her happy childhood. More than sixty years later the pain of separation and loss is still there.[53]

Conclusion

The years 1939 to 1941 were painful but ones in which the bare fact of hanging on in the face of terrible adversity brought a glimmer of confidence that the war might one day be won and that a new China might re-emerge. As time went on, the self-confidence and hope for a happy outcome drained away in the GMD areas and in occupied China, whereas the growth of the CCP started to bring into question what a new China, if there was one, might look like.

[52] Xiao Hong, 'North China', in Howard Goldblatt (trans.), *Selected Stories of Xiao Hong* (Beijing: Panda Books, 1981), pp. 175, 176.
[53] Interview with Ye Jiaying, May 7, 2009, Vancouver, British Columbia, Canada.

Readings

Reading 1: Dai Wangshu, 'Written on a Prison Wall'[54]

Dai was one of the best known of modern poets. He was imprisoned for a time by the Japanese.

If I die here, friends, do not be sad,
I shall always exist in your hearts.
One of you died in a cell in Japanese occupied territory.
He harboured deep hatred, you should always remember.
When you come back dig up his mutilated body from the mud,
Hoist his soul up high with your victory cheers.
And then place his bones on a mountain peak, to bask in the sun
and bathe in the wind.
In that dark damp dirt cell that was his sole beautiful dream.

Reading 2: Song Meiling, 'The Seven Deadly Sins'[55]

Song's denunciation of many of the people she knew in Chongqing.

The war is shown in to high relief many of our shortcomings. Now is the logical and psychological moment for us to correct them. All other nations of the world have found it necessary and politic to institute immediate reorganisation and reforms when the shadow of war has approached; responsible officials are galvanized into action to estimate the possible consequences of incompetence in hostilities and to prepare the necessary house-cleaning measures to meet all emergencies. Now that war is upon her, China should do likewise. She must be swift and lavish in action, slow and miserly in talk, in order to avoid laying herself open to charges of laxity or indifference.

In a lengthy disquisition, Song Meiling then lays out the sins (paraphrased here):

Self-seeking: Enrichment at the cost of the people, profiteering, squeeze, graft – the most vicious of the sins.
Face: Unwillingness to reveal ignorance, leading to 'monumental and fatuous decisions' and camouflaging of incompetence.

---

[54] In Joseph Lao and Howard Goldblatt (eds.), *Columbia Anthology of Modern Chinese Literature* (New York: Columbia University Press, 1995), p. 514.
[55] Madame Chiang Kai-shek, *China Shall Rise Again* (London: Hurst and Blackett, 1941), pp. 38–48.

Cliquism: Reliance on closed circles of colleagues, based on ties of locality, education, or political interest – a 'dry rot in the administration'.

Lack of self-discipline: Indolence, indifference, inefficiency – all products of lax education.

Evasion of responsibility: Ignorance, incompetence, even obstructionism, all to avoid taking responsibility – has created 'an army of paid unemployables'.

Defeatism (*meiyou fazi*): Indecision and do-nothingness – the easy way out of any situation.

Inaccuracy (*chabuduo*): Casual, slipshod, lazy – 'the phraseology of the time-server and the slovenly'.

Reading 3: Ai Qing, 'Lifting'[56]

Ai Qing was one of China's most famous poets. This poem was written in June 1940, after one of the many raids on Chongqing. In the 1950s, Ai Qing was labelled a 'rightist' and spent almost twenty years in internal exile.

请你们让开
请你们走在人行道上
我们把他们抬起来
请你们不要推挤
请你们站在街旁
让我们把他们抬起来
请你们不要叫嚷绕
请你们用静默表示悲哀
请你们让我们抬起来
这是一个妇人
她的脑盖已被弹片打开
让她闭着眼好好睡
愿她过一阵能慢慢地醒来
让我们抬起她送回他的家
让她的家属用哭泣与仇恨
这是一个服务团的团员
灰色的制服上还卦得有他的臂章
你们认识他么 – 他的脸已蒙上了土灰
无情的弹片打断了他的勤劳的臂
请你们让开，请向他表示悲哀
他已为了减少你们的牺牲而被残害
请你们不要挤，这里还有更多的

56 Ai Qing, June 11, 1940. Reprinted in Ai Qing, *Xuanji*, Vol. 1 (Chengdu: Sichuan wenyi chubanshe, 1986), p. 378.

他们都是伤兵住在兵医院里
他们在前方受了伤躺在床上
等着伤好了再上战场
现在无耻的敌人已把医院炸倒
现在他们已收到了更大的创伤
请大家让开
让我们抬起他们来
请大家站在旁边
让我们抬着臾床的走来
请大家记住
这些都是学债

Please make way
Please walk on the pavement
Let us lift them up 让
Please don't push
Please stand aside
Let us lift them up
Please don't make a noise
Please show your sorrow quietly
Let us lift them up
This is a woman
Her skull split open by shrapnel
Let her close her eyes and sleep well
As if in a while she may wake up
Lift her up and take her to her home
Let her family arrange [a funeral] in tears and hatred
This is a man from a fire warden
His armband still hangs on his grey uniform
Do you recognise him – his face is covered in dust
The callous shrapnel has broken his hard-working arms
Please make way, please show him your grief
He suffered to lessen your losses
Please don't push, there are many more here
They are wounded soldiers from an army hospital
They were in bed after being wounded at the front
Waiting to recover before going back to the battlefield
Now the inhuman enemy has bombed the hospital
Now they have suffered even worse wounds
Please make way
Let us lift them
Please stand aside
Let us carry away the stretchers
Please everyone remember
These are all blood debts

Reading 4: Francis Hsu, 'China's New Social Spirit'[57]

These tremendous changes, though chiefly a result of war and therefore tempo-rary, may have a permanent effect on the social structure. Conscription, war dev-astation and new opportunities have combined to drive or induce young people away from home and shatter the last stronghold of patriarchal authority, that is the financial control over the younger generation. Old-style courtesies, such as the literary habit of addressing people as 'kindly brothers' and so on in letters my persist for some time, but state legislation, not family authority, will be the main spring of the country's law and order. This will gradually come about even in remote areas.

Moreover, the new opportunities in industries and commerce, and the break-ing up of the literati as a distinct group, have given rise to a middle class whose final ambition will be in trade and factories and other such ventures. To that extent the new development will make the scholastic professions sounder and the official ranks 'cleaner'. The adventurous elements and intelligentsia of the country will no longer look to officialdom as their main route to personal fortune and salvation. The scholars in, their turn, will tend less to despise manual work.

How far the civic status will be separated from the occupational status will still be uncertain. As far as one can see, the lower officials may continue for long to be regarded by the higher officials as personal servants and to be treated in any way they like. And the illiterate peasants may continue for long to be regarded by the officials as their subjects in an autocratic sense. But at least within the newly bor middle class the emphasis among its occupations will be not so much that one is higher or lower than another as that it is different, as for soldiers, they will be gradually recognized as an important element of the nation and not as outcasts.

Reading 5: Liu Guosong, An Orphan's Life[58]

The celebrated Taiwanese painter grew up during the war and was edu-cated in the National Revolutionary Military Orphan School.

Like many other young people of his generation, Liu Guosong's childhood and youth passed during the convulsive period of smoke and fire of the War of Resistance. He was born in 1932 in Yidu (Shandong), the year after Japan occupied Manchuria. His father was a soldier who felt it his duty to protect his country. From a young age Liu moved around, far away from home, following his father as he moved with the army, bobbing around from place to place. This tough existence gave him an independence of spirit, a self-confidence and an ability to cope with difficulties. It enabled him to be at home wherever he went, and able to adjust to any new circumstances.

[57] *Asia*, September 1942, p. 508.
[58] Taibei guoli meishuguan, *Liu Guosong huaji* (Taibei: 1992), p. 12.

When he was six, after the war had been going for more than a year, he was struck a heavy blow. His father had risen to the rank of battalion commander, a courageous young man much respected by his subordinates. In 1938, when the Japanese were attacking Wuhan, his father was killed in a battle to the death. For a time, Liu, his mother and his younger sister were plunged into great gloom [literally, 'sad clouds and strands of mist']. They drifted around from place to place for the duration of the war, to Hubei, Shaanxi, Sichuan, Hunan, and Jiangxi. He wrote about this difficult time: 'My mother and we two children lived a rootless life. I collected firewood in the hills, she worked spinning thread, and we and we had to eat spoiled rice that we boiled in salt water. When we were so cold that we could not sleep, we wept together in silence.'

Films

The Children of Huangshi. Director Roger Spottiswoode, 2008.
Inn of the Sixth Happiness. Director Mark Robson, 1957.
Shanghai Triad. Director Zhang Yimou, 1997.
Lust, Caution. Director Lee Ang, 2007.

4   Grim Years: 1942–1944

Events

At the end of 1941, Japan attacked the United States and within the next few weeks took Hong Kong, the Philippines, Malaya, Singapore, and Indonesia. The United States entered World War II and joined the Allies in an all-out war with the Axis powers (Germany, Italy, and Japan). The Japanese attack on Pearl Harbor was a tremendous success, but as Admiral Yamamoto, commander-in-chief of the Japanese Navy recognised at the time, it was also the beginning of the end for the Japanese imperialist enterprise. American outrage brought the country's full might against Japan. This meant active involvement in China.

The two years that followed the start of the Pacific War were marked in China by a combination of optimism and pessimism. On the optimistic side, China now had determined foreign allies, the United States, Britain, Australia, Canada, and the USSR, who would take the war to the enemy and increase the likelihood of Japan's defeat. On the pessimistic side, the political unity that had been so important at the beginning of the war was gone, inflation was gaining ground, and morale was seeping away. A new wave of refugees fled into China from Hong Kong.

During 1942 and 1943, there was little fighting in China itself. The Japanese armies were fully engaged in the occupation of Southeast Asia and in planning their attack on their ultimate goal, India. To deny them this prize, Chinese troops fought beyond China's borders in the Burma campaigns. They were led by the senior US commander in China, General Joseph Stilwell, who was embroiled at the same time in bitter disputes with Chiang Kai-shek that eventually led to his recall from China.

The United Front was in its death throes. The Guomindang (GMD) and the Chinese Communist Party (CCP) were effectively split, the split exacerbated by mutual sniping and, on both sides, serious covert operations against each other. The CCP was still relatively weak in military and economic terms, but its propaganda offensive was increasingly successful; it convinced many people that the communists were tough, decent, patriotic, and courageous people. The CCP presented itself as both revolutionary and deeply traditional. One of Mao Zedong's favourite books was the heroic saga, *Romance of the Three Kingdoms*, tales of bold, clever, brave, sometimes tragic heroes. He and his generals fitted the mould of these heroes – informal, tough, and humourous men destined to appeal to the common people. At this stage of the war, CCP forces were involved mainly in guerrilla fighting, and this form of warfare was by definition flexible, responsive, and non-doctrinaire. The party had achieved a close identification between the people and the army.

Meanwhile, in Chongqing, war weariness had set in. Economic problems were increasing as inflation took hold. Shortages worsened; the last direct route to the sea, by plane to Hong Kong, was cut after the island fell to the Japanese on Christmas Day 1941. The only way to bring in goods and passengers now was by plane over the Himalayas or through Xinjiang from the USSR; these were privileges afforded only to the very few.

The morale of the people who had fled to the west was not good. At the beginning of the fifth year of the war, despondency was setting in. It was hard to imagine that the war would ever end; there was little sense of a future. The war had gone beyond a stalemate, beyond stagnation, into a permanent, dragging nightmare. People were exhausted, fed up, self-doubting, querulous, and irritable. The sense of unity, the common cause that marked the early part of the war, had given way to grim competition for survival. Apathy and lassitude crept over those who lived in the dank murk of Chongqing. The prevailing mood paralleled the climate, grey and gloomy. There was little the government or anyone else could do to cheer things up or to raise morale. After five years away, the people from downriver were suffering from homesickness, manifested by a longing for their own foods. The deep devotion of Chinese to their regional cuisines means that when they cannot eat this food, they feel a sense of deprivation and even depression. The in-comers had a particular dietary problem – the love of the Sichuanese for fiery hot food. The Sichuanese pride themselves on eating the hottest food in China (a view contested by the Hunanese). The in-comers from northern and eastern China had scarcely eaten hot food before, and most never got used to it.

The food problems of unoccupied China were irritations, nothing remotely compared with the hunger on the North China Plain, where one of the worst famines in China's awful history of famines unfolded slowly throughout 1942. This long, drawn-out catastrophe was the worst manifestation of China's wartime suffering.

Gu Yuan, Unterstützt unsere Armee, die Armee
des einfachen Volkes; Holzschnitt, 1944

**4.1. Support our army. (*Holzschnitt im neuen China*. East
Berlin, 1976, p. 82.)**

Topics and Case Studies

Social Dislocation and Decay

In 1942, society in the unoccupied parts of China was showing signs of
dislocation and decay. Social patterns were changeable and fluid. The

old stability was gone and had not been replaced in a systemic way. Ad hoc social patterns were evolving to take the place of the missing family. Young people made their own marriages and grandchildren were born, all without reference to the family elders. The family separations had now gone on so long that they seemed permanent; they brought freedom for the young but also feelings of guilt at the breach of fundamental social obligations. The most fundamental obligation concerned the death of parents.

Ritual Failure   The most important duty of a son was to see his parents laid safely to rest. There was a whiff of sacrilege at the failure to carry out the proper rituals of burial and mourning for parents. Many of the refugees had to go through this sad ordeal. Lao She was devastated that he did not even know that his mother had died until a long while after her death far away in Beiping [Reading 1]. The Ji family managed to bury the patriarch of their family after he died in Hankou in 1938, but it was not a proper burial because it was not in their native Fenyang, nor could the family pay the regular respects to their dead patriarch because they soon had to flee again.[1] The Jis were a gentry family, but the need to respect the remains of a parent was felt just as powerfully at every level of society. Zheng Zhonglin from a village near Xuzhou, joined the army with his father in late 1937. For four years they served together, first in the regular army and then as GMD guerrillas in southern Jiangsu. Then his father was killed in the fighting. His body was cremated. Zheng took the ashes home by train; travelling in white mourning clothes, he was not interfered with by the Japanese. He buried the ashes in the clan graveyard, as a filial son should. This was the last time he was able to perform his filial duties. He went back to the army and never went home or saw his mother or grandmother again. More than forty years later, his abandonment of his family still haunted him, a burden of grief and sorrow that nothing could lighten.[2]

The topic of the improperly buried dead is hard to discuss in any society, even more so in China given the great importance of proper burial and the amount of care that people took before they died to ensure a decent burial, including the purchase of their own grave sites and coffins. The spirits of improperly buried people were believed to haunt their

---

[1] Ji Chaozhu, *The Man on Mao's Right* (New York: Random House, 2008), p. 16. The body was taken home after the war – but during the Cultural Revolution, the tomb was destroyed (p. 163).

[2] Zheng Zhonglin, 'Fuzi bing', in Situ Fu (ed.), *Kangzhan suiyue* (Taibei: Zhongyang ribao, 1985), pp. 32–39.

living descendants, begging them to make sure that their remains were found and brought home.

Many wartime families did not know whether they should be mourning or not. Soldiers often died without a record of their death being made. Often, their families were not notified. There was no efficient means of notifying families of the death of a soldier, no military cemeteries in which they were buried. During the fighting, bodies were disposed of in temporary, often haphazard ways, in shallow graves or mass pits.[3] Families were kept in long-term suspension, not knowing whether a soldier was alive or dead. The saddest wartime notation was *shizong* ('lost trace'). This might mean that men had been blown to bits in fighting, had been buried in a mass grave, or as at Nanjing, their bodies thrown into the Yangzi. It might even mean that they were still alive but had deserted their families – there was no means of telling. The pain for the family in not knowing what had happened created an unending grief that prevented families from coming to terms with loss.

The failure to perform less significant but more joyous rituals, for the birth of a son, a wedding, the seventieth birthday (*qishi dashou*) of a parent, or the sweeping of the graves at the Qingming Festival, brought a different kind of sadness and underlined the sense of separation and loss that the war brought. For millions of people, it was impossible to celebrate the happiest festival of all, the New Year, at home for at least eight years.[4]

The inability to celebrate joyous occasion helps to explain why, when a suitable occasion arose, one particular birthday was celebrated with extravagance close to ostentation. In early 1942, the mother of Bai Chongxi turned ninety, a prodigious age for a woman in China at the time. Bai was particularly devoted to her because she had been widowed quite young and had dedicated her life to her son. A huge celebration was organised in Guilin, with a succession of banquets and opera performances over several days. Many of China's senior generals attended the birthday, taking time off from the war and flying in from Chongqing for the occasion. Chiang Kai-shek did not go in person, but he sent a donation of 10 million yuan, a sum that, although it reflected the inflation that already gripped unoccupied China, was still enormous. There was

[3] Drew Gilpin Faust's brilliant study of the way in which military deaths were handled in the American Civil War shows how the carnage of the war produced systems of notification, burial, commemoration, and pensions in the United States. *The Republic of Suffering* (New York: Knopf, 2008).

[4] The Chinese New Year is celebrated according to the lunar calendar and usually falls in February. The New Year according to the Western calendar is not important.

some criticism that such a lavish celebration should be held in wartime – although given how rare such a birthday was, there was not much danger that it would set a precedent.[5]

Some family rituals did not occur regularly but also were critically important. These included the division of property within a family (*fenjia*), a complex process that required personal attendance to ensure one's own interests, and decisions about major investments, such as businesses, schools, shrines, and graveyards. The family members who were in exile could not participate in such matters for the duration of the war. What they often saw as skewed outcomes produced enduring bitterness among family members. This skewing could not be blamed on the invader – but it *was* a by-product of the occupation.

Fear and Social Erosion   In the occupied areas, different pressures ate away at social cohesion. Chronic fear made people timorous, more concerned for themselves than for their families or communities. The threat of arrest or even death was sporadic and unpredictable, but it never went away. In the cities and towns, the Japanese and their agents were always present.

In the rural areas, the Japanese 'mopping-up' raids, undertaken on the pretext of destroying support for guerrillas, continued and even increased. The raids might stimulate further resistance – or they might have quite the opposite effect. There was an inherent contradiction in the relationship between peasants and guerrillas. The peasants were the 'water in which the guerrillas swam' – but they were also the ones who bore the brunt of retaliation once the guerrillas were gone. The savagery of the 'mopping-up' operations produced various states of mind. Defiance was one, but passivity and chronic anxiety were common too, along with a sense of hopelessness, negativity, and a lack of any sense of a future. Peasants in north China in the middle years of the war were inward-looking (*zisi*). They felt frightened (*kongju*), weak (*nuoruo*), helpless (*wuju*), and hopeless (*wunai*). Their chief concern was self-preservation (*shengcun zhuangtai*). The only choice that occurred to many peasants was to passively accept the Japanese presence rather than actively resist.[6] This is far from the conventional CCP presentation of fearless resistance, but it was often the reality – coping behaviours learned from bitter experience where resistance was futile and led to reprisals. In many places these behaviours became

---

[5] Cheng Siyuan, *Bai Chongxi zhuan* (Beijing: Huayi chubanshe, 1991), pp. 222–224.
[6] Jiang Pei, *Huabei 'zhiyun' shiqi zhu qunti xintai kaocha, 1941–42* (Third International Conference on the Sino-Japanese War, Hakone, November 2006), p. 15.

118   The Chinese People at War

entrenched; in the next two decades, they served peasants well in the early, turbulent years of communist rule. Their chief concern was to survive and hang onto their property, already more than many peasants could manage.

Towards the end of the war, a new menace came to threaten the rural populations of north China – poison gas and biological warfare. Poison gas was used against peasant resisters in north China, especially to flush people out of the networks of tunnels dug in parts of the North China Plain. And during the war, the Japanese carried out biological research at six places in China, the most infamous Unit 731 (*Qisanyao budui*), near Haerbin, in Manchuria. There, prisoners of war were used as human guinea pigs. Neither chemical nor biological warfare was ever talked about openly; the rumours of what was going on made it seem all the more horrible.

Eviction and conscription   Expropriation of land brought virtual social extinction to some communities in north China. From late 1941 to late 1942, Japanese forces cleared land in Hebei and Shanxi and along the Great Wall where it bordered Manchuria. The aim was to create exclusion zones to prevent guerrilla actions. The local people were evicted and their land confiscated. Altogether, 42,000 square kilometres of land were cleared and turned into 'no man's land (*wuren qu*)'. In the twelve months of the operation, more than 100,000 young people and their families were sent to Manchuria.[7] The original communities ceased to exist.

The conscription of labourers in the occupied areas, to work in China or in Japan, was another cause of social breakdown, especially in the last three years of the war. The men taken away had to abandon their families, usually with no preparation, because they were often press-ganged. They received no wages and could not send any money home to their dependents – who were not only destitute but also uncertain as to whether their men were alive or dead. The exact numbers of men taken is hard to tell, but it was certainly in the millions over the duration of the war. Labour recruitment was a large-scale business.[8] The issue of forced labour has remained alive until the present; some of the conscripts have launched lawsuits in Japan against their former 'employers', where the companies still exist.

[7] Chen Jianhui, *Wurenqu* (Beijing: Zhongyang biance chubanshe, 2005).
[8] Ju Zhifen, 'Labour conscription in north China, 1941–1945', in Stephen MacKinnon, Diana Lary, and Ezra Vogel (eds.), *China at War*, pp. 227–246; and Zhuang Jianping, 'Japan's exploitative labour system in Qingdao, 1933–1945', *ibid.*, pp. 267–264.

14 反对日本兵,到处抓壮丁。   胡一川

4.2. Press-ganged labourers. (*KangRi zhanzheng shiqi xuanchuanhua*, Beijing, 1990, p. 14.)

Dislocation, Depression, and Disease In unoccupied China, the problems of social dissolution were less dramatic than these examples but often severe. For refugees, a constant anguish was the lack of information about family members in the occupied areas. Feelings of despondency, depression, and even doom were widespread. The psychological malaise was noted by a psychiatrist, Dr. Leslie Cheng, in Chengdu. He applied his Western psychological knowledge to states of mind that would be classified in pre-psychiatric China not as illnesses but as sadness, misfortune, or weakness. Cheng found less war neurosis than he had expected; many people were coping well with the stress of war, and Cheng saw a 'great capacity for humor and laughter'. But he saw many cases of breakdown, particularly in people between thirty-five and forty-five years of age who were overwhelmed by feelings that they were growing old with no hope for the future[9] [Reading 2].

The psychiatric disturbances noted by Dr. Cheng had their parallels in physical health. The social breakdown of war helped to create the conditions for breakdowns in physical health. Epidemic diseases spread quickly in the chaotic conditions of war as people moved around and lived in temporary, often unsanitary conditions. Here is a list of major wartime epidemics[10]:

	Disease	Provinces
1937	Cholera, dysentery	Lower Yangzi Valley
	Plague	Fujian
1938	Cholera	Hubei, Hunan, Jiangxi
	Malaria	Hubei
	Relapsing fever	Northwest
1939	Cholera	Hubei, Shaanxi
1940	Plague	Fujian, Zhejiang, Jiangxi, Hunan
1941–44	Malaria	Yunnan

Non-epidemic disease also took a heavy toll. People who had moved inland might succumb to tuberculosis in the fetid climate of Sichuan. A 1943 estimate claimed that 5% of college and high school students in Chongqing were suffering from active tuberculosis, this in a city that only had one tuberculosis sanatorium with sixty beds.[11]

Those who fled to the countryside from the more advanced cities could not find medical help and might die of diseases that elsewhere would be curable. The mother of distinguished historian Yang Tianshi died when he was only three of an illness that could not be cured in the village to which the family had fled but which in their city home in Yangzhou would have been easily treated.

[9] Jean Lyon, 'War casualties on the psychological front', *China at War*, XIII, 3 (September 1944), pp. 33–37. Dr. Cheng himself had turned to religion after the death of his wife.

[10] Statistics of the National Health Administration, cited in Yip Ka-che 'Disease and the fighting men: Nationalist anti-epidemic efforts in wartime China, 1937–1945', in David Barrett and Larry Shyu (eds.), *China in the Anti-Japanese War* (New York: Peter Lang, 2001), p. 174.

[11] C. K. Chu, 'Modern public health movement', in H. F. MacNair (ed.), *Voices from Unoccupied China* (Chicago: The University of Chicago Press, 1944), p. 29.

Ba Jin's novel, *Ward Four*, modelled on Chekov's *Ward Six*, is a bitter commentary on wartime China. In the novel, the sufferings of patients in a miserable makeshift hospital are metaphors for the ills of society.[12] The book, published just after the end of the war, makes dismal reading, especially since it is written by a man once so optimistic about change and a new, free society. It was tempting to interpret the rise in disease with a medical metaphor, making physical disease a parallel with the political and military disasters that had fallen on China. The temptation increased when the state of the economy was added in.

Alongside the unravelling of the social fabric, the economy of unoccupied China was in tatters – and the clearest sign was rampant inflation.

Inflation One of the most damaging social effects of the war came from inflation. Given the dramatic decrease in government revenues after the Japanese occupation of most of the revenue-producing regions of China and the huge increase in military expenditures, the government resorted to printing money to pay for the war, apparently oblivious to the effect this would have on all those living within the monetary economy. Non-monetary causes of inflation were also clearly present – scarcity of goods, disruption of trade and communications, destruction of goods and of the means of production, drastic reductions in imports and exports, and the influx of refugees – but these factors accounted for far less of the inflation than did the cavalier use of the printing press.[13]

During the first years of the war, the pace of inflation in the unoccupied areas was noticeable but slow. From the beginning of 1942, it burst into full, malignant force. The Indian government representative in Chongqing K.P.S. Menon, quoted a graphic representation from a local newspaper of the effects of inflation in terms of purchasing power[14]:

In 1937	100 dollars could buy 2 cows
In 1938	100 dollars could buy 1.5 cows
In 1939	100 dollars could buy 1 calf
In 1940	100 dollars could buy 1 calf
In 1941	100 dollars could buy 1 hog
In 1942	100 dollars could buy 1 ham

---

[12] Ba Jin, *Ward Four: A Novel of Wartime China* (trans. by Haili Kong and Howard Goldblatt) (San Francisco: China Books, 1999).

[13] Arthur Young, *China's Wartime Finance and Inflation, 1937–1945* (Cambridge, MA: Harvard University Press, 1965), XXXX, p. 299.

[14] Krishna Menon, *Twilight in China* (Bombay, India: Bharatiya Vidya Bhavan, 1972), p. 213. Things got much worse. In 1945, 100 dollars could buy 1 fish; in 1946, 1 egg; in 1947, half a packet of matches.

In 1943   100 dollars could buy 1 chicken
In 1944   100 dollars could buy 1 bag of rice

Another way of looking at inflation is to look at the rise in price of one product. These are figures for rice in Quanzhou (Fujian)[15]:

	Price of rice per 100 shijin (50 kilograms)
1938 May	7 yuan
1939 early	8 yuan
1939 end	15 yuan
1940 fall	30 yuan
1941 end	80–90 yuan
1942 July	150 yinyuan (silver dollar)
1942 end	400 yinyuan
1943 Sept	900 jinyuan (gold dollar)
1943 end	1,200 jinyuan
1944 early	1,400 jinyuan

Inflation hit unequally. Peasants, still 80% of the population, were little affected unless they lived near urban markets, in which case the value of their produce rose, and they did well. They also had the capacity to barter goods, which people who were not producers could not. Workers who were paid by the day kept pace with inflation. People on fixed incomes or salaries were affected most drastically. This number included lower-level civil servants, the lower ranks of officers, common soldiers, teachers, and workers paid by the week or month. Wen Yiduo was supporting a family of eight. His monthly salary as a professor at Xinan Lianda could only feed this family for ten days. He dealt with this situation by teaching in a middle school, where he was paid in rice, and by carving seals.[16]

Inflation hit hard at people depending on remittances; by the time the money arrived, it would be worth less than when it had been sent. And it wounded the sense of self. This plaintive comment from an army major stationed on the Yichang (Hubei) front in early 1943 shows what was happening to the defenders of China[17]:

---

[15] Peng Tianhua, 'Kangzhan qijian Quanzhou de mihunag ji qi heimu', *Quanzhou wenshi ziliao*, 13 (1982), pp. 55–56.

[16] Hsu Kai-yu, *Wen I-to* [*Wen Yiduo*] (Boston: Twayne, 1980), p. 155. Seals are used in China instead of signatures. Seal carving is one of the high arts, and Wen was an accomplished practitioner.

[17] Young, p. 319.

I have no face any more. Although I may get leave to visit my wife in Wanhsien [Wanxian, up the Yangzi], I cannot do so because I am unable to maintain her on my $175 [about US$4] monthly salary. Even she herself earns $500 a month as a teacher. She will simply tell me: 'What sort of a husband are you?'

This story of a man whose income had not kept up with inflation is a small example of the social impact of inflation and the sense of inadequacy and failure that came over men who were unable to care for their families or to send them remittances. This was often the final straw that broke already loosened or damaged relationships – especially in cases where women were less dependent than they had once been and less inclined to put up with failings in their husbands.

The economic and social problems generated by inflation were what obsessed much of the population in the cities of unoccupied China. People were not starving. In Chongqing, the government took the management of staples seriously. It saw to the provision of grain, first to the armies and to civil servants and then to the urban populations. Land tax was collected in kind from landowners, and grain was purchased compulsorily from farmers, usually in return not for cash but for government bonds. There were large schemes to bring new land under cultivation, as in Huanglongshan. These methods provided an adequate supply of grain but not much else in the way of foodstuffs.[18] The grain-purchase schemes also had the effect of disturbing, if not destroying, traditional grain markets and infuriating the people, usually landowners, who had most benefited from them in the past.

The government did what other nations at war do to cope with food shortages: It promoted new foods. The British used the German word *ersatz* ('substitute') to describe substances such as coffee made from chicory or acorns. In China, the ancestor of the pot noodle was born. The Ministry of Food developed a range of dehydrated foods – soup powder, crystallised soy sauce, powdered eggs, powdered cabbage, rice bricks, corn bricks, wheat bricks, tea essence, and ginger essence candy. These were intended initially for army use only but gradually spread into the general population.[19] These delicacies joined America's Spam and Britain's Woolton Pie (a meat pie with carrots substituted for meat, named for the Minister of Food) in the race to the culinary bottom. The difference was that neither in the United States nor in Britain had good food been an integral part of social life; wartime substitutes might be

---

[18] Chang Tao-hsing, 'The food situation in China', *Asiatic Review*, XLI, 148 (October 1945), pp. 196–200.
[19] *China Newsweek*, 117 (December 14, 1944), pp. 8–9.

acceptable to the undiscerning consumer in those countries, but not to the serious eaters of China.

These concerns about food were complaints rather than signs of malnutrition or starvation. At the northern end of unoccupied China, the economic problems were much starker – and catastrophic. The famine that struck Henan was one of the greatest tragedies of the war.

The Henan Famine   Henan is one of the poorest provinces in China, often visited by famine. In 1942–43, a combination of war and natural disaster triggered a famine that took the lives of over three million people; another three or four million were forced to flee.

The frontline between Chinese and Japanese forces ran through the province, the Chinese in the west and the Japanese in the north, south, and east. In 1942, the spring and summer rains failed, locusts came, and there was virtually no harvest. In the past, such natural disasters would have triggered government intervention – the releasing of grain from state granaries. This time the local authorities had no surplus grain, and there was no railway or water access from outside. What stored grain there was went to the troops; the requisition of grain for the military was reduced, but only slightly.[20] There was virtually no relief work at first, except for efforts of missionaries in the southern and western parts of the province.[21] The people of Henan could either flee or sit at home and wait to die.

The famine-hit area had already been weakened in 1938 by the effects of the Yellow River flood at Huayuankou. Fugou, directly south of the breach in the dike, was devastated by the flood, with almost the entire county under water. It was beginning to recover when it was hit by locusts and then by drought. As the famine took hold in late 1942, people were driven to desperate tactics to survive[22]:

Parents sold their sons and daughter, husbands sold their wives, brothers sold their sisters, people were changed into commodities, there was a human market. As people were separated from their flesh and blood forever, the wails and anguished calls brought tears to the eye.

This evocative language is a conventional way of describing the horrors of famine, but this does not make the tragedy less real. Equally evocative

---

[20] Zhang Zhonglu, '1942 *nian Henan dazai de huiyi*', in Song Zhixin (ed.), *1942: Henan da jihuang* (Wuhan: Hubei renmin chubanshe, 2005), p. 145.

[21] Erleen Christensen. *In War and Famine* (Montreal, Canada: McGill-Queens, 2005). Christensen's father was a missionary doctor in southern Henan.

[22] *Fugou xianzhi* (Zhengzhou: Henan renmin chubanshe, 1986), p. 93.

is the string of three-character phrases used to describe conditions in Gongxian in the hills of west Henan[23]:

Gou bu jiao, ji bu zhao, jingshui ku, heshui gan, shu luo ye, cao mai gu, tian wu yun, huangfeng qi.

Dogs do not bite, chickens do not call, wells dry up, rivers run dry, trees drop their leaves, weeds and crops wither, the sky is cloudless, the yellow wind blows.

In Sishui, west of Zhengzhou, the famine victims ate grasses, wild plants, fruit peel, peanut shells, tree bark, and even earth; they burnt cloth and made a paste of the ashes. They ate their livestock. Some of these 'foods' had disastrous consequences – poisoning, edema, bleeding, pain, and even death. Many peasants sold their land for prices so low that the money received hardly dented the crises of individual families. In the end, the population fell during the famine from 95,000 to 61,600: 30,000 people fled, and 3,400 died of hunger.[24]

In the unoccupied parts of the province, where county authorities were still functioning, they and local gentry pleaded for government help, but there was almost none available. They resorted to traditional means of trying to relieve drought. In Gongxian, the magistrate prayed for rain at the Temple of the Dragon King, hoping that the ceremonies would give the people some mental relief (*anding minxin*).[25] In a small town in Tanghe, in the northwest of the province, a 'human market (*renshi*)' had emerged by the end of 1942. On market days, girls were brought in for sale. Most of them were from refugee families. The traders in human beings (*ren fanzi*) bought the girls to be prostitutes or servants.[26]

The cities and towns of Henan fared little better than the villages. Intrepid American journalist Theodore White went into the region in February 1943, to Zhengzhou, the epicentre of the famine.[27]

When we awoke in the morning, the city was a white sepulcher peopled with grey ghosts. Death ruled Chengchow [Zhengzhou], for the famine centered there. Before the war it held 120,000 people; now it had less than 40,000. The city had been bombed, shelled and occupied by the Japanese, so that it had the half-destroyed air of all battlefront cities. Rubble was stacked along the gutters, and the great buildings, roofless, were open to the sky.

[23] Liu Qingzhao, '*Minguo sanshiyi nian Gongxian zaiqing ji jiuzai*', *Henan wenshi ziliao*, 19 (1986), p. 166.

[24] Wang Yuguan, '*Yijiu siernian dacaozai zhi Sishui*', *Henan wenshi ziliao*, 19 (1986), pp. 160–165.

[25] Liu, p. 157.

[26] Jin Shilun, '*Tanghe de renshi*', in Song, pp. 209–211.

[27] Theodore White and Annalee Jacoby, *Thunder Out of China* (New York: William Sloane, 1946), p. 170.

The famine dragged on into 1943, long after the drought had broken. A Canadian missionary, Bill Simpson, reported from Zhengzhou in April 1943[28]:

We have had a lovely spring with occasional rains just like today and the compounds and countryside look very beautiful. The barley is nearly ripe and the wheat is in that luxuriant blue-green stage just after it has blossomed, One sees a beauty deeper than the colour of the waving grain when one realizes that the harvest will mean solid cereal food again for hungry stomachs that have been constantly filled and refilled with leaves, weeds, cottonseed cake and various other things unfit for human consumption. The sad thing is, though, that many who planted will not be here to reap. Thousands have died and none of those who fled last autumn when they realized what lay ahead have as yet returned, and most of them will never return. Some villages are reported to be devoid of people, and in most of them the population has dwindled a fourth to one half of what it was last year.

This was sadness almost beyond grief, an awful victory for nature and for the war that allowed the famine to run on and on without any help being given to its victims.

Rural Instability

Shandong/Gaomi   In the occupied areas, rural instability became the way of life during the war. The situation in Shandong was an archetype of what was happening throughout north China. Shandong had a long tradition of fighting, of resisting outside control, and of rebelling against injustice. It was the province of the Liangshanbo heroes, fighters, drinkers, and carousers. It was also the province of the great strategist of the Three Kingdoms period, Zhuge Liang, as well as the home province of Confucius and Mencius. Shandong people did not scare easily. In modern times, their most famous exploits were as Boxers, in the anti-foreign movement at the end of the nineteenth century. Japan had long coveted Shandong and had made three previous incursions into the province (1914, 1920, and 1928).

Early in the war, Shandong descended into chaos. Most of the provincial elite disappeared, and the society was effectively decapitated; the government, military, and much of the rural elite fled before the invading Japanese, led by Governor Han Fuju, who withdrew his armies rather than resist. He was soon executed by Chiang Kai-shek to encourage others to resist.[29] The Japanese put in a puppet provincial government in

---

[28] Quoted in Christensen, p. 128.
[29] Diana Lary, 'Treachery, disgrace and death: Han Fuju and China's resistance to Japan', *War in History*, XIII, 1 (January 2006).

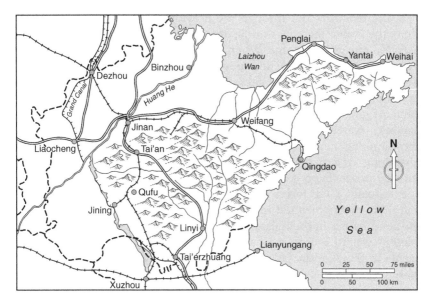

Map 4. **Shandong**

Jinan, while the remnants of the GMD government, under He Siyuan, former head of the civil government, withdrew into the salt flats and marshes of the Yellow River delta, with a motley crew of supporters, marines, leaderless soldiers, students, and bandits. He kept a government operating until the end of the war, but it had no fixed location, no income, and no authority.[30]

The CCP had high hopes for Shandong and sent capable organisers to Shandong from Shaanxi, intending to establish a strong base area there. But relentless attacks from Japanese forces, coupled with internal divisions, meant that the base area did not achieve the coherence and solidity that had been anticipated until well into the war.[31]

Japanese control over Shandong was partial, concentrated along the two railway lines, along the major roads, and in large towns. In small towns and villages, control fluctuated, occasionally Japanese, more often puppet, and sometimes autonomous. On the coast, the major ports, Qingdao and Yantai, were strongly held, but lesser ports, such as Penglai, were largely left alone so long as they did not upset the Japanese.

---

[30] He Zichuan, *Yige chengshi aiguo de Shandong xuezhe* (Beijing: Beijing chubanshe, 1996), pp. 323–334.

[31] Dagfinn Gatu, *Village China at War: The Impact of Resistance to Japan* (Vancouver, British Columbia, Canada: UBC Press, 2008), p. xi.

In the hills that run through the province and in the marshy lands along the rivers, there was no Japanese presence and seldom even puppets. No one was in charge. When Liang Shuming, the philosopher who had run a rural reconstruction movement in Shandong, went on a secret trip in 1939 trip to visit the sites of his former activities, he found a chaotic situation in which the men called 'guerrillas' – local militias, remnants of government armies, communist 8th Route Army troops, and bandits – were 'merged in kaleidoscopic patterns of alliance, vendetta, accommodation and rivalry'.[32] In effect, there was civil war in rural Shandong. At a time when there was a clear national enemy, the guerrillas were producing not organised resistance but chaos and confusion.

Eventually, CCP forces came out on top. As the war went on, more and more young men left the coastal towns and cities and went to join the communists in the hills. One motivation was to join the revolution; another was to escape the danger of being taken as forced labour by agents working for the Japanese. The Shandong Base Area emerged as a loosely connected collection of hill and coastal base areas that the CCP leadership in Yan'an sought, with mixed results, to bring under direct control.[33]

The chaos in Shandong had a crippling impact on rural society, so pervasive and so continuous that only very remote, self-sufficient areas could escape. Rural social structures were so stressed that they often were close to falling apart. Families were dislocated by the departure of young men to the armies and to the guerrillas. The accompanying shortage of agricultural labour created economic distress. Rural markets faltered, credit dried up, and livestock was seized. Peasants reverted to subsistence farming; there was a decline in cash crops in favour of food crops.[34]

The dislocation of rural society intensified as the Japanese turned to more and more brutal ways to deal with 'communists' (all guerrilla activity was labelled 'communist'). The 'three-all strategy (kill all, burn all, destroy all)' was used with hideous ferocity. Villages were subjected to collective punishment – the people killed, the buildings burnt, and anything material destroyed [Reading 3].

---

[32] Guy Alitto, *The Last Confucian* (Berkeley: University of California Press, 1979), p. 303.

[33] Elise Devido, 'The survival of the Shandong Base Area, 1937–1943', in Feng Chongyi and David Goodman (eds.), *North China at War: The Social Ecology of Revolution, 1937–1945* (Lanham, MD: Rowman and Littlefield, 2000), pp. 173–188.

[34] Ramon Myers, *The Chinese Peasant Economy* (Cambridge, MA: Harvard University Press, 1970), pp. 278–282, describes the situation in Shandong and Hebei, documented from Japanese sources.

The anguish of the Shandong peasantry is described in vivid detail in Mo Yan's novel, *Red Sorghum* (*Hong Gaoliang*), an earthy description of the marshy areas of northeastern Gaomi, where he grew up. Gaomi is on the railway between Jinan and Qingdao. In the war, the county town was tightly controlled, but the rural areas were not, especially in the summer when the sorghum (*gaoliang*) grew well above the heads of men, a sea of sweet-smelling red. At the start of the war, the peasants were poor but quite cheerful, their spirits buoyed by drinking great quantities of *gaoliang* wine. The war brought disaster on disaster. In 1939, the Japanese built a road across the county and demanded thousands of days of free labour to build it. The mules that were crucial to cultivating the *gaoliang* were seized. Most difficult of all for the locals was that once the *gaoliang* was up, it provided perfect cover for guerrillas, and that summer they came to attack the newly built road. They brought with them the guarantee of reprisals.

A local bandit, Yu Zhan'ao, is the hero of the novel. His wife, sur-named Dai, inherited a distillery from her first husband. Yu was hardly an upright character – in fact, he had killed Dai's leprous husband – but his strength, his boldness, and his love of Gaomi redeemed his failings; in rural Shandong, tough, strong men were the traditional heroes. He and the passionate and beautiful Dai organised a daring operation to blow up a bridge on the new road, after 'devils' (Japanese troops) skinned their foreman alive. The operation failed because their supposed allies failed to turn up. Dai was killed in the fighting. The operation brought retribution from the Japanese army on their village; the village was burnt out, and the villagers either died or survived to live in abject terror, no one able to trust anyone any more, their old world was gone forever. Yu ended up in a Japanese forced-labour camp in Hokkaido.[35]

Mo Yan's account closely parallels the war in Gaomi and other counties. To the west of Gaomi, in the central massif, Linqu was hit by a disaster that could not be blamed directly on the Japanese occupation – a four-year drought that started in 1940 and gradually reduced the county to destitution and famine. Almost half the population of about 350,000 left, most fleeing to relatives in Manchuria. Over 100,000 of those who stayed died of starvation; only 80,000 people were left at the end of the war. No help came to the county for the duration of the war.[36]

[35] Mo Yan, *Hong Gaoliang* (Beijing: Zuojia chubanshe, 1995). It is translated into English by Howard Goldblatt as *Red Sorghum* (London: Penguin, 1993). The film *Honggaoliang* came out in 1987, starring Jiang Wen as Yu and Liu Xiaoqing as Dai, two of the biggest names in Chinese cinema. Their own love affair made the film a huge event, as *Cleopatra* was because of the Burton-Taylor romance.

[36] Thomas Gottschang and Diana Lary, *Swallows and Settlers* (Ann Arbor: University of Michigan, 2000), p. 117.

Socioeconomic Disruption: The Qiaoxiang

The upheavals of the war took many forms, some less severe than others but still difficult for the people who went through them. One of the less severe but still traumatic upheavals was what happened to the communities from which the Overseas Chinese came, the *qiaoxiang*. The war brought international isolation to China; most links to the outside world were broken. The Overseas Chinese were cut off, severely affecting the areas in China from which they came. The major *qiaoxiang* were in Guangdong and southern Fujian (Minnan).

Xiamen, the port city for Minnan, lies on an island in the far south of Fujian. It developed as a port in the late nineteenth century, outpacing the much older port city to the north, Quanzhou (Marco Polo's Zaitun). Xiamen became the centre of the migrant trade to the Nanyang (Southern Ocean, i.e., Southeast Asia) and also one of the main exporters of foodstuffs from China; the Amoy Canning brand of sauces and pickles was world famous. Xiamen was a favourite haunt of foreign diplomats and businessmen, who lived on the idyllic island of Gulangyu across the harbour from the city. For Britain, Xiamen was an outpost for Hong Kong; for the United States, its close connections to the Philippines made it important. For Japan, it was the link between Mainland China and Taiwan, a colony of Japan since the Sino-Japanese War (1895); most of the Chinese population of Taiwan came from southern Fujian.

Another attraction of Xiamen to foreigners was that the city and the province behind it had a long-standing tendency to ignore whatever central government was in power. Xiamen and Fujian went through the first two and a half decades of the Republic in a state of semi-autonomy but paid for this autonomy because the government provided little in the way of maritime defence for the province. In early 1938, the island of Jinmen (Quemoy), only two kilometres from Xiamen, was taken. Xiamen people looked on in horror as refugees flooded in from the island, full of stories of brutality and violence, including stories that women were being taken from the 'lost island (*wangdao*)' to Taiwan 'to satisfy the pitiless lust of the savage army'.[37] Only a few months later, in May 1938, a contingent of Japanese troops landed on Xiamen Island and captured the city. The ferocity of the assault, in which several hundred people were killed, shocked the city. In panic, almost two-thirds of the city's people fled. The population declined from 260,000 before the war to 88,000 in 1941.[38]

[37] *Xingguang ribao*, February 26, 1938.
[38] *Xiamen KangRi zhanzheng*, p. 572.

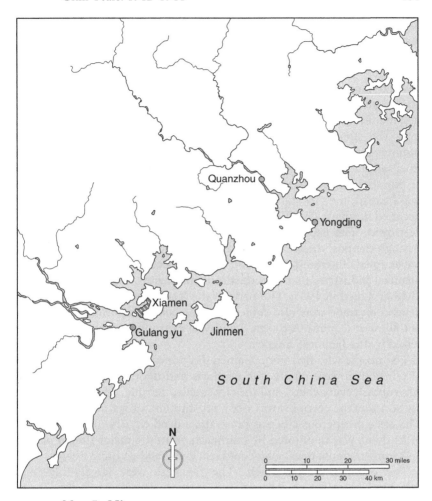

Map 5. **Minnan**

Many of the refugees fled first to Gulangyu; the island was not occupied until the start of the Pacific War. From there, some went on to Hong Kong and to the Nanyang. Others moved inland. Xiamen University, set up by Tan Kha-khee (Chen Jiageng), the rubber baron of Malaya, moved into the interior, to Changting. The city government withdrew inland, to Zhangzhou. With it went all the professionals and business people. Within a brief moment, all those who could afford to flee had gone, and only the poor remained in the city.

The refugees were distributed, in quite an orderly fashion, throughout the interior of the province. Local social organisations were instructed to pay for the costs of receiving the refugees, and uncultivated land was taken over to settle them on, a move that indicated the acceptance by the provincial government that the Japanese occupation would be a long one.[39]

What happened to Xiamen after the exodus had little of the horror that accompanied the occupation of Nanjing. There were rumours of atrocities, including one that fat young men and plump girls were disappearing from the streets and reappearing cooked in butchers' shops.[40] The rumours were ghastly, but there was little likelihood that they were true; salacious stories associated with cannibalism are a recurrent theme in popular culture. Xiamen did not in fact suffer atrocities or bombing. Instead, the city started to die. The port was blockaded, and trade declined dramatically. Without its trade, Xiamen's economy was almost destroyed. The exports of tea, sugar, and fruit that had once poured through the port dried up, and the city was increasingly cut off from its unoccupied hinterland, which had not been occupied. The transport and financial industries that depended on the migrant trade withered after 1938 and died in 1941. The parts of the Xiamen economy that did not depend on trade were also ruined. Fishing collapsed; fishing boats were not allowed to put out to sea. Land was expropriated, and crops were seized by the Japanese military.

The people who fled from Xiamen did not come back. By 1940, nine of ten houses were empty, the windows and doors smashed in. There was rubbish everywhere, and the city smelled terrible. The only flourishing sector of the economy was vice – prostitution, drugs, and gambling.[41] The once prosperous city was prostrate, a dead city (sishi). The process of its dying was monitored by journalists from the major Fujian papers and some national ones, who could still come and go quite freely.

The occupation was harsh. The Japanese were largely invisible; they used as agents of occupation Taiwanese. Xiamen had the largest concentration of Taiwanese on the Mainland. They were Japanese subjects, but their forebears came from Fujian, and they spoke the local Minnan dialect. By 1940, there were almost 11,000 Taiwanese in Xiamen, or one in eight of the population. Most of them had come to stay – they arrived as families.[42]

The war was like a multiple amputation for Xiamen. Only the torso remained; the limbs, the connections to the Nanyang and the hinterland,

[39] *Nanfang ribao*, August 26, 1939; *Fuxin ribao*, September 26, 1939; *Yongchun ribao*, September 23, 1939.
[40] *Dacheng ribao*, June 27 1940; and *Yangguang ribao*, July 9, 1940.
[41] *Zhongnan ribao*, July 23, 1940; and *Fujian ribao*, December 11, 1940.
[42] *Dacheng ribao*, November 29, 1940.

were severed. The war was a disaster for Xiamen and a disaster from which the city did not recover until the 1980s – the first time that trade flows reached the levels they had in the pre-war period.

Xiamen's neighbour, Quanzhou, had a different experience of war. The city and its region got through the war with little direct damage. The Japanese did not pursue their occupation northwards. The rugged coast, fringed by reefs, and the hills just inland made an attack on Quanzhou difficult; the Japanese settled instead for a naval blockade.[43]

Quanzhou was not occupied, but the appearance of an easy passage through the war is illusory; the city was turned inside out by the war. From its earliest history, Quanzhou had faced outwards. It was the home region of the hundreds of thousands of people who emigrated to Taiwan and to the Nanyang. They went out to trade and to work in the plantation industries (i.e., rubber, timber, and coffee). They sent money home in the form of remittances, which became one of the major sources of income for the region, especially as income from the traditional local sources, tea and porcelain, declined.

Many of the able-bodied men were away more or less permanently in the Nanyang. They went on their own, leaving their parents, their wives, and their children at home. Those who did well acquired second, 'little' wives abroad. The family members at home did some farming but did not depend on farm income; the bulk of their expenditures were covered by remittances from the men abroad. This money paid for living expenses and for the construction of houses, some of them mansions, depending on how well the men had done away. The families of the emigrants led agreeable, relaxed lives. One of their main occupations was to maintain the family and clan shrines, to keep the sense of local ties going, and to make sure that those outside never forgot home. For the rest, they did a little farming, entertained each other, and gambled enthusiastically.

This pleasant life came to an end with the war. The local economy staggered. The naval blockade made two of the major forms of local employment almost impossible – fishing and smuggling. Family connections with the Nanyang were strained after the occupation of Xiamen in 1938. Some money still got through, but visits from family members abroad almost stopped. After the start of the Pacific War in 1941, all connections with the Nanyang were broken; no letters got through, there was no news of family members abroad, and remittances stopped completely. The collapse of remittances was not the result of direct Japanese action but of the rupture of a system that depended on an intricate web

---

[43] O. J. Caldwell, 'Japan's failure in Fukien [Fujian]', *Amerasia*, IV, 2 (April 1940), pp. 83–85.

of connections based on trust – and on the smooth working of the inter-national postal system. It did not involve direct transfers but the deposit of money in money shops (*qianguan*) in the places where the emigrants were working. The recipient at home was then notified by post and col-lected an equal amount at home, in Chinese currency, from a local part-ner of the money shop.[44]

Without the remittances, the lives of family members at home fell apart. The loss of income left them with only two ways to support them-selves – selling their possessions or going out to work, something they had never expected to have to do. The family and community relation-ships that had been oiled by money from abroad atrophied.[45] The war was a time of intense insecurity, poverty, and anxiety, all eating away at the fabric of a society that had once been self-confident, cheerful, and optimistic.

The anxiety was compounded, for the duration of the war, by the fear that Japanese armies might land at any moment. Their first landing was dramatic. At 6 a.m. on July 16, 1940, Japanese marines landed at the fortress of Yongningzhen, south of Quanzhou. Warships off shore first shelled the town, including the huge mansions built with money from businesses in the Philippines. They took the Ming fortress, killed a num-ber of people, and then withdrew the same day.[46] This incursion turned out to be the last. Japanese troops never came ashore again, although their planes were overhead often, and gunboats periodically shelled the coastal communities from the sea. Each time the Japanese were sighted, the local people raced for the caves in the headlands. They lived in a state of chronic tension and anxiety. They also had to put up with the increased presence of Chinese troops on the front line with the Japanese, something they had lived without for a very long time.

What Fujian went through during the war was replicated in the other *qiaoxiang*, particularly Zhongshan and Taishan counties in Guangdong. In the emigrant villages, men were away for years at a time in North America, leaving parents, wives, and children behind. The families lived from remit-tances. After the war started, the remittances and the visits home dwindled and then stopped. The *huaqiao* families had to learn to fend for themselves. Many of them barely survived, farming, taking any job that came up – a life remote from the previous ease as the pampered relatives of men work-ing themselves to the bone abroad. The family ties were almost destroyed. Helen Yu was born in China in 1937, just after her father had returned

[44] Interview with Zeng Kunluo, Jinjiang Chidianzhen, May 14, 2005.
[45] Interview with Chen Shubi, Huang Ruilian, Quanzhou Fengzhouzun, May 15, 2005.
[46] Interview with Xing Tianying, Yongningzhen, May 16, 2005.

to Canada. She and her family eked out an existence in Zhongshan over the eight years of the war. They never heard a word from their father; not a single letter got through from Canada. She first met her father in 1964, when she came to Canada herself – at the age of twenty-seven.[47]

Denise Chong's family was divided for even longer, between Taishan and Canada. Her grandfather, Chan Sam, had two wives, one at home and the other, May-ying, in Vancouver. Chan Sam was reasonably prosperous in the early 1930s. He went back and forth to China several times, and on one trip he left two of his Canada-born daughters in China. His third daughter was born in Canada and his only son in Taishan, at about the same time, one to each wife. He never managed to get home again, never saw his longed-for son. The war kept him in Canada, with May-ying. They heard that the second of their three daughters had died mysteriously in 1942 after she had encountered a unit of Japanese soldiers. They dared not voice the horror of what she might have been through before she died. After the war, the Civil War in China kept him from going home. He stayed in Vancouver, sending money whenever he could to the family at home. Only in the 1980s did his third daughter, Way-hing, and her daughter, Denise, make their first visit to the village. The family had been divided for fifty years.[48]

The experiences of the *qiaoxiang* do not seem so terrible when compared with the sufferings that people went through in other parts of China, but for the families of Overseas Chinese, the war was still a long, drawn-out ordeal. The old, comfortable order had come to an end – and though they could not know this at the time, it was not going to be restored for more than forty years. The start of the war was the beginning of the separation of the overseas communities from home that continued under the communist government until the 1980s – when what seemed like a miracle happened, and after five decades of separation, the old ties were revived. It was amazing that they could be revived, that there was enough toughness of spirit and resilience to keep the ties alive, even when they seemed quite dead.

Coping Mechanisms

As the war dragged on, some people sank into apathy and depression, fearing that it would never end. Others were consumed by bitterness.

[47] Interview with Helen and John Yu, Vancouver, British Columbia, Canada, August 25, 2008.
[48] Denise Chong, *The Concubine's Children: Portrait of a Family Divided* (Toronto, Montreal, Canada: Viking, 1994).

Between these two extremes, people found many ways of coping with the situation.

Some coping mechanisms are universal. Substances – opium, alcohol, cigarettes – provide relief, and in wartime China, all were present. In unoccupied China, opium smoking was not encouraged, but opium was still widely available. In the occupied areas, opium was virtually a government monopoly; Chinese leaders made bitter denunciations of the Japanese for trying to reduce the Chinese to abject slaves to drugs. Pu Yi, the restored emperor, presiding over a mini-palace in Xinjing (Changchun), the new capital of Manzhouguo, found his own escape in drugs.

Alcohol consumption was considerable, less in the urban population than amongst peasants, especially in north China, where some of the strongest home brews in the world are distilled. And cigarette smoking was almost universal amongst men and gaining ground with women. But substances were only an aid to coping with uncertainty, grief, and anxiety. Other mechanisms involved digging deep into the Chinese tradition, finding new solutions and new ways of living or short-term ways of relaxing and relieving the pressure of the war.

Stoicism

疾风知劲草患难见交情
Adversity reveals true strength

The greatest cultural inheritance that the Chinese had to rely on in adversity was stoicism, the belief that China, with her turbulent history, her sometimes harsh social systems, and her frequent natural disasters, had taught her people to suffer patiently. One of the commonest of sayings is 'Eat bitterness and suffer hardship (*chiku nailao*)'. It implies that when things get tough, as they undoubtedly will, the best way to get through them is to accept them, to hope that things will get better, and in the meantime to endure them. The trait is described in a negative way as 'fatalism' and in a positive way as 'stoicism'.

The war was the time above all to see this state of mind in operation. The hardships that came upon China were accepted, and people kept going through tragedy and upheaval without complaining very much and without giving in either to the occupiers or to despair. This stoicism impressed Allied foreigners living in China as much as it confused the Japanese, who had assumed at the start of the invasion that the Chinese, being rational people, would understand that they had been defeated and would embrace the new rulers. Instead, the Chinese relied on a combination of new nationalism and ancient culture. They recalled the cultural heroes and heroines who had endured horrors and even death rather than succumb to the enemy. Hua Mulan was one. The strategist Zhuge Liang and the general Yue Fei, both of whom died fighting for righteous causes, remerged as models of people prepared to die for their country rather than surrender.

The ability to endure – and to endure with grace and humour – was one of the chief coping mechanisms, one that was hard for foreigners to analyse. Sometimes the ability to endure was misinterpreted as a lack of feeling, a dull, insensate ability to suffer without complaint, or resignation in the face of adversity, or as an inability to stand up for themselves. These misinterpretations were unfair and showed a misunderstanding of what endurance meant.

Endurance was not enough on its own to live through hard times. Other measures had to be brought into being.

Survival Mentality   The rise of the survival mentality, the idea of looking after oneself at the cost of concern for others, was a drastic change in Chinese social norms, one that persisted long after the war. The need to survive in the turbulence of war brought a constriction in the family circle, in the number of people one individual could care for or be concerned about. This was the phenomenon described later by Edward Banfield as 'amoral familism', the inability to think beyond the immediate, nuclear family. It is a mentality borne of extreme poverty and insecurity, when the extended family and broader social connections are either absent, through separation or death, or too demanding in time and money. Each small unit strives only to look after itself in a dog-eats-dog world where you either survive or die. The mentality was not a question of choice, or of moral turpitude, but a reflection of living in impossibly difficult circumstances that did not allow a person to care for anyone except the immediate family. During the war, the survival mentality became ingrained. It was a product of the havoc caused by fighting, natural disasters, and occupation that came with the war.

There were winners in these battles for survival, the individuals who came out on top or did well, but there were more losers. The losers eventually turned to any force that promised stability and authoritative control. This was the appeal of fascism in Europe and of the CCP in China. Both promised stability and security. In China, the CCP offered a community of mutual reliance and a new creed that appeared to put the poor and the benighted at the top of its concerns. The creed came along just when earlier faiths appeared to be faltering.

Religion   Many people turn to religion in times of war and crisis for consolation and guidance, and they pray for divine help; war intensifies the need to appeal to metaphysical powers. In China, religion seemed to offer little comfort during the war. Prayers to Buddhist and Daoist deities for divine intervention were not answered, nor did local deities associated with folk religion help much to mitigate the disasters the war brought. In unoccupied China, the religious activities of temples were restricted by the loss of their facilities; most were taken over by schools, hospitals, and government departments.

The one religion that flourished during the war was Christianity. At the top of the GMD, Song Meiling proclaimed her Christian faith fervently and frequently and praised Christianity's focus on social service. In the occupied areas, missionaries had extraordinary opportunities to help the communities in which they lived: They could offer sanctuary to local people in danger when Japanese armies came in, and they could provide medical care. Their help won them sudden spurts of conversion. In Jiangsu, the Canadian Jesuit missionaries made thousands of converts in the short weeks of the Japanese occupation in May 1938, far more than they had ever made before.[49] Some of the conversions stuck beyond the immediate crisis that drove desperate people to the protection of the missionaries. The help from missionaries did not last. By the middle of 1942, most missionaries from Allied countries had either left the occupied areas or had been interned. The German, French, and Italian missionaries who remained made little impact.

If religion was not a major help, other parts of the Chinese tradition were.

Humour   Black humour, gallows humour, and self-deprecation are well-tested ways of coping with anguish and misery. Humour makes people laugh, and it lets them mock the people whose actions have produced their current misery. It releases tension and makes the unbearable ridiculous.

Humour is a powerful cultural marker; it is strongly entrenched in some fortunate cultures, amongst them the British and the Chinese. The ability to laugh through adversity could be summed up in one of the catch phrases of the war in Britain – Mrs Mop's 'It's being so cheerful wot keeps my going', repeated in every instalment of *ITMA* and passed on again and again by ordinary people to each other.[50] During the war,

---

[49] Diana Lary, 'Faith and war: Canadian Jesuits and the Japanese invasion of China', *Modern Asian Studies*, XXXIX, 4 (2005), pp. 825–852.

[50] *ITMA* (*It's That Man Again*) was the BBC's wartime comedy show, a linear predecessor of the *Goons* and *Monty Python*. *ITMA* and Winston Churchill's speeches were the two broadcasts that no one ever missed.

foreigners from non-laughing societies living in China were astounded at the way Chinese could react to dreadful situations with laughter and smiles, with humour rather than despair. Lin Yutang noted how little some foreign experts appreciated the spirit of many Chinese, including their sense of humour[51]:

> The serious students of China's affairs are not only a sad lot, but they usually manage to miss the subtle, indefinable human quality of the Chinese people and Chinese politics, which carries with it a sense of convincing reality.

Humour is often carried by jokes, and there were unofficial anthologies of jokes in wartime China, told and retold. An unexpected source was the traitor, Han Fuju. Han's coarse, often crude, and always banal jokes lived on after his execution for treachery in 1938. Han's jokes were nothing if not self-deprecating; they celebrated his own ignorance. One of his most famous jokes was about the diplomatic quarter in Beijing: 'There are so many huge embassies in *Dongjiao minxiang* [the diplomatic quarter]. Almost every country in the world has one. Only our China does not have one, it's too unfair.'[52] Han's jokes were retold throughout unoccupied China and not only by the unsophisticated. Jian Youwen, one of the best known historians of modern China, was a master exponent of Han's jokes and a performer much in demand at social gatherings. In Guilin, professional performers such as Ouyang Yuqian relied on Han's jokes and his stammer to pack in audiences, as in this comment on Chiang Kai-shek's efforts through the New Life Movement to instil discipline on China, including making pedestrians walk on the right-hand side of the street[53]:

> I ... I ... I am ni ... ni ... ninety-nine thousand nine hundred and ninety-nine percent in favour, bu ... bu ... but I am one percent not in favour. Wh ... wh ... why? If a ... a ... all the pedestrians walk on the right, what will the left side of the road be used for?

Any occasion could be turned into an excuse for humour. The wedding in January 1944 of the philosopher Liang Shuming was a surprising one. He was a fifty-year-old widower, and his bride was a spinster school teacher. They fell in love and decided to marry in a public celebration in a Guilin hotel. The wedding was followed by a raucous, bawdy party at which dubious poems were recited by some of China's leading intellectuals, and the bridegroom sang arias from Peking operas.[54]

---

[51] Foreword to George Kao, *Chinese Wit and Humor* (New York: Sterling Publishing, 1946).

[52] Shen Yunjia, '*Wuzhi zhong de yumo*', in *Siwei yu zhihui*, Vol. 1, 1998, p. 48.

[53] Diana Lary, 'Treachery, disgrace and death: Han Fuju and China's resistance to Japan', *War in History*, XIII, 1 (January 2006).

[54] Guy Alitto, *The Last Confucian*, pp. 311–314.

Perhaps the greatest benefit of humour was in the way it changed attitudes towards the enemy. Mocking the enemy made them seem stupid, incompetent. These jokes included aspersions to height and sexual capacity, all guaranteed to make the enemy look ridiculous rather than threatening.

Poetry Educated men in China have always written poetry as a way of expressing their deepest, often most painful feelings. Although usually a practice associated with the scholar elite, there were also famous military poets, most famous of all Yue Fei, the Song general who wrote 'Manjianghong'. During the war, generals and politicians wrote classical poetry in huge quantities and practiced calligraphy to restore some tranquillity to their spirits. Intellectuals wrote even more.

Some of the poets stayed with traditional themes – nature, love, drinking – but others were moved by the plight of the people. Yu Youren, one of the elder statesmen of the GMD, wrote about the sufferings of orphans, in 'The Fatherless Child'[55]:

> In the East village the house is burnt
> And people have fled from the West suburb.
> My father went out to fight the barbarians,
> But when did he die on the battlefield?
> There was a young girl in our neighbor's house on the left
> And a little boy in the right-hand neighbor's house
> But the mad brigands took them away.
> I cannot tell what they wanted to do with them
> How many orphans has the battlefield made?
> How many tears are shed for the fatherland?
> Who will defend our fatherland?
> And the poor young ones of the fatherland?

This was a traditional form of poetry. Modern poets, working in the new language, also were hard at work throughout the war, the most famous being Wen Yiduo, Dai Wangshu, and Ai Qing. Their works helped them to cope with the war, as it helped their readers cope. Chinese war poetry was not the anti-war poetry of Wilfrid Owen or Siegfried Sassoon but deeply patriotic, anguished, and inspirational.

Escape from the War: Departure, Nostalgia, camouflage China has traditions of avoiding conflict. One was to become a hermit, getting right away from the world and its horrors. Closely linked to complete withdrawal was the practice of Daoism, which allowed one to escape psychologically and spiritually without leaving the turbulent world. In

[55] Lu Qian, 'Chinese poetry in wartime', *Asiatic Review*, XLI (October 1945), p. 75.

every period of conflict in China's long history, some people chose to escape rather to engage in the conflict. At the end of the Ming Dynasty, in the seventeenth century, Bada Shanren, the greatest of all Chinese painters, fled to the mountains and became a hermit. He was a connection of the Ming royal family, and this form of escape was one of the few means of survival. Another Ming artist with imperial family connections, Shitao, became, after the Qing conquest, a monk, escaping into a monastery and emerging only late in life to rise to great fame as a painter. Other Ming loyalists fled the Qing occupation and sailed across the sea to Taiwan. The most famous of those was Zheng Chenggong, founder of the first Chinese settlements on the island.

There were new patterns of escape in the Resistance War. At the beginning of the war, affluent people who wanted to get away from the turmoil went abroad or into the safety of the foreign-controlled areas of China. Shanghai's foreign concessions and Hong Kong filled up with people who preferred to sit out the fighting close to China rather than fleeing to the interior. Life in these havens was strange and isolated and became more so after the start of the Pacific War. Hong Kong almost closed down under the Japanese, the population falling to less than 500,000. Shanghai came to be known as the 'orphan island *gudao*'. There was cautious passive resistance and a common refusal to collaborate actively,[56] but in many ways life went on as normal. Shanghai's hectic social life continued, business continued, though at a much lower level, and residents tried to ignore the Japanese.

But Shanghai was not the same. There was an odour of cowardice to the behaviour of those who stayed in the safe havens; their reluctance to share the sorrows of the nation was criticised in the same way that people who left England for America during the war were seen as running away.[57] Those who stayed on were slightly shame-faced and seldom talked, after the war, about what they had done then. These havens were only for the affluent; the poor could not afford to live in the concessions, unless they were able to move in with relatives.

Another way of escaping from an unbearable present is to pretend it does not exist and to retreat into the past, steeping oneself in nostalgia. This nostalgia is not the common form of sentimental regret for what has been lost. It is the deliberate creation of a lovely past that is quite

---

[56] See Nicole Huang's important study, *Women, War, Domesticity: Shanghai Literature and Popular Culture in the 1940s* (Leiden: Brill, 2005).

[57] Ironically, the writers who brought the China war to life, in *Journey to a War* (London: Faber and Faber, 1938), Christopher Isherwood and W. H. Auden, left England for Hollywood when war came to Europe.

different from the horrible present. This is a exaggerated reaction of people who are profoundly unhappy; it may even involve the creation of imaginary worlds. A penetrating description of such a personality comes in Elias Canetti's novel about a sinologist living in Berlin, so absorbed in the Chinese past that he is oblivious to the Nazis who are taking over the world outside his apartment.[58] In China, some people who stayed in the occupied areas, drifted back into the past, especially in Beiping, a city that had never really left the imperial age. They sank back into the past and lived in a haze of beautiful memories, of detached beauty. They blocked the war and its horrors out.

Another form of retreat learned well in difficult times is to camouflage oneself, to withdraw into an obscurity so complete that one becomes almost invisible. During the war, many of China's celebrated artists and performers did this. They could not bear to move into the interior, but they would not have anything to do with the Japanese. Qi Baishi, the celebrated painter, was almost eighty at the start of the war, too old to leave Beiping. He put up a sign on his gate: 'No orders for paintings accepted'. He did sell pictures discreetly, to support his enormous family; some of them (such as 'The Crab') were guarded anti-war allegories.[59] Mei Lanfang, the greatest player of female roles in Peking opera, did not go to Chongqing, but he did refuse to perform for the Japanese – and grew a moustache to make sure that he could not play his female roles. He lived in Shanghai, trained students, and studied English but did not perform in public until just after the Japanese surrender.[60] Butterfly Wu (Hu Diedie), the most famous actress of her generation, spent much of the war in Hong Kong in a retirement from which she emerged after the war. Novelist Zhang Ailing (Eileen Chang) spent the war in Shanghai, writing in exquisite prose about romance and intensely personal anguish, as if the war and the outside world did not exist.

The reverse of camouflage was escape in clear view. This is what some young writers in Manchuria did. They wrote publicly, but in code, subtly speaking for the cause of women, indirectly attacking the Japanese. Mei Niang and her friends pulled it off; they became immensely popular without the authorities noticing how subversive they were.[61] They paid

---

[58] Elias Canetti, *Auto da Fei* (London: Jonathan Cape, 1982).

[59] T. C. Lai, *Ch'i Pai Shih* (Kowloon: Swindon, 1973), pp. 99–103.

[60] Zhang Changfa, *Mei Lanfang nianpu* (Nanjing: Hehai daxue, 1994), pp. 137–151. For an extravagant version of the life of Mei Lanfang, see the 2008 movie *Forever Enthralled* 梅兰芳.

[61] Norman Smith, *Resisting Manchukuo: Chinese Women Writers and the Japanese Occupation* (Vancouver, Canada: University of British Columbia Press, 2007).

an awful price later on, when, in the 1950s, they were attacked for having 'collaborated' with the Japanese.

Conclusion

This period of the war seems, in terms of China's society, to have been almost the worst of the war. The rate of increase in the indices that mattered to daily life – prices, scarce commodities – speeded up. Family separations lengthened. The disaster of the Henan famine underlined how terribly vulnerable the peasants of China now were. No one could help them when a natural disaster struck. China was at a very low ebb.

Readings

Reading 1: Lao She, 'My Mother (Wode muqin)'[62]

Lao She's mother was a Manchu from a farming village outside Beijing. Her youngest son adored her but let her down when he refused an arranged marriage and when he went to England. In the war, he let her down again when he fled to the southwest.

After war broke out on July 7th [1937] I fled from Jinan. Beiping had been occupied by the devils, as [foreign armies had occupied it] in 1900, and the son whom Mother cared about so much had run off to the southwest. I could imagine how much she missed me, but I could not go back. Whenever I received a letter from my family, I did not dare to open it at once, I feared, feared, feared that there would be bad news in it. People can live to eighty or ninety. As long as you have a mother alive you can still feel a bit like a child. When you lose your mother you are like a flower in a vase, with colour and a scent, but no roots. People whose mothers are alive have secure hearts. I feared, feared, feared that a letter from home would tell me that I was now a plant without roots.

Last year [1942] I found no mention in the letters from home about how my old mother was doing. I was worried and fearful. I wondered if everything was alright, and it was just that my family, knowing that I was off on my own, didn't want to bother me. My mother's birthday was in September, so halfway through August I sent off a letter of congratulations, reckoning that it would get there before the great day. In the letter I poured out my best wishes; after that I stopped worrying. On December 26th, when I came back from a meeting of the Cultural Army, I found a letter from my family. I did not dare open it. When I was alone I opened it. My mother had already been dead for a year.

---

[62] First published in April 1942 in *Banyue wencui*; reprinted in *Lao She wenji*, Vol. XIV (Beijing: Renmin wenxue chubanshe, 1989), pp. 250–251.

My life was given to me by my mother, and my growing up to be an adult came through her blood and sweat in caring for me. Being able to become a not entirely bad person was due to her efforts. My character and my patterns of behaviour were passed on to me by her. She never had any good fortune in her life. Even when she was dying she still only had coarse food to eat. Ah, what else is there to say? My heart hurts. My heart hurts.

Reading 2: 'War Casualties on the Psychological Front'[63]

Case histories of the psychological effects of war:

... a government office worker in Chungking [Chongqing]. During the terrific continuous bombing of the wartime capital in the summer of 1940, this man lost his wife and two children. After that the man became more and more of a recluse, lost his interest in his work and gradually fell into a state of complete inactivity. Now he simply sits or lies still, refusing to be a part of life at all.

... a wife of a middle school teacher. The man and his wife and two children had been living in North China, and fled as the invader approached, taking all their most prized possessions with them. They reached the city of Loshan [Leshan] in Szechwan [Sichuan] Province, and took rooms in a hotel while they looked for permanent quarters. While they were out house hunting the city was attacked by Japanese bombers. ... when the family returned to the hotel they found it ruined and all of their possessions completely destroyed. The loss of her household possessions – the materials evidence of her former security – seemed to unbalance the mind of the wife. The family moved to a country place not far away, where they were looked upon as strangers and 'down-river' people. The wife began to think she was being persecuted. People were laughing at her, she thought. Eventually the persecutions she imagined became until she finally convinced herself that the neighbours had killed her two children. She was taken to the insane asylum, and there, mercifully, she died.

Among the students, separation from their home seems to be one of the main causes of psychological upset. ... They seldom hear from their families and each new battle on the war fronts of China starts an epidemic of worry and all its resultant ailments (headaches, insomnia, loss of appetite).

Reading 3: 'A Devastated Village in Longkou, Shandong'[64]

There are now accounts of mopping up in many villages in the occupied areas. Few are contemporary records. The Japanese army did not publish accounts; peasants were too terrified to write down the details. But

---

[63] Jean Lyon, pp. 33–35.

[64] 'Zhonggong Longkou shiwei dangshiwei', Longkou dangshi ziliao, III (November 1990), pp. 190–191.

memories survived; over the last two decades, many have appeared in *Materials on History and Literature.*

Shanxitou Village

On March 30th, 1942, towards evening, five or six hundred Japanese soldiers suddenly rushed in to Shanxitou Village, which lies on the road between Xiheyang and Fengyi. Shanxitou was a small village, with only seventy or eighty households. The arrival of so many Fascist soldiers was like an explosion. The sounds of shooting did not stop. Inside the village and outside, up on the hills and in the woods. People were screaming, horses neighing, chickens squawking, dogs barking. As the Japanese soldiers rushed into every house, the people were panic-stricken. The village was gripped by horror.

When the peasants coming back from their day's work got to the entrance of the village and saw what was happening, they abandoned their animals and their tools and fled. Some of the young men in the village had already managed to escape as the soldiers were coming in, but the majority of the villagers were stuck in the village.

The arrival of the Japanese turned the quiet, peaceful village into a nightmare. Fires were lit all over the village. All the chicken and geese – about four hundred – were seized and roasted over the fires. The pigs and goats were all slaughtered. All the grain stored in the houses was taken, the finer grains for the Japanese soldiers' own stomachs, the coarse grains for their animals. They were so careless that the ground was covered in split grain. The seizures meant that the village, already short of grain, would face famine in the spring.

At nightfall the soldiers turned on the women like wild animals, and raped ten or twenty women. Some of the women were unable to move for days after their ordeal. The saddest case was the pretty new wife of Zhang Zhongshun, who was raped to death.

Towards dawn the Japanese soldiers cleaned out all the valuables in the village, and took five of our young men to carry them away.

Films

Red Sorghum (Hong gaoliang). Director Zhang Yimou, 1987.
Forever Enthralled (Mei Lanfang). Director Chen Kaige, 2008.

5   Turning Points: 1944–1945

Events

The Course of the War

During the last year of the war, the power balance within China shifted
decisively. The Guomindang (GMD) government and its armies were
critically weakened, and the Chinese Communist Party (CCP) and its
armed forces grew rapidly in strength. The United States, the GMD's
main ally, had real doubts about its future capacity, while in the last week
of the war the CCP acquired a potential international ally, its fraternal
socialist brother, the USSR.[1]

By late 1944, the tide of war in Europe had turned. The German
armies were on the defensive, thrown back from the USSR and North
Africa and losing ground against Britain and the United States in
Western Europe after the Normandy landings in June. Italy was effectively out of the war. In Europe, towns and cities under German control
were being subjected to tremendous Allied bombing. In the Pacific, US
naval and air forces were winning victory after victory against Japanese
forces. Japan's cities were coming under ferocious bombing. In the
largest raid, in March 1945, a firestorm created by bombing almost
destroyed Tokyo and killed nearly 90,000 people. The Americans
seemed to be taking retribution for Pearl Harbor. The end of the war
was very close.

In May 1945, Allied victory was proclaimed in Europe. Three months
later, Japan surrendered unconditionally. The war that had convulsed
the world ended sooner than had been expected, brought to an end in
Asia by the dropping of two atomic bombs on Japan. Before the end
of the war, however, Japan's last ground campaign – ironically called
Campaign One – brought terrible damage to China.

---

[1] There is no single word in Chinese for 'brother', only 'older brother' (*gege*) or 'younger
brother' (*didi*). The USSR saw itself as China's older brother, the source of what became
a difficult relationship.

The Ichigo Campaign

玉石俱焚

Stone and jade are both destroyed in the fire[2]

The Ichigo Campaign lasted from May to December 1944 was the largest Japanese campaign in China. For China, it was almost the greatest military debacle of the war, the worse because it came when defeat for Japan already seemed inevitable. The strategy behind the campaign was a mystery. The strategic justification for the campaign, to link Japanese troops in China and Indochina (Vietnam) and to create a land connection all the way from Manchuria to Singapore, was specious, negated by the wild terrain in the border region between China and Indochina and by the absence of rail or road links.

More than a million soldiers fought in the campaign, over 500,000 on the Japanese side (the largest number deployed in any Japanese campaign) and even more on the Chinese side. The Japanese attack started in Henan and then pushed south through Hubei, Hunan, Guangxi, and into Guangdong. Then the Japanese armies attacked from Guangxi into Guizhou, threatening Chongqing from the rear. The Chinese armies fell back in a series of disastrous defeats. The casualties were enormous, almost 100,000 killed or wounded on the Chinese side, over 60,000 on the Japanese side.

The GMD armies were devastated by Ichigo. Veteran soldiers had been at war for seven years without home leave, and the men were dispirited and exhausted. The newer soldiers were conscripts, in poor condition. None of the soldiers was well equipped, and many were hungry. Even though much of the fighting was in fertile areas, the army supply system was an early casualty of the campaign. In the ranks, there was little stomach for fighting.

弃甲曳兵而走

Abandoning weapons and running

The result of the poor shape of the soldiers was massive desertions or disorganised withdrawals. The United States was furious with what it saw as the incompetence of the GMD military. The US air force installations in Hunan and Guangxi had to be destroyed to prevent them from falling into Japanese hands. As the campaign drew to a close, the GMD once again took the dreadful resort of a scorched-earth action – the beautiful city of Guilin was burned out by its own defenders.

---

[2] 玉, jade, stood for China; 石, stone, stood for Japan.

This campaign underlined the demoralisation and exhaustion of the GMD armies. It looked as if the Japanese strategy was to destroy them, to wipe them out before the war ended, and to leave the field to the CCP armies in the north – who were not attacked in the campaign and for whom Ichigo was a huge and unexpected bonus. Since Japan launched her occupation of China in the name of containing communism, the Ichigo strategy seems a contradiction; it remains one of the most inexplicable campaigns of the entire World War II.

The Rise of the CCP

At the start of the war, the main body of the CCP was a small, exhausted group of people hunkered down in Yan'an in the remote, rugged hills of Shaanxi. They had just escaped from the jaws of annihilation on the Long March. Their location in the northern hills meant that the main communist forces barely had to engage in large-scale, positional warfare against the Japanese – in which they probably would have been defeated. CCP forces seldom engaged the Japanese armies directly; throughout the war, the bulk of the fighting and the great majority of Chinese casualties were from the GMD armies.

Six years after the start of the war, the CCP's military situation had undergone a sea change. The CCP came into the last two years of the war as a strong force with a major base in Shaanxi, significant areas of control in various parts of north China, and a large army. On the political side, Mao Zedong was now unchallenged, growing in stature as a strategist and an ideologue of great ability. Three of his four 'commonly read' articles, 'In Memory of Norman Bethune (*Jinian Bai Qiuen*)', 'Serve the People (*Wei renmin fuwu*)', and 'The Foolish Old Man Who Moved the Mountain (*Yugong yishan*)', were written during the war. These articles were short, pithy, and inspirational. They could be read and understood by the barely literate as well as by intellectuals. They were learned by heart by all communists. They showed the confidence of the CCP and its leader and the conviction that the future belonged to them [Reading 1].

The CCP's greatest strength was now its armies. Its armed forces were a mixed lot in origin, ranging from tough and disciplined pre-war Red Army soldiers to former GMD soldiers to former bandits and militiamen. It was a hard task to make these disparate groups in to a disciplined, united armed force – which is where the skills of the CCP's formidable generals were so important. The Ten Great Marshalls (Zhu De, Peng Dehuai, Lin Biao, Liu Bocheng, He Long, Chen Yi, Luo Ronghuan, Xu Xiangqian, Nie Rongzhen, and Ye Jianying) all served in key positions during the war. They were not only excellent tacticians and strategists

Map 6. **China, 1945**

but also inspirational leaders.[3] In terms of the quality of its armies, the CCP now outshone the GMD, whose armies had more generals but fewer who could inspire their men. The CCP forces were still poorly armed and equipped, but they could fight. By the end of the war, the CCP's army had brought the CCP to a position from which it could challenge the GMD, at least for shared control of China.

---

[3] These men were as famous in China as any generals in the West. All but one were southerners, who moved to north China with the Long March. Four of the six were persecuted in the Cultural Revolution.

5.1. **Election of a village head.** (*Kangri zhanzheng shiqi xuanchuanhua*, no. 109.)

The CCP made parallel gains on the political and organisational fronts, especially in rural north China. According to a senior Japanese staff officer, Samukawa Yoshimitsu, by late 1944 the Japanese army could claim firm control over only seven of the 400 counties nominally under its control; 139 were under CCP control. In the remaining 295, 67% of the total, control fluctuated, with the population largely pro-communist.[4]

The CCP's policies were still not very radical. They called for reform rather than out-and-out class warfare; the party promoted policies such as rent reduction and minor land redistribution. The GMD meanwhile had not been able to maintain control of the guerrilla units in the occupied areas that had previously been loyal it. The last these places had seen of the GMD was now seven years earlier.

The CCP showed a remarkable ability to rise to the occasions provided by the shifting situation in the war to provide leadership and to get people organised for resistance, for production, and for education. In his path-breaking study, Dagfinn Gatu gives full credit to this ability[5]:

[4] Cited in Dagfinn Gatu, *Village China at War* (Vancouver, British Columbia, Canada: UBC Press, 2008), pp. 30–31.
[5] Dagfinn Gatu, pp. 358–359.

... assertions by many historians that wartime developments strongly favoured the growth of the CCP is a gross simplification; it only addresses novel opportunities opened up to the CCP, chiefly the weakening of the GMD, while ignoring the enormous difficulties, hazards and dangers that [were] conditions imposed on the CCP movement. Besides, harnessing advantageous circumstances required commensurate abilities.

The CCP also showed its strength in making allies of members of local elites who were not actively collaborating with the enemy. The cooperation of these people, mostly members of the lower levels of the elite, was essential in popular mobilisation. In the base area in southern Henan, the CCP co-opted much of the lower elite, people who shared the sense of desperation that the war had brought – but, by ideological standards, were class enemies.[6] Through a long period of trial and error, the CCP honed its organisational skills throughout the areas it controlled in north China.

The CCP drew strength from the redeployment of Japanese forces in north China and from the behaviour of those who remained. As the fighting shifted to south China and to overseas, there were fewer and fewer Japanese troops on the ground. Those left behind became more insecure and even paranoid about guerrilla attacks. This mentality produced greater violence against civilians and brought more reprisals for real or perceived threats. 'The populace of North China was so antagonised that they were a vast source of anti-Japanese manpower' – and went to the only people who seemed willing and able to lead them in resistance – the CCP.[7]

The CCP was also winning the propaganda war against the GMD. The party identified itself with peasant culture, using peasant art forms – woodcuts, folk songs, and traditional dances – to show its interconnections with the masses.[8] The GMD was associated much more with high culture, poetry, calligraphy, and landscape painting; the early successes in war propaganda had withered. The common touch and the CCP leaders' apparent lack of moral turpitude endeared them to foreigners who came to visit Yan'an. The glowing accounts from these visitors were quite different from the irritable reports now coming out of Chongqing, which showed the GMD as corrupt, inefficient, and unwilling to fight.

---

[6] Odoric Wou, *Mobilizing the Masses: Building Revolution in Henan* (Palo Alto, CA: Stanford University Press, 1994), pp. 375–379.

[7] Lincoln Li, *The Japanese Army in North China* (Tokyo: Oxford University Press, 1975), p. 232.

[8] The film *The Yellow Earth* (*Huang tudi*), which launched the revolution in Chinese filmmaking in the early 1980s, gives a vivid picture of the activities of a song collector.

At home and abroad, the CCP's reputation rose as the GMD's sank, making it more and more possible to conceive of the CCP as a viable participant in national government.

The Soviet Arrival

In early August 1945, the Soviet Union entered the war. Soviet troops crossed the northern border of China into Manchuria. The intervention was too late to bring about the defeat of the Japanese because it came just after the first atomic bomb had fallen on Hiroshima and just before the Nagasaki bomb. But it was enough to get Japanese soldiers and civilians to flee in panic from Manchuria. There were historical scores to be settled. Within living memory, Japan had defeated Imperial Russia in Manchuria (1905), humiliating the Russian nation and precipitating the first revolution there. In their rush to escape Russian vengeance, the Japanese abandoned armaments, trucks, food supplies, and industrial equipment. The Soviets shipped much of the industrial equipment back to European Russia as spoils of war. The intention was to use the equipment to replace what had been destroyed by the war in the West. Other materiel – weapons, trucks, and military supplies – gradually found its way into the hands of the Soviets' rather distant allies in the socialist cause, the CCP – which now found itself equipped to take on the GMD forces.

Topics and Case Studies

By 1944, the war had been going on for so long that it seemed it might never end. The hope that the Japanese might be defeated was still faint. A dismal 'new normal' was depressing but tolerable. What could not be tolerated with even the slightest equanimity was that the war would suddenly get much worse, as it did in 1944.

A New Wave of Losses

The last year of the war brought new waves of refugees and another round of material losses to China. The war moved into the southernmost provinces that had largely escaped the direct impact of the fighting. Their cities and towns had been bombed but not annihilated. They were now hit with a vengeance, victims both of the Japanese attack and of the scorched-earth strategies of their own forces. Hunan, Guangxi, and Guizhou were visited by a wave of losses that replicated with a dreadful symmetry those that had befallen other places earlier in the war. In June

Map 7. **Guangxi**

1944, Changsha fell to Japanese forces, a hugely symbolic loss because Changsha had been defended successfully three times at earlier stages of the war (though burned down in 1938 by its defenders). Fire now consumed another great city of southern China.

The Great Fire of Guilin   A massive conflagration is the ultimate symbol of destruction. Buildings are consumed by flames; people are incinerated. The survivors are displaced, denuded of all their possessions. This was the fate of Guilin in the autumn of 1944.

The destruction of Guilin was a tragedy for the city's inhabitants and for those who had sought refuge there during the war, many of China's most prominent intellectuals and artists. It was also a great cultural loss for China. Guilin was one of the most beautiful cities in the country, its lovely buildings set in a wonderful, almost surreal landscape of limestone crags and bright green paddies.

The Guilin fire was an act of self-immolation. The fire was a desperate tactic of scorched earth ordered by army commanders who were themselves from Guangxi. To stem the remorseless southern advance of

5.2. Evacuation from Guilin. (Cai Dizhi, in *Woodcuts of Wartime China, 1937–1945*, 1946.)

the Japanese armies, they fired their own home. In early October, wild rumours had the Japanese forces very close to the city. There were still huge numbers of troops to defend northern Guangxi (about 170,000), but morale had collapsed. Even the execution of a senior commander who withdrew his troops from the border with Hunan, Chen Munong, could not stem the tide of defeatism.[9] The local commander, Wei Yunsong, ordered the evacuation of the city in mid-October. Most of the civilian population fled; a great flood of refugees poured south to Liuzhou and west, up the new railway line in to Guizhou[10]:

Along the road straggled lines of war's most miserable creatures – refugees. Households reduced to awkward bundles, the roots plucked up and strewn helplessly by big winds. Women of all ages and with hobbled feet and loads on their backs and on children. An occasional column of dejected retreating soldiers. On the tracks just outside the city and at the south station three stalled refugee trains. Cars of all types were crawling with people like bees on a comb, inside and outside on the rods. Movement was blocked by a derailment up the line. People waited mostly with unsmiling patience. Some had taken [to walking] along the ties, walking hopelessly in search of safety.

[9] *Guangxi tongzhi dashiji* (Nanning: Guangxi ren minchubanshe, 1998), p. 232.
[10] Harold Isaacs: *CBI Roundup*, 1944. Isaacs was near Guilin to cover the destruction of the US air bases.

Kweilin [Guilin] was a dead city, dead as only a teeming Chinese city suddenly emptied can be dead. Shops, houses, hotels, cafes and whorehouses were boarded up.

Military discipline amongst the units detailed to remain for the 'defence to the death' of the city collapsed. Many of the soldiers deserted, too demoralised and disorganised to think of fighting – and also wanting to get home to protect their own families, whom they had not seen for seven years. The troops who did not flee went on the rampage, looting away until the city was stripped bare.[11] Virtually every house in the city was turned upside down by the looters. Then the city was fired, supposedly to open up a field of fire or, alternatively, to prevent the Japanese from profiting, but just as likely to cover up the evidence of the looting. The city burned for ten days with no effort to extinguish the flames. Japanese troops arrived weeks later, on November 11, to find an empty, gutted, blackened city; only the natural beauty surrounding it survived.

The main flood of refugees, some of whom had fled from Hunan and some of whom were Guangxi people, poured westwards up the new railway line into Guizhou. As they fled, they were strafed from the air by Japanese planes. Eventually, Japanese ground forces caught up with the streams of refugees. There was wild chaos in which huge numbers of people died, either mown down from the air by bombing or strafing, or killed by Japanese forces, or crushed in stampedes. A Chinese officer who tried in vain to maintain some order on the railway line claimed that in the border area between the two provinces, 100,000 refugees and local people were killed.[12] This figure is imprecise and quite probably an exaggeration, but even if the real number was much smaller, it was still a horrible disaster. The fact that the civilians were not protected by their armed forces showed how low military morale had sunk. The rout marked the collapse of what had been one of the finest armies in China, the Guangxi Army. Even its brilliant strategist, Bai Chongxi, was powerless to prevent the disintegration.

The last terrible campaign of the war hit hardest in southern China. In the north, the main effect of the fighting was a realisation that the focus of Japanese attention had shifted away from the north. And it was understood that as brutal as the campaign was, the likelihood was that Japan would win the campaign but lose the war. The time had come to prepare for the end of the war.

[11] Huang Mengnian, '*Rijun jinfan Guilinji*', *Guangxi wenshi ziliao*, 25 (1987), pp. 91–98; Chao Wei, '*Guilin jiaotu kangzhan qinliji*', *Wenshi ziliao xuanji*, XL (1963), pp. 181–189.
[12] Cao Fuqian, '*Xiangguiqian dakuitui qinduji*', *Wenshi ziliao xuanji* (1963), pp. 191–197.

War's End in the Occupied Areas   As the end of the war drew near, people in the cities of northern China that had escaped the direct impact of war began to fear what would happen to them in the next while. Some joined late resistance efforts, others rewrote the history of their own behaviour in the war, but most kept quiet, stuck in a sullen state of anxiety. They were in the same kind of situation that the French in occupied France were in early 1944; knowing that the Germans would soon be defeated, the resistance surged up, and people who had lived with the Germans suddenly became anti-German. In China, people described as members of the 'wind faction (*fengpai*)', those who survived by watching which way the wind was blowing and adjusting their allegiances accordingly, started to distance themselves from the Japanese and to make discreet overtures to the GMD or CCP.

The horror of war finally reached some of the occupied cities; they were bombed, something they had escaped at earlier stages of the war. The bombs came not from Chinese planes but from the enormous new US B29 bombers that could reach Japan and occupied parts of China from fields in India, Guam, and the Marianas. Wuhan, the Yangzi city that had been the temporary capital of China six years earlier, was nearly destroyed by allied bombing. These raids, coupled with the news, garnered through rumour rather than the press, of the terrifying raids on Tokyo and other Japanese cities, convinced people that the war was almost over.

谣言满天飞
Rumours flying everywhere

Outside the cities and towns still held by the Japanese and their associates, the political and military situations were complex. Some areas were already under CCP control; others were shifting back and forth between different forces. The film *The Devil on the Doorstep (Guizi laile)* captures the terrible uncertainty of the peasants in a small village close to a Japanese fort about what will happen to them if and when the Japanese depart and the mysterious guerrilla leader, known only as 'I (*wo*)', who comes in the night, takes control.

Social and Economic Dissolution

Physical destruction was one facet of the accelerating decline and dissolution in China. Social dissolution was another. As people came to perceive that the war might soon be over, they came too to make an accounting and to realise how much they had lost. With the sense of loss came a realisation that there could be no going back to the world they had known before the war – if they were old enough to remember it. The fears were unspoken, and they were not addressed by political or intellectual leaders, except in the communist camp. Even there, talk about revolution was muted. No one knew what the post-war world would be like. The great writer Mao Dun described the utter dejection that dominated Chongqing before the end of the war [Reading 2]. Old social relationships had gone, and there was nothing to replace them except confusion and atomisation.

The economic crisis was another facet of dissolution gnawing away at the fabric of society. In 1944 and 1945, it degenerated from a chronic, debilitating crisis to an acute one in which people were involved in an all-consuming battle for daily survival. Inflation was the surest sign of the economic crisis and an omnipresent monster.

Inflation The spiralling inflation made life almost impossible for anyone reliant on money.[13] Late in the war, the rate of inflation galloped away as the government printing presses worked harder and harder.

Issue of Banknotes by Four Government Banks, 1937–1945, for July in Each Year[14]	
1937	1,445,000,000
1938	1,754,000,000
1939	3,193,000,000
1940	6,250,000,000
1941	11,296,000,000
1942	25,308,000,000
1943	52,505,000,000
1944	129,057,000,000
1945	462,327,000,000

The issuing of banknotes was the prime cause of the accelerating inflation, now careening towards hyperinflation (monthly price rises of over

[13] For a detailed description of the inflationary process, see Chang Kia-ngau, *The Inflationary Spiral: The Experience in China, 1939–1950* (Cambridge, MA: MIT Press, 1958).

[14] Arthur Young, *China's Wartime Finance and Inflation* (Cambridge, MA: Harvard University Press, 1965), pp. 363–365. After 1942, the central bank took over all issuing responsibilities.

50%). K.P.S. Menon's depiction of inflation, presented in Chapter 4, shows the acceleration in the rise of prices at the end of the war[15]:

In 1937	100 dollars could buy 2 cows
In 1944	100 dollars could buy 1 bag of rice
In 1945	100 dollars could buy 1 fish
In 1946	100 dollars could buy 1 egg

These are figures for rice in Quanzhou[16]:

	Price of rice per 100 shijin (50 kilograms)
1938 May	7 yuan (Chinese dollar)
1944 early	1,400 jinyuan
1944 late	5,000 jinyuan
1945 early	10,000 jinyuan

These astronomical numbers miss one aspect of inflation, a weighty one, and that was the government's reluctance to print large-denomination notes. People had to take bags, suitcases, or even wheelbarrows to collect their wages and salaries. As the rate of inflation increased, they had to spend their money as quickly as possible, running not walking to the market or to the shops, buying necessities first and then anything else that was for sale, whether they needed it or not – they might be able to sell it later for a better price. By the end of the war, average prices in Chongqing were more than 2,500 times the pre-war levels.[17]

Inflation hit unevenly. Workers who were paid by the day were poor but did not get noticeably poorer, but for people on fixed incomes or salaries, the situation was now terrifying They were oppressed with anxiety over whether they would be able to eat or not and despairing as they saw their bank savings evaporate. The political consequences for the GMD were huge. Inflation ate away at the confidence and eroded the trust of the people whom the GMD saw as its natural constituency – the middle class, merchants, and the military.

[15] Krishna Menon, *Twilight in China* (Bombay, India: Bharatiya, 1972), p. 213.
[16] Peng Tianhua, '*Kangzhan qijian Quanzhou de mihuan geji qi heimu*', *Quanzhou wenshi ziliao*, 13 (1982), pp. 55–56.
[17] Young, p. 327. Prices rose another 2,500 times over the next three years.

The indignity of inflation was exacerbated by the increasingly wide-spread activities of hoarders, profiteers, and black-marketeers. For these people, the raging inflation was a godsend. Scathing local and foreign comments made little impact [Reading 3]. Scarcity of most consumer products had already encouraged the rampant black market; inflation played even more into the hands of the profiteers. Now they could get even higher prices for their goods if they waited only a few hours.

Many salaried people felt that they had no choice but to get into the black market themselves and speculate; their salaries came nowhere near to keeping up with inflation. The transactions they had to involve themselves in – running round the markets, checking prices, haggling, counting out hundreds of bills – were preoccupying and time-consuming. They became the centre of peoples' lives, and they left little time for political thoughts or concern for others.

The loss of morale and of nationalist spirit was almost total. People who had started the war willing to abandon their homes and families in the name of the nation now tacitly accepted that money had become the only yardstick of success.

The abuses triggered by inflation started at the top. Chongqing was alive with rumours about how much money the relatives of Chiang Kai-shek, especially his sister-in-law, Song Ailing, and her husband, Kong Xiangxi, who ran the government's financial affairs, had made through their access to the highest levels of government and administration. These rumours were by their nature unprovable, but they were widely believed, and they made those who were suffering from the inflation indignant. A foreign commentator summed up the feelings of many local people: The real problem was the baleful influences from downriver, the Shanghai obsession with money.[18]

The values of Shanghai have been transplanted to Chungking [Chongqing]. To get rich quickly, to have a beautiful mistress (or at least one who compares favourably with Hollywood standards), to be able to give dinners in which shark's fin, already almost unobtainable, will be served as a delicacy, to ride in a motor-car and be able to say that your income can be measured in millions are the hallmarks of the most exquisite taste.

The later years of the war were a golden age for anyone who had access to US dollars. As the Chinese currency (*fabi*) depreciated, the value of the dollar went up. After 1942, US currency poured into China through Lend-Lease projects and through support for US operations in China.

[18] Robert Payne, *Chungking Diary* (London: Heinemann, 1945), p. 99.

The change in the market exchange rate between Chinese and American currencies was startling[19]:

Date	Rate: Fabi per US dollar
1937 July	3.37
1940 December	17.6
1942 December	49
1943 December	84
1944 December	570
1945 July	2,925

Put another way, a person could buy almost a thousand times as much with dollars in 1945 as with the same dollars in 1937. The exchange rate made people who could get a hold of dollars very rich – and produced a rapacious currency market in which many of the players were government officials and army personnel – anyone who dealt directly with Americans.

Inflation also hit the urban economy of occupied China. A price index for Beiping was 100 in 1937 and 1,790 in April 1944. The price of grain increased by an even higher percentage.[20] And inflation was only one financial problem; beyond it, there was great anxiety about what would happen to the wartime currencies when the Japanese were defeated, an anxiety felt equally strongly in Taiwan and Hong Kong.

Conscription   Peasants were insulated from the worst effects of inflation because they produced what they ate, and they could exist in a barter economy. But they were vulnerable to conscription. In unoccupied China, this was conscription to serve in the armies; in occupied China, it was conscription to work as a virtual slave in Japan, Korea, and Manzhouguo.

The demand for recruits for the GMD armies far outstripped the supply of volunteers; in the later years of the war, there were no more patriotic recruits. Conscription became the norm in unoccupied China. By law, all men between eighteen and forty-five years of age were liable for conscription; only sons and the physically or mentally disabled were exempted. In practice, only poor peasants were conscripted, 14 million of them during the course of the war. Quotas for new recruits were assigned to specific counties and villages, and military teams went out to

---

[19] Young, p. 265.

[20] Zhang Quan, *KangRi zhanzheng shiqi lunxianqu shiliao yu yanjiu* (Nanchang: Jiangix chubanshe, n.d.), p. 131.

enforce them. This was a golden opportunity for corruption; any family with the means bought out their sons, either by paying a substitute or by bribing recruiting officials.

Conscripts were rounded up in villages, dragged off, often roped together, to army camps and to battlefields. They were expected to walk to their military bases, sometimes hundreds of miles. Those who could deserted; those who could not were subjected to persistent mal-treatment in training and on the way to their units. When Chiang Kai-shek heard how badly recruits were being treated, he apparently broke down, wept, shouted at the head of the conscription board. 'You are murdering my soldiers!' – and ordered the immediate execu-tion of one recruiting officer.[21] Whether the story is true or another example of how Chiang dealt with publicity disasters (as with Han Fuju and the Changsha commanders in 1938) by executing scape-goats, it could not cover up the disgraceful sight of poor young men being maltreated in the name of fighting for their country. The mal-treatment was a symbol of a fundamental loss of morale – and of the fact that by the last years of the war it was the poor who were paying the price of resistance.

The circumstances of the men taken by Japanese recruitment agents in north China (mainly in Shandong and Hebei) were equally awful. After the start of the Pacific War, Japan's need for soldiers increased dra-matically. Japanese men were conscripted into the armies, and Chinese labourers were conscripted to take their places in factories and mines and on farms in Japan, Korea, Mongolia, and Manchuria. The demands of the Japanese recruiting systems were huge, the numbers actually brought in 1944 lower than the target, but still enormous[22]:

	Planned	Actual
1942	907,000	1,087,350
1943	800,000	1,009,050
1944	700,000	476,350
1945	410,000	51,970
Total		2,624,720

[21] F. F. Liu, *A Military History of Modern China* (Princeton, NJ: Princeton University Press, 1956), pp. 135–138.

[22] Ju Zhifen, 'Labour conscription in north China', in Stephen MacKinnon, Diana Lary, and Ezra Vogel (eds.), *China at War* (Palo Alto, CA: Stanford University Press, 2007), p. 218.

There was no pretence that these men were voluntary workers. They were picked up in villages and marketplaces by puppet troops, kept in internment until they could be shipped to Japan, treated abominably, and never paid. Their treatment was the ultimate statement of the prevailing racist attitude towards Chinese.

This anti-Chinese racism had a concomitant aspect – the turning of the tables on white people who had previously embodied racial superiority in China.

The Collapse of Western Prestige

Since the Opium War, Westerners in China had lived in varying degrees of luxury and privilege, protected, except for brief periods, by the unequal treaties that put them outside Chinese law. Almost all had servants. Their children went to special schools. Some, especially missionaries, made great efforts to adapt to China and learned Chinese. Others, notably diplomats, merchants, and the treaty-port foreigners, did not. J. G. Ballard spent the first sixteen years of his life in Shanghai without learning a word of Chinese or eating any Chinese food.[23] Most resident Westerners stood apart from Chinese life, ineffably superior.

This sense of superiority did not survive the war. By the end of the war, Western prestige had been so eroded that it was virtually destroyed. The coup de grace was delivered by the Japanese. The first Westerners to slide into the abyss were allied (i.e., British, American, Canadian, Australian, and New Zealand) civilians, who from early 1942 on were interned in camps. Axis foreigners (i.e., Germans, Italians, and Vichy French) rode high under Japanese rule but were brought down with a sickening bump at the end of the war, now citizens of defeated countries, along with the great number of Japanese who had often lived in China for many years.

There were other, stateless foreigners. These included nearly 20,000 European Jews, most in Shanghai, who had fled overland from Western Europe at the start of the Nazi persecutions. Tens of thousands of White Russians were in China, the largest concentrations in Manchuria, where they had lived comfortably with the Japanese for fifteen years. As the war drew to an end and the threat of the Soviet arrival loomed, they fled south into China Proper, preferring anything to falling under Soviet control.

---

[23] J. G. Ballard. *Miracles of Life: Shanghai to Shepperton* (London, Fourth Estate, 2008).

The only foreigners whose prestige increased during the war were Americans. The substantial aid given to the government of China after Pearl Harbor and the American political influence in Chongqing meant that Europeans were sidelined. The new power in China was the United States.

The Weixian Camp   After Pearl Harbor, Allied citizens in China became enemy aliens, subject to internment. Over the next few months, they were herded into makeshift camps. The largest camp was the Weixian (*Wei hsien*) Camp in Shandong, opened in 1942. It was housed in a former mission compound. More than 2,000 Allied civilians, missionaries, business people, and teachers were held there. For the first time, different groups of foreigners who had previously lived quite separate lives were lumped together.

The camp was crowded, the buildings were almost derelict, there was never enough to eat, and the food that there was monotonous and of low quality. The climate was harsh, too hot in summer and too cold in winter.[24] The inmates were not maltreated, as Allied prisoners of war were elsewhere in Asia. There was no physical brutality, no rape. For the inmates, however, their incarceration was miserable and tedious. They had to learn to manage without servants, to do their own chores. The single people lived together in dormitories; the families were crowded into tiny rooms. They spent much of their day in endless queues for food, lavatories, or showers.

The most famous inmate of Weixian was the Flying Scotsman, Eric Liddell, the athlete hero of *Chariots of Fire*, who refused to race on a Sunday in the 1924 Paris Olympics. He died of a brain tumour just before the end of the war; despite the large number of doctors in the camp, there were no facilities for them to operate on him. Most of the internees survived. They were treated immeasurably better than Chinese prisoners of war, who were either killed or sent to Manchuria, Japan, or Korea as forced labour. For many internees, though, there was deep sadness that their lives in China had come to an end.

The Japanese authorities may have hoped that interning their white enemies would win them favour with the Chinese people, taking conviction from their claims that the war was an anti-imperialist war designed to save Asia for Asians. But the Chinese had suffered enough from the Japanese to be quite incapable of regarding them as saviours. The only racism they perceived was aimed against Chinese.

---

[24] The conditions at Weixian are described in a charming book based on the diaries and recipes of Lilla Eckford, who assuaged her hunger by writing out all the recipes she had ever used. Frances Osborne, *Lilla's Feast* (London: Black Swan, 2004).

Overseas Chinese

One of the almost unseen but permanent changes brought about by the war was the identity shift of many Overseas Chinese. The overseas communities were cut off from China for the duration of the war. This added to the decline in contacts during the pre-war depression, which had made travel back and forth to the *qiaoxiang* too expensive. Personal contacts were eroded, now seemingly to the point of extinction. The decline in visits and then the drying up of remittances altered the dynamic of the relationships between those abroad and those at home. The war changed allegiances and identities. In several countries, men of Chinese origin served in the armed forces of their country of settlement. In Canada, many young Chinese Canadians insisted on enlisting. When they were demobilised at the end of the war, they pressured the Canadian government to grant franchise rights to Chinese Canadians, thus making them all full citizens.[25]

A few Overseas Chinese went in the opposite direction. They returned to China at the beginning of the war to fight in the resistance. Some of them stayed permanently. Hua Lifang was one of 3,200 drivers and mechanics who were inspired by patriotic fervour to leave the Nanyang to work on the Burma Road in 1938. He left his wife and son behind. He was unable to get home at the end of the war and settled in Kunming, where he married again.[26] He did not forget his first wife, but over the next few decades, there was never a possibility of going back to the Nanyang. Eventually, in the late 1980s, his first wife came to join him. 'He now lives a happy life with his two wives'.

The enforced separations of Overseas Chinese and their families during the war and in the Civil War that followed was the end the old *huaqiao* world. China's seclusion in the Mao era made it permanent. By the time full connections were resumed in the 1980s, there had been enormous changes. Travel was controlled by passports and visas, making the informal travel arrangements of the past impossible. Many of the second and third generations of Overseas Chinese had changed their identities and now felt settled where they were. And the long disruption in remittances meant that they no longer played a crucial economic role in the *qiaoxiang*

---

[25] Ng Wing Chung, *The Chinese in Vancouver* (Vancouver, British Columbia, Canada: University of British Columbia Press, 1999), p. 44; and Judy Maxwell, *A cause worth fighting for: Chinese Canadians debate their participation in the Second World War.* Master's thesis, University of British Columbia, 2005.

[26] In Qian Qishen, *Huaqiao yu KangRi zhanzheng* (Beijing, 1995), p. 6.

A New World in Birth

In the midst of all the misery just described, there were parts of China where the mood was very different – the CCP-held areas. The scent of victory was in the air in the rural areas of north China where CCP control was strong; a new society was already in birth. Local leaders felt emboldened to start serious social and economic reform – distributing the land and possessions of local men who had worked for the Japanese and now were without protection as the Japanese withdrew to fewer and fewer strong points. In Huangxian (Shandong) in early 1945, the Japanese and their supporters were blockaded in the port city and two other towns by CCP forces, unable to leave except by boat. The local CCP already had its own county administration, and much of the peasant population was organised in a production drive. Communist forces picked off isolated units of 'puppet' troops and seized weapons. The end seemed close, and the CCP clearly was the winner. Party membership expanded rapidly.[27]

There was a convenient overlap between men who could be labelled traitors because of their association with the Japanese and men who owned large amounts of property. They could be attacked without specifically engaging in class warfare, still not an open CCP policy. This virtual class warfare was popular because taking traitors' property glossed over the fact that in single-surname villages, common in northern China, the rich had blood ties to the poor.

These last months of the war were a time of great excitement for the young people now flocking to the CCP. There seemed to be real promise – of an end to occupation, an end to oppression, and an end to the old – the promise of the 'Communist Internationale', now joining the songs of resistance as one of the most often sung songs. The Chinese version, translated by the communist martyr Qu Qiubai, proclaimed that 'the old world has been beaten into fallen flowers and spilt water (*jiu shehui dege luohua liushui*)'. These hopes seemed to justify some of the suffering of the war and to make the sacrifices seem worthwhile.

Conclusion

殘兵敗將
Scattered soldiers, defeated generals

The last year of the war was the worst year of the war for the GMD and its supporters. The military defeats, the inflation, and the corruption

---

[27] '*Zhonggong Lungkoushi weiyuanhui*', in *Zhonggong Longkoushi dangshi dashiji* (Longkou, 1990), pp. 84–85.

all added up to a massive loss of morale and of legitimacy. For the CCP, it was the reverse. The decline of the GMD, the arrival of a (doubtful) ally in the form of the USSR, and the CCP's growing popular success all meant that the party could look forward to even greater success once the war was over [Reading 4].

The stage was set for what many Chinese and foreign observers most feared as the outcome of the Resistance War, a Civil War. The costs that this would exact on Chinese society were not factored into the equation. Perhaps the wartime costs already were so great that further costs seemed immaterial.

Readings

Reading 1: Mao Zedong, excerpt from 'Serve the People' (1944)

We hail from all corners of the country and have joined together for a common revolutionary objective. And we need the vast majority of the people with us on the road to this objective. Today, we already lead base areas with a population of 91 million (population of the ShanGanNing region), but this is not enough; to liberate the whole nation more are needed. In times of difficulty we must not lose sight of our achievements, must see the bright future and must pluck up our courage. The Chinese people are suffering; it is our duty to save them and we must exert ourselves in struggle. Wherever there is struggle there is sacrifice, and death is a common occurrence. But we have the interests of the people and the sufferings of the great majority at heart, and when we die for the people it is a worthy death. Nevertheless, we should do our best to avoid unnecessary sacrifices. Our cadres must show concern for every soldier, and all people in the revolutionary ranks must care for each other, must love and help each other.

Reading 2: Mao Dun, 'Frustration'[28]

Mrs. Chang seemed to be listening with only half an ear. Her eyes gazed vacantly. After a while she queried softly. 'Will there really be victory this year so that all of us can go home?'

'Naturally that's what everyone hopes.'
'Then it's not definite?'
'I'm afraid it won't be so soon.'
'Next year, maybe?'

[28] Mao Tun (Dun), April 26, 1943. Reprinted in *Spring Silkworms and Other Stories* (Beijing: Foreign Languages Press, 1956), pp. 253–254.

'That's more likely. But it's no use asking me. I don't know any more about it than you do. The optimists figure it shorter, the cautious think it'll take a little longer. Actually they're just like you and me. No one can predict for sure. It isn't some tangible object that we can measure exactly.'

Mrs. Chang listened silently. Then she sighed and said: 'If I knew that we had to spend the rest of our lives here, I could settle down to it. But we don't know how long we'll be here. I'm always thinking about going home, but nobody knows when that day will come. That's the hardest part of all. Every day is harder to face. Even the weather tortures you here. One day you're sopping wet, the next day you're scorched.'

'We've stuck it out so long. Just be patient a little longer....'

'Everyone is trying to be patient,' Mrs. Chang interrupted, 'It's easy enough to say, but when it affects you personally, how can you help being aggravated? Like the weather, for instance – turning so hot all of a sudden. Is it any wonder I'm upset?'

Reading 3: K.P.S. Menon, 'Chongqing'[29]

Menon was the head of the Indian Office in Chongqing for three years and later the first Indian ambassador to China.

With all its drawbacks – its fogs and mists, mud and slush, smells and steps and dust, flies and sand-flies and mosquitoes, malaria and typhus and cholera – Chungking [Chongqing] has a fascination of its own. It is a city with character. It has an individuality of its own.

On the seamy side of Chungking much has been written. The pests of the earth are here – hoarders, racketeers, black-marketeers, financiers who care more for their own finances than the finances of the country. Ministers who have invested tons of gold in their personal accounts in the U.S. banks, and officials living on the fat of the earth while the people are eating the roots of grass and bark of trees. Their names will perish in the dust, and, not being an absolute believer in non-violence, I hope retribution will overtake them and their successors in this world, if not in the next. But Chungking will live, a rock of resistance which for seven years stood four square to the winds that blew.

Reading 4: Theodore White, Thunder Out of China[30]

White's analysis of wartime China is one of the English-language classics of the war. He was at the time firmly pro-communist, believing the Communist Party to be reformers rather than revolutionaries.

---

[29] Krishna Menon, *Twilight in China*, pp. 165–166.
[30] Theodore White and Annalee Jacoby, *Thunder Out of China* (New York: William Sloane, 1946), p. 201.

Though their enemies denounced the Communists' beliefs and attributed to them every shameful excess they could imagine, no one could deny that they had wrought a miracle in arms. In six years the Communists have thrown out from the barren hills [of Shaanxi] a chain of bases that swept in an arc from Manchuria to the Yangtse [Yangzi] Valley. Rarely in the history of modern war or politics has there been any political adventure to match this in imagination or epic grandeur. The job was done by men who worked with history as if it were a tool and with peasants as if they were raw materials; they reached down into the darkness of each village and summoned from it with their will and their slogans such resources of power as neither the Kuomintang [GMD] nor Japan imagined could exist. The power came from the people – from the unleashing of the internal tensions that had so long paralyzed the countryside, from the intelligence of masses of men, from the dauntless, enduing courage of the peasant.

Film

The Devil on the Doorstep. Director Jiang Wen, 2000.

6   The Immediate Aftermath of the War: 1945–1946

Wandering between two worlds
One dead, the other powerless to be born[1]

Events

The end of the eight-year Resistance War came on the same day that the Pacific War ended, August 15, 1945, the day Japan announced her unconditional surrender. The events that precipitated the end of the war took place not in China, but in Japan, where the dropping of the second atomic bomb on Nagasaki forced the Japanese government to surrender. The end of the war was sudden, but the process of surrender of Japanese forces that followed was painfully slow.

The formal surrender of Japanese forces in China took place in Nanjing, at 9 a.m., on September 9 – 9.9.9.[2] Another ceremony was held in Beiping on October 10 – the thirty-fourth anniversary of the Wuchang Rising that precipitated the 1911 Revolution. Japanese troops were ordered to surrender only to Guomindang (GMD) forces, not to Chinese Communist Party (CCP) forces. Little by little, GMD forces took over places that had been occupied. They were not always the liberators local people had expected [Reading 1]. The surrenders were long and drawn out. In Xiamen, GMD troops did not arrive to take surrender until October 3. Japanese troops stayed on at their posts until they could surrender to the GMD, in the last cases not until early 1946. In Hong Kong, to the surprise of many Chinese inhabitants, Chinese troops did not arrive at all; the British resumed control in September.

The spoils of war were huge. GMD forces took control of a vast stock of Japanese weapons, trucks, horses, aeroplanes, ships, and other

---

[1] Matthew Arnold, *Growing Old*. Quoted by K. P. S. Menon, in *Twilight in China*, p. xi.
[2] The choice of 9.9.9 seems to echo the end of World War I, at 11 a.m. on November 11 – 11.11.11. The repetition of numbers was echoed in the opening of the Beijing Olympic Games: at 8 a.m. on 8.8.08.

materiel for waging war. In Manchuria, the USSR took over Japanese war equipment and passed some of it to the CCP. The treatment of Japanese military officers and government officials was dictated by the Allies. A number were put on trial in Tokyo for war crimes, but the emperor, Hirohito, in whose name the war had been waged, was tacitly exonerated.

At the end of eight years of war, many of China's people were worn out, dispirited, almost beyond sadness. On the day that the news of Japan's surrender arrived, there were spontaneous demonstrations in most of the cities of unoccupied China, but thereafter there were few popular celebrations to mark the end of the war [Reading 2]. China was exhausted, and the immediate problems were enormous. There was no peace bonus for China. The looming Civil War meant that there was no disbandment of troops and no reduction in military expenditures. There was no economic boost from the return of formerly productive Manchuria and Taiwan. Instead, inflation surged ahead, after a brief respite, guaranteeing continued economic misery for much of the population.

The GMD government did not distinguish itself in the immediate aftermath of the war. It seemed ill prepared and uncertain. Despite the length of the war, there were few clear-cut plans for the coming months. It was as if the government was surprised by the victory because it had become convinced that the war would go on forever.

In unoccupied China, one of the first issues was the return of refugees to their homes, the longed-for 'victorious flow to the east after the victory (*shengli dongliu*)'. Virtually all the people who had moved west in 1937 were determined to go back east; there was very little affection for Sichuan or gratitude for the hospitality the province had provided. In addition, there were millions of refugees further north and in the south and southwest. The government estimated in late 1945 that 42 million people had ended the war away from home in the terse phrase 'fled to another place (*liuli taxiang*)'. Most of the refugees had to make their own way home. The government set up organisations to help returnees but in the end helped fewer than 2 million.[3]

For many refugees, there was no home to go to. The flooded areas in the Yellow River Valley were largely uninhabitable; the areas in northern China from which the people and villages had been cleared (*wuren qu*) could not support people. Until the land was reclaimed, the peasant refugees could not return. They were among the millions of people who were permanently displaced by the war.

---

[3] Zhang Genfu, *Kangzhan shiqi de renkou qianyi* (Beijing: Chaoyang ribao chubanshe, 2006), p. 49.

6.1. Nanjing residents welcome GMD troops. (*Zhonghua minguo kangRi zhanzheng tulu*, Taibei, 1995.)

6.2. Victory celebration. (Zhang Henshui, *Bashiyi meng*, 1946, p. 269.)

In most of the occupied areas, the departure of the Japanese was welcomed, although less so in the areas that had been under Japanese control for a long while. In Manchuria, the Japanese departed at speed as the region's original colonisers, the Russians (now Soviets), arrived.

The puppet emperor of Manzhouguo, Pu Yi, did not get away; he was arrested by the Soviets and taken to the USSR.[4] Manchuria's economy collapsed with the departure of the Japanese; factories and mines closed, and hundreds of thousands of migrant workers from north China lost their jobs. The Soviet looting of industrial plants over the following months stripped Manchuria of much of its industrial capacity.

Taiwan was the target of mainland China's wrath. The departure of the Japanese ended 50 years of colonial rule, a longer period than most peoples' lifetimes. Taiwan was almost totally disconnected from China, and the Taiwanese were treated by the incoming Chinese almost as enemy aliens. The economic effects were quick and devastating. There was an immediate loss of jobs for Taiwanese in government, education, the armed forces, and the security services; these jobs either disappeared or were given to in-comers from the mainland.[5] The economic ties between Japan and Taiwan were broken, leading to further job losses to the island where much of the agriculture was devoted to supplying Japan. The economic losses led to major social dislocation and disintegration and, just over a year later, to mass protests in February 1947 (*Ererba*). The protests were put down with great ferocity. This left an indelible well of hatred, alienation, and anger. The Taiwanese independence movement can be said to date from *Ererba*, although it was another four decades before it flourished openly.

The CCP came out of the war massively stronger than it had entered it. The party controlled much of rural north China, although none of the major cities, and had significant armed forces in the north and north-west. There was no doubt that it would contest the GMD government for power over at least parts of the country. Most of the population – and China's allies – hoped that the two sides would come to some agreement, as they had in 1937, just before the start of the war, in the Second United Front. General George Marshall, described in flowery terms as 'a midwife delivering the peace child to China', failed in his mission (December 1945–January 1947) to stave off civil war. It floundered on obduracy on both sides. By the time Marshall left China in disgust, the Civil War had started.

This was the grim aftermath of the war. New issues of political and military control pushed the losses of the war into second place. But they were still there – and enormous in scale.

---

[4] His life is portrayed in Bernardo Bertolucci's 1987 film, *The Last Emperor*.
[5] Decades after the end of the war, Taiwanese were still claiming for back wages and pensions against the Japanese authorities for whom they had worked.

Topics and Case Studies

Casualties

兵連禍結

Ravaged by incessant warfare

In the aftermath of the war, the massive scale of loss of life gradually became clear, although the actual figures did not. Statistics were published, but they were usually partial, vague, or unreliable. For the whole country, figures of 20 million to 30 million for wartime deaths, military and civilian, were widely cited, figures so huge that they almost beggared comprehension. According to official statistics collected in 1947, the total population of China had declined since the last collection of nationwide statistics in 1936; in 1936, the population was given as 479,084,651; in 1947, as 461,006,285.[6] These statistics are almost certainly not accurate, given the circumstances in which they were collected, but they do show a decline of over 18 million, a sharp decline given that natural growth in the population had been rising rapidly before the war.

This vast numbers of casualties is a concomitant of the size of China's population. In war as in peace, population figures for China are always huge, so huge that they seem almost unreal. The figures for a single province are easier to grasp. In the province of Guangxi, nearly a million people died, about 1 in 14 of the population[7]:

Guangxi Wartime Casualties

	Wartime casualties
Civilians killed by the enemy	211,080
Military deaths	Over 500,000
Deaths from illness	282,256
Injured	433,823
Missing (*shizong*)	58,456

Guangxi's tragedy was concentrated. Most of the civilian deaths occurred in the last eleven months of the war, between September 1944

---

[6] Hou Yangfang (ed.), *Zhongguo renkou shi*, Vol. 6 (Shanghai: Fudan daxue chubanshe, 2001), pp. 266, 296.
[7] Shen Yiju, *Guangxi KangRi zhanzheng shigao* (Nanning: Guangxi renmin chubanshe, 1996), p. 324.

and August 1945. During the same period, much of Guangxi's stock of public buildings, bridges, and roads was destroyed, some by bombing and some by pre-emptive destruction.

The military casualty statistics were clearer than the civilian statistics. The official count was that just under five million officers and men were dead or wounded after eight years of war – although this figure counted only deaths registered by the army and so would omit many paramilitary casualties, such as irregular fighters and men in local militias.[8] Figures for civilian casualties were less reliable. There are no detailed statistics. During the war, the internal chaos meant that on the government and CCP sides very little collection of statistics went on; in the occupied areas, statistics were collected in some places but not in others. One source of statistics is missing. To date, there are few casualty statistics from the Japanese side; there is no equivalent to the detailed Nazi statistics, the source that revealed the full horror of the Holocaust.

China's military losses were staggering, on the same level as those in many European countries in World War I. The scale of loss was beyond anything the country had experienced before, except during the Manchu conquest three centuries before. The grief at the losses found no expression at the time. There was little public mourning for the military dead, very few remembrance ceremonies – or later memorials. Very few of the surviving soldiers got medals, and very few of the widows and orphans got pensions. For the whole war, fewer than 10% of the men killed or wounded who were considered pensionable actually received pensions.[9]

The scale of loss should not encourage cold or cynical assumptions that death and loss on a massive scale make individual losses less important, as in Josef Stalin's chilling observation that 'one death is a tragedy, a million deaths are a statistic'. Callousness about death has been a characteristic way of thinking for Chinese governments, who have seldom blinked at huge population losses.[10] But, at ground level, every person who died or was lost during the war was a member of a family, and the loss was felt. The sense of loss could never disappear so long as part of a family survived because the dead continued to exist along with the living in the generational numbering system and in the way family members referred to each other. This was especially the case with males. Even if

[8] Zhang Ruide, *Kangzhan shiqi de guojun renshi* (Taipei: Institute of Modern History, 1993), p. 105.
[9] *Ibid.*, p. 106.
[10] This applies equally to the Qing government in its suppression of the Taiping Rebellion in the mid-1980s and to the communist government in the human-made famine of the early 1960s and the Cultural Revolution.

Laoda, the eldest son, was dead, his younger brothers would always be Laoer, Laosan, Laosi – second, third, and fourth brothers. No society was less likely to be indifferent to the deaths of individual sons.

Women and girls were traditionally less mourned than men. Women could be mourned only by their marital families, not by their natal families. Mourning for young women could be perfunctory. The exception was older women – so long as they were mothers. In no society is the mother more adored than in China, and the loss of a mother was the occasion for great grief and prolonged mourning. Under the old imperial system, officials had to take two years' leave to mourn a parent, either mother or father.

The losses of family members were felt in economic terms, too. At the war's end, there was a shortage of labour in many rural areas – at a time when demands to help relatives under the old social system of mutual dependency had risen sharply. The family had to continue to care for the dependents of the dead. With a reduced amount of labour and no outside aid, the problem of getting enough food to eat intensified after the war.

The loss of civilian lives was scarcely discussed publicly, in the press, or by government. In the immediate aftermath of the war, it was impossible to be certain about who had died and who was simply lost. Over the next few years, as refugees made their way home, some of the lost reappeared; many did not. In the meantime, there were no casualty lists, no telegrams to families, and no formal notifications.

Displacement   By the end of the war, up to a quarter of China's population had been forced to flee at some stage of the war.[11]

Refugee Numbers, 1937–45

Province/city	Number of refugees	% of population
Wuhan	534,040	43.56
Henan	14,533,200	43.49
Hunan	13,073,209	42.73
Shanxi	4,753,842	41.06
Suiyuan	695,715	38.20
Jiangsu	12,502,633	34.83

(continued)

[11] Cited in Ch'i Hsi-sheng, 'The military dimension 1942–45', in James Hsiung and Steven Levine (eds.), *China's Bitter Victory* (Armonk: Sharpe, 1992), p. 180. The figures have been rearranged by order of magnitude.

(continued)

Province/city	Number of refugees	% of population
Nanjing	335,634	32.90
Shandong	11,760,644	30.71
Hubei	7,690,000	30.13
Hebei	6,774,000	23.99
Zhejiang	5,185,210	23.90
Guangxi	2,562,400	20.37
Beiping	400,000	15.45
Shanghai	531,431	13.80
Guangdong	4,280,286	13.76
Anhui	2,688,242	12.23
Manchuria	4,297,100	12.12
Chahar	225,673	11.08
Tianjin	200,000	10.00
Jiangxi	1,360,045	9.55
Fujian	1,065,469	9.25
Total	95,448,771	26.17

These figures are approximate, as the large number of noughts indicates. The total figure is not an exact proportion of the whole population; several provinces are missing, those in the interior that did not produce any refugees (i.e., Shaanxi, Sichuan, Guizhou, Yunnan, Xikang, and Xinjiang). The list undoubtedly includes people who were refugees more than once. But, with all these caveats, the figure is still horribly high. The proportions reveal the severity of fighting and the effect of the scorched-earth strategy. The highest proportions of population forced to flee were from cities and provinces in the thick of fighting (i.e., Wuhan, Hunan, Shanxi, and Jiangsu) or those directly affected by pre-emptive destruction (notably Henan).

Material Loss   The material losses that China suffered were huge. War-related destruction in China's cities was less than the devastation that came on the cities of Japan, Germany, or the Soviet Union. The cities of unoccupied China were bombed; the occupied ones generally were not. Infrastructure in the occupied areas destroyed at the beginning of war had largely been repaired by the war's end, usually by the invaders. And the Japanese left behind a huge investment in industrial and mining plant, in addition to their war material, although much of this was soon lost to China when the plants in Manchuria were dismantled and shipped off to the Soviet Union. The Japanese armies also left behind some very unwelcome weapons, chemical ones, stockpiled in various parts of Manchuria and buried at the end of the war. More than six decades after the end of the war, these hidden dumps still cause anxiety and occasional casualties.

China did not suffer the level of losses of historic buildings and structures that many European nations did. Most of her national landmarks survived the war – the Great Wall, the Forbidden City, the Temple of Heaven. The great imperial buildings of occupied Beiping were scarcely damaged at all. The occupation of Nanjing involved the massacre of huge numbers of inhabitants but not the destruction of the city's historic landmarks. Across the nation, very few major temples were destroyed in the war. But many cultural treasures disappeared during the war, either destroyed in bombing or stolen; these losses have been seen, in retrospect, as attacks on the fabric of Chinese culture.

The most extensive were losses of books and manuscripts. The first major loss came in 1932, when the Commercial Press in Shanghai was burnt down in the first Japanese attack on the city; with it was lost a treasure trove of modern manuscripts. Between 1931 and 1945, over 20 million volumes disappeared from public libraries, university collections, and private houses, either destroyed because of their 'anti-Japanese' content, burnt in bombing, or purloined. Half of these were considered to be 'important or valuable'.[12] The most valuable was one of the four surviving copies of the *Sikuquanshu*, the great repository of Chinese literature; it was removed to Tokyo from Shenyang.

The most celebrated and most mysterious cultural loss was the fossilised bones of Peking Man. They disappeared from Beiping in late 1941. They had been moved from the research institute in the Peking Union Medical College and stored for safe keeping in the US embassy. When the Pacific War started, US marines were ordered to remove them from Beiping and ship them out of China. The fossils got as far as the coast, but then they were lost, either thrown away accidentally, taken away to Japan, taken away to New York, or hidden in western China. The search for the fossils is still on. Another terrible loss was a secondary one. The Buddhist frescoes looted from Turfan in the early twentieth century by the German explorer Albert von Le Coq were already lost to China. They were completely destroyed by bombing in Berlin late in the war.

Other cultural artefacts survived. The major treasures of the Palace Museum (*Gugong*) – scrolls, bronzes, ceramics, and jades – were shipped

12 Dai Xiong, '*Kangzhan shiqi Zhongguo tushu sunshi gaiyao*', *Minguo dangan*, 3 (2004), p. 119.

inland in 1937 in thousands of cases.[13] They were stored in caves and temples for the duration of the war. They were returned to Nanjing at the end of the war and eventually taken to Taiwan, where they now form the bulk of the Palace Museum collection.[14] The collection of Shang (the first historic dynasty) artefacts excavated at Anyang in the 1930s was also saved. Three hundred packing cases filled with bronzes, jades, and oracle bones were moved to Sichuan at the start of the war. They too ended up in Taiwan, where they are housed at the Institute of Language and History in the Academia Sinica. One loss emerged only six decades later. The Japanese built a small airport at Anyang on what turned out to be the site of part of the Shang capital. Since the airport remains in operation, present-day archaeologists have not been able to excavate there.

Private losses of possessions and property were enormous and largely unrecorded. The greatest losses were caused by bombing and scorched-earth actions. Other losses were of property abandoned or entrusted to relatives or friends by people who fled at the start of the war. It was not possible to quantify most losses – they were incalculable. In a period of hyperinflation, it was impossible to put monetary value on possessions, let alone to establish whether they were really lost or not. Lost property was seldom retrieved; after eight years, it was hard to find or, if found, to repossess. Property expropriated in the occupied areas by the Japanese was confiscated at the end of the war as enemy property and not returned to their original owners. There was seldom compensation for such losses, given that few Chinese families had insurance at the time and that even those who did might not be covered for damages caused by acts of war. People simply had to accept loss – with resignation or with bitterness.

Four decades later, after China launched the policy of 'reforming and opening up (*gaige kaifang*)' in the 1980s, many people tried to recover property lost in the war or later during the early stages of communist rule under the Policy of Restitution (*Luoshi zhengce*). Some succeeded; others did not.

However great the loss of property, it was less painful than the loss of family and friends. At the war's end, the great hope in the hearts of millions of people was for family and friends to be reunited at last.

[13] Many of the treasures had been sent to London the year before, for what was then the greatest exhibition of Chinese art ever assembled. Almost a thousand artefacts were shown, including 175 paintings and 350 pieces of porcelain. *Illustrated Catalogue of Chinese Government Exhibits for the International Exhibition of Chinese Art in London* (Shanghai: Commercial Press, 1936).

[14] Liu Beifan, *Gugong cangsang* (Hong Kong: Sanlian shudian, 1988). See also Jeanette Shambaugh Elliott and David Shambaugh, *The Odyssey of China's Imperial Treasures* (Seattle: University of Washington Press, 2005).

Family and Community Reunions

In late 1945 and early 1946, China saw tremendous flows of people as those who had fled from the Japanese joined the reverse flows, the 'victorious return to the east'. Families had been separated for the duration of the war. While the war was still on, the separation seemed interminable; no one knew when the war would end. Once the war had ended, people began to hope to see their relatives again. The problems of travel were so enormous that the hope was still remote.

The return home was less chaotic than the initial flight but still very difficult, given the shortage of transportation. The return from Sichuan was delayed by the low winter water levels in the Yangzi. There was no way to get large numbers of people back to Nanjing except by boat. It was nine months before the GMD government was re-established in Nanjing in May 1946. In that month, the China-born Canadian diplomat Chester Ronning managed with great difficulty to get passage on a steamer leaving Chongqing. When he went to board the boat, at anchor in the Yangzi, he was shocked at the chaotic embarkation, especially given that the passengers were privileged people who had been able to get tickets that were as rare as hen's teeth[15]:

Swarms of sampans surrounded the ship, each laden with people and piles of bundles. Passengers were using ropes to haul their baggage up themselves. On every deck, relatives were shouting instructions to relatives below. As each sampan was cleared of baggage, the people started crawling up to the overcrowded decks, assisted by ropes and the hands of their families.

Some enterprising people took circuitous routes to get round the jams on the Yangzi. The Yu family took two months to get back to Nanjing from Chengdu, leaving the warmth of Sichuan at the end of 1945 to move into the chill of winter. They travelled north by road to the LongHai Railway, east along the railway to Xuzhou, and then south to Nanjing. The road part was by mule cart or, for one stage, as unofficial passengers on top of the load of a military truck. Unlike many other people, they had some financial resources (US dollars) from the father's position at the Nanjing Theological Seminary, so their journey was relatively 'easy'.[16]

The reunions with family and colleagues were often warm, but eight years had elapsed, and major changes had taken place in family relations and circumstances. The first major film produced after the war,

[15] Chester Ronning, *Memoir of China in Revolution* (Beijing: Foreign Languages Press, 2004), pp. 192–193.
[16] Interview with John Yu, Vancouver, British Columbia, Canada, August 25, 2008.

The Spring River Flows East (Yijiang chunshui wang dongliu), came out in 1947. It dealt with the unhappy reunion of a devoted wife who had stayed in the east during the war and her profligate husband who had become successful and corrupt during the war. Its success stemmed from its reflection of the difficulties of reunion, far from uncommon in a society that had undergone so much disruption and dislocation.

The wartime separations shaped the structure of families. Joseph Lee was born in Hong Kong in 1940. His father, a sailor, was away for the next nine years, taken all over the world with the Blue Funnel Line, on vessels that transported troops and then refugees. He was out of touch for most of the time, and his wife, who had retreated to Macao, where she worked as a teacher, assumed that he was dead. When he returned, the family was reunited, and a second child, Fatima, was born in 1951.[17]

For many families, there was no reunion. For them, the return flows confirmed the gradual, sad realisation during the war years that their lost relatives would not be coming back and that even their remains might not be found. Fang Zhenwu was a celebrated GMD general and anti-Japanese activist who ran afoul of the GMD leadership and was forced into exile in Hong Kong. He disappeared under mysterious circumstances at the end of 1941 and was almost certainly assassinated by GMD special agents. When he did not reappear at the end of the war, the last hope that he might have survived was gone. His family had to accept that he was dead.[18]

The retrieval of the remains of the dead was a painful issue. In traditional culture, there was a powerful convention that if a person died away from home, every effort had to be made to get the remains home for burial, even if only the bones could be brought home. At the end of the war, millions of people were missing, some still alive but out of touch and others dead. Their families had no way of commemorating those who were almost certainly dead. In Britain a way was found to commemorate men whose fate was unknown, with the Tomb of the Unknown Soldier. In the tomb were the remains of an unidentified soldier, with the inscription 'known only to God'. He symbolised all those who had died and gave some comfort to the families who had no grave for their sons. China did not have the comfort of such a tradition.

Return of Refugees to the Eastern Cities   In the Months after the end of the war, as the refugees returned to the great cities of eastern China,

---

[17] Interview with Fatima Lee, Toronto, Ontario, Canada, October 4, 2008.

[18] Fang's grand-daughter, Anson Chan, later became chief secretary of Hong Kong and a strong proponent of democracy and the rule of law.

bad feelings towards those who had stayed and lived under Japanese rule came to the surface. The people who had stayed seemed to be *de facto* unpatriotic, almost contemptible. And these people themselves often feared the return of people who might feel embittered after eight years in the interior. The returnees wanted what they had abandoned back – and they were not feeling very charitable to their relatives and colleagues who had spent comparatively comfortable years living under Japanese rule. Some of the returnees wanted to take out the stored-up fury of eight years of exile on those who had stayed at home. Many people had left at the start of the war, but far more had stayed and had gradually taken over the houses, possessions, and jobs of those who had left. There had been some underground resistance in the big cities, but nothing on a scale to seriously bother the Japanese.

In Hong Kong, those who had fled were close by – in Guangdong or in Macao. They returned quickly, and life resumed. The British reassumed sovereignty, the institutions that had closed down reopened, and life went on. By a general consensus, the war was forgotten.

In Shanghai, the situation was more complex. Shanghai was the magnet of wealth and prosperity in the eyes of the returnees. Shanghai had been the site of the first patriotic battles in the war, but the people who had fought in them had either died or retreated. Now the millions who had stayed in the city during the war or even fled there from other parts of the country held their breath in trepidation. They were right to do so; Shanghai was treated almost as a conquered city, invaded by a horde of carpet-baggers. Some of the new arrivals were people from Shanghai who wanted to reclaim their property and not only recover their own possessions but also seize things that had never belonged to them. Then there were people who had no prior connection to Shanghai. Leaders in the carpet-bagging were officials and army officers, who commandeered houses and cars and any other property that appealed to them. Suzanne Pepper described how this process was seen by those on the receiving end[19]:

The Chinese word for 'take-over (*jieshou*)' is neutral, implying nothing more than to take and receive. But as public experience grew with KMT [GMD] application it became popular to substitute one of several homophonous phrases (with different characters) meaning to plunder, seize openly or rob poor.

Nowhere was carpet-bagging more acute than in Taiwan. The first stage was the requisitioning and disposition of Japanese property – tens

---

[19] Suzanne Pepper, *Civil War in China* (Berkeley: University of California Press, 1978), p. 8. I have added the characters.

of thousands of houses; agricultural land, about 20% of which had been Japanese-owned; and schools, factories, government buildings, and museums. The property included much of the centre of Taibei, where the colonial-era buildings, in a variety of styles from Greek classical to French chateau, are still to be seen. The requisitioning of Japanese property was presented as the spoils of war, but with it came the confiscation of Taiwanese-owned property, on the grounds that the Taiwanese had lived with the enemy. The process gratified the newcomers from the mainland and made the Taiwanese feel that they had been reoccupied, not liberated.[20]

Permanent Separation   Many families did not know if their relative were still alive but unable to come home. These families were separated for much longer than the war. There were people who could not go home for political reasons. Supporters of the GMD or members of the old elite feared returning to their homes in rural areas already under CCP control. Although the CCP was still clad in the robes of reformers, land reform had begun in some of the areas it controlled, and the returnees might now be classified as class enemies. At the same time, supporters of the CCP whose homes were in the south, the majority of the old revolutionaries who had made the Long March, could not go home after the end of the war in case they were labelled as 'communist bandits (*gongfei*)'; the looming Civil War made this a real possibility. These people had now been away from home for at least eleven years. Some communists, the most famous Deng Xiaoping, never went home.

There was no home-coming for the bulk of GMD soldiers; many were separated permanently from their families. Immediately after the war ended, the GMD started to move large numbers of troops back to the east and up to Manchuria. For a few soldiers, the redeployments took them back to their homes with their units.[21] For most, though, the end of the war simply extended their separations from home. The Guangxi troops had been away from home since late 1937, eight years. Now their separation was lengthened. It lasted until 1949, when hundreds

---

[20] A moving account of this process comes in *City of Sorrows* (*Beijing chengshi*), the masterpiece of Taiwanese filmmaker Hou Xiaoxian.

[21] Few soldiers had a reunion as strange as Jacques Guillermaz, long-time French military attaché in China. At the end of the war, he landed with Free French forces in the south of France. His unit recaptured his home village. His mother, who had not seen him for almost a decade, believed that she had heard his voice at the door the night before – but still fainted when she saw him. Jacques Guillermaz, *Une vie pour la Chine* (Paris: Lafont, 1989), p. 126.

of thousands came back, in flight, at the very end of the Civil War, with the People's Liberation Army (PLA) hot on their heels. These men were designated 'GMD bandits (*guofei*)'. The men who had been heroes of the early resistance to Japan were either killed, imprisoned, or sent for 're-education' in labour camps.[22]

In 1949, most of the GMD armies were taken with the retreating GMD to Taiwan. They could never go home and settled reluctantly in Taiwan, often in abandoned Japanese military facilities. Some of them married local women, often without telling them that they had families on the mainland. There were recriminations thirty years later when it became possible to go back to China – and to uncomfortable reunions with the families they had left behind. Bai Xianyong's work, *Taibei ren* (*People of Taibei*), gives sympathetic portrayals of these old soldiers and must be based on the lives of soldiers from his father's (Bai Chongxi) forces.

Overseas Chinese families had already been cut off from their families at home for the duration of the war. Little bits of news had filtered through about relatives at home, but not enough to feel in close contact. Now the looming Civil War made it seem dangerous for those abroad to come home. After 1949, China was isolated from the rest of the world, and Overseas Chinese, many of them staunchly anti-communist, dared not go home or be in touch with their families except through clandestine means.

All these continuing separations were a sign of how damaging the war was to Chinese society. The question, then, was whether this damage was reversible – and in the short run if there would be recriminations against those who had attacked China or worked with the attackers.

Treatment of Collaborators, Re-establishment of Communities

Immediately after the war, no one was quite sure what the government would do with those who had collaborated actively with Japan – who would be punished and who would escape punishment. Some of the major collaborators were put on trial, and several were sentenced to death. Wang Jingwei's closest colleagues, Zhou Fohai, Chu Minyi, and Chen Gongbo, were executed, as was Liang Hongzhi, Wang's predecessor in the Nanjing regime. Wang's widow, Chen Bijun, was sentenced to a long term in prison. Beyond these trials, though, the government did not seem to have a clear-cut policy on how to treat lesser collaborators.

---

[22] *Dangdai Zhongguo di Guangxisheng* (Beijing: Dangdai Zhongguo chubanshe, 1992), p. 46.

One thing that stood out, however, was that the scale of official vengeance was quite limited.[23]

There were reasons for this confusion. One was the general war weariness; another the recognition that another war was brewing. The GMD needed as many people as it could find to restore the pre-war economic and social situation. The CCP had the same needs as the party extended its hold over parts of north China. Both were willing to ignore dubious wartime activities provided that they were not too egregious. And then there was the scale of the problem. Vast numbers of people had lived under the occupation, compromising, surviving, and keeping their heads down; it was impossible to hold them all accountable.

In the rural areas, the treatment of collaborators was often achieved without reference to a legal system or a formal tribunal. In the communist-held areas, the CCP was trying a new form of punishment; through a process of 'settling accounts', the judgement of the masses was passed on men who had actively collaborated with the occupiers. Since these men were often members of the local elite, the process blended in with class struggle [Reading 2].

In one particular sense, those who had stayed in the occupied areas were all punished – and that was in the way in which the currency situation was handled. All currencies used in the areas under Japanese occupation had to be converted to the national currency (*fabi*). The process was chaotic, there was no standard exchange rate, but the result was usually the same: The rate set meant that the occupation currencies became worthless. In Hong Kong and Taiwan, the issue is still alive; elderly people have held onto notes and to their bank books to prove what they once owned. Their hope for compensation has not died.

Social and Economic Reconstruction

百废俱兴
Picking up the pieces

At the end of the war, China's society and economy were in a terrible state. Parts of the society were completely shattered and others heavily damaged; in a few areas, the society had survived relatively intact. The economy was in a state of near total collapse. Poverty was almost

---

[23] There are parallels here with what happened in France after the war. A veil was drawn over much of what happened in the German-occupied parts of France. The veil was not lifted until Marcel Ophuls' film, *Le chagrin et la pitie* (*The Sorrow and the Pity*) came out in 1969.

universal, and in some parts of China, many people were near starvation, especially amongst those cast loose from their families.

The need for revival and reconstruction was massive – but there were no solutions on the GMD side about how this would be done. There were some government reconstruction projects, but none came close to restoring the pre-war economy. Instead, the revival or not of the economy was determined by the new structures of the society in which the economy functioned. And inflation had dramatically changed the ability of people to act in the economy.

New Social and Economic Strata   The inflation of the last years of the war produced a dramatic reconfiguration of China's social and economic hierarchies. At the top of the system, a few people were much richer than they had been before the war – senior government officials, army officers, and some business people all kept ahead of inflation, helped in doing so by the government that wanted to ensure their loyalty. These people were concerned mainly with making money to look after themselves and their families. There was no question of rebuilding businesses – or for that matter, of trying to stop the inflation.

The members of the merchant and entrepreneurial elite, the pre-war hope for China's modernisation, now found themselves powerless unless closely connected with the GMD. They were unable to recoup their pre-war status. The inflation and political insecurity made it very difficult to resume pre-war operations. Those who made the effort were beaten back by extremely adverse conditions – including the state of the international markets, which took years to recover from the war. The inability to export crippled many of the light industrial operations in the coastal cities. Some entrepreneurs looked for better places to do business and gradually moved all or parts of their operations to Hong Kong.

At the other end of the economic spectrum, the situation of workers and day labourers had scarcely changed; they were paid by the day and usually were more or less current with inflation. They and the peasants who lived near cities and towns were in a stronger situation economically than they had been before the war. Peasants who produced items to sell on the urban market – vegetables, meat, eggs, and oil – were always ahead of inflation. Peasants who did not market their good were either self-sufficient in food or as mired in poverty as they had always been; inflation was irrelevant to them.

The people who were really caught by inflation were people who had once been comfortable – professionals, salaried workers, and intellectuals; they were now near destitution and panic-stricken. Their income came in slowly, often by the month; they could not keep up with inflation.

This unhappy middle, once the burgeoning middle class and the hope for China's modernisation, was all but abandoned by the GMD government in the period just after the end of the war. Since this was one of the GMD's largest constituencies, the loss was critical.

Some experts saw the post-war economic and financial crisis as fundamentally connected to the size of China's population. 'The sweeping destruction and derangement of the war period in China were superimposed upon a broader, deeper, and more permanent disequilibrium. At the basis of China's economic problems lies an enormous pressure of men against resources.'[24] Given that the most obvious sign of economic disaster was war-induced inflation, however, it would have been difficult to take such a long-term, almost abstruse approach to the miseries of the present.

Disappearing Elites   The status of the old rural elite was undermined by the war; at its end, there was great difficulty for its members in recouping their pre-war status. Those who had fled had suffered financial losses during the war, and they had not been able to fulfil their duties of care to their communities. They had been replaced, for the duration of the war, either by Japanese nominees or by local people who had been 'thrust up by the masses' – that is, put in by the CCP. The CCP's rural cadres were not to be sidelined after the war; they had organised the people, raised their political consciousness, and taken over local leadership. Members of the old elite might just as well not go home, and many did not. The members who had stayed and had collaborated, to whatever degree, with the Japanese were hopelessly compromised after the Japanese departure. They had not only lost their sponsors, but they also had not fulfilled traditional obligations. They were despised and reviled. The disgrace of these elite members may explain the willingness of their peasant clansmen to attack them during the land reform.

Some small but once-powerful elites were wiped out by the war. Manchus, many of whom had worked enthusiastically for the Japanese, enjoying a reprise of their former influence as part of the ruling race of the Qing Dynasty, were completely discredited at the end of the war. Many Manchus who had worked closely with the Japanese were arrested and imprisoned. Less compromised Manchus had long tried to hide their identity by changing their names. The family of actor Ying Ruocheng was one example. Not until the 1980s, in a new and more open atmosphere,

---

[24] George Woodbridge, *UNRRA: The History of the United National Relief and Rehabilitation Agency*, Vol. II (New York: Columbia University Press, 1950), p. 405.

did he reveal to his colleagues in the Beijing Arts Theatre that he was a Manchu.

Another lost elite was the Western one. The end of the war revealed the extent to which the elevated status of Westerners had been damaged by the war. The mystique of white superiority had been broken in the Japanese internment camps, and with the exception of the Soviets in Manchuria and the Americans close to the GMD, white superiority in China was done for. The foreign-owned properties and businesses expropriated by the Japanese were not recouped, except in the only remaining bastions of white power in China, the colonies of Hong Kong and Macao.

Economic Reconstruction: Redirecting the Yellow River   The Yellow River is one of the most potent symbols in Chinese history; failure to control it is a sign that a government is about to lose the mandate of heaven, the right to rule. After the Japanese had withdrawn, it was essential for the GMD to reassert its control over the river and to heal the breach at Huayuankou that in 1938 had created such massive disruption and destitution. The government was determined to 'close the gap and return the river to its original bed (*dukou guigu*)'. Closure of the breach was identified as an urgent task before the government returned to Nanjing; it was named as one of the major projects in China for the United Nations Relief and Rehabilitation Agency (UNRRA).[25]

From May 1946 to March 1947, 10,000 labourers worked under UNRRA supervision to close the huge breach, a kilometre across. A much larger number, up to 200,000, worked on repair of the dikes along the old course of the river through Shandong. The total cost was listed at 592 billion *yuan*, a mind-boggling figure and a reflection not only of the huge cost but also of the spiralling inflation.[26]

The undertaking was bedevilled with political problems. The Yellow River was effectively the border between GMD- and CCP-controlled areas in a burgeoning Civil War. Much of the old river bed itself was under communist control, as were the 400,000 peasants who had settled on the fertile soil of the dry bed and were farming there.[27] Their interests

[25] UNRRA carried out major projects all over the world during its brief existence from 1943 to 1949. The projects were to provide relief for those areas liberated from Axis occupation.

[26] '*Huang He dukou futi gongchengju*' (1947), *Huang He Huayuankou helong jiniance* (Commemorative volume for the closing of the breach at Huayuankou on the Yellow River). Nanjing: Second Archives 568.

[27] George Woodbridge, Vol. II, pp. 430–437; and O. J. Todd, 'The Yellow River reharnessed', *The Geographical Review*, XXXIX (1949), pp. 38–56.

were ignored despite talks among the GMD, the CCP, and the US special advisor George Marshall in mid-1946. These peasants were destined to support the CCP, which did seem concerned about their fate when the waters of the redirected river flowed over their homes and fields.[28]

The work went ahead quite rapidly, even, towards the end, when the workers came under shelling from the north bank of the river. On May 4, 1947, the prime anniversary of Chinese nationalism, a lavish ceremony was held on the dike at Huayuankou; the ceremony was not a commemoration of the hundreds of thousands who had died when the dike was opened but rather a self-congratulatory celebration of the closure of the breach.[29] There was a sense of unreality to the ceremony and to the grandiloquent term used for the closure – 'uniting the dragon (*helong*)'. The gorgeous volume that recorded the ceremonies gives no indication that the area was about to fall to the CCP and that the GMD and UNRRA had, in effect, performed a major service to the CCP. Far from re-establishing their own credibility, they had performed a mammoth task that the CCP would sooner or later have had to undertake itself.

Repatriations

At the end of the war, there were hundreds of thousands of Chinese in Japan and Korea, taken there as forced labour during the war. These men were repatriated quite soon after the end of the war. The process seemed fairly straightforward because most came from Hebei and Shandong. They were brought across the Yellow Sea by ship to Tianjin and Qinhuangdao, passed briefly through reception centres set up by the government, and then sent on to their villages. Their return was actually less simple than it seemed. The returnees were returning to war-torn areas. In Shandong, much of the rural areas was already in CCP hands, and the towns and cities were contested. This situation prevented the returnees from getting any kind of rehabilitation or compensation. There was no effort by any Chinese authorities to raise the questions of payment of back wages or of compensation for the maltreatment the labourers had endured. Only decades later did a few of the survivors make claims in Japanese courts – usually without success.

Allied civilian internees in China were released at the end of the war, thin, weary, but in nothing like the state of Allied prisoners of war who emerged from camps in Japan and other parts of Asia, where they had

---

[28] Zhao Fuhai, *Lao Zhengzhou* (Zhengzhou: Henan chubanshe, 2004), pp. 133–135.
[29] *Huang He Huayuankou helong jiniance.*

been systematically maltreated. Their countries made arrangements for the internees to be repatriated quite rapidly. For some of them, this meant going 'back' to unknown countries. J. G. Ballard first saw England when he was fifteen years old. The only Allied civilians not repatriated were White Russians, who had no desire to be sent to the Soviet Union. Those in Manchuria fled southwards as their 'compatriots' in the Red Army came in; those in Shanghai made their arrangements to leave slightly later, when victory of the Chinese communists seemed more certain. By 1949, most of the White Russians had left China, migrating as displaced persons to the United States, Canada, and Australia. The vibrant communities that they had created disappeared.

Enemy repatriation was a huge problem. In late 1945, China was faced with how to deal with the defeated Japanese soldiers and civilians – there were 1.6 million Japanese civilians in Manchuria alone and large numbers in China Proper, as well as Koreans and Taiwanese. The process went more smoothly than could have been expected, certainly more smoothly than the repatriation of Germans and Volksdeutsch from Eastern Europe.[30] There were no massacres of defeated Japanese, although those still in China lived in a state of terror at the prospect of the kind of violent reprisals that occurred in Eastern Europe against Germans. The devastation of the atomic bombs may have created the feeling in China that Japan had already been punished. The United States certainly put heavy pressure on China to repatriate Japanese rather than attacking them.

The repatriation took place from many ports; the largest operation was at Huludao, a small island off the coast of Liaoning Province. It became the staging post for one of the largest repatriation movements ever known. In early 1946, a joint decision by China and the United States was made to move Japanese citizens in Manchuria to Huludao. Repatriation from the island started in May 1946, and by the end of the year, over 1 million people had been sent to Japan. Another 50,000 followed over next the two years. A total of 13,441 trains were used to ship people to Huludao, as well as 800 boat trips.[31] In all, 2,020,345 Japanese were repatriated from China, along with 75,363 Koreans and 44,118 Taiwanese.[32] This number did not include the half million Japanese soldiers in Manchuria and Mongolia, who fell into Soviet hands and were

---

[30] Volksdeutsch were people of German origin settled in Eastern Europe from the eighteenth century.

[31] China.org.cn, 5.5.2005.

[32] Hsu Long-hsuen and Chang Ming-kai, *History of the Sino-Japanese War* (Taipei, Taiwan: Chungwu, 1971), p. 571.

taken as forced labour to Siberia. The last of them were not released until the 1990s.

Japanese Orphans   As Japanese civilians fled in panic from the incoming Soviet forces in Manchuria, many of them had to abandon their children. Those left behind were mainly girls born between 1942 and 1945. These children were brought up in Chinese families. They grew up speaking only Chinese and answering to Chinese names. Some of them always knew that they were Japanese by birth; others did not discover their origins until they were adults. In the 1980s, once China reopened to the outside world, the Japanese government sent officials to find the lost children, now in their forties. Several thousand were taken to Japan to meet their families. The reunions seldom worked. The elderly parents and their adult children did not share a common language, and the children, who had been brought up to think of themselves as Chinese, and therefore to hate the Japanese, found adjusting to Japan almost impossibly difficult. It was a sad, belated footnote to the war.[33] In 2006, a class action by the orphans, now in their sixties, won them compensation from the Japanese government for having abandoned them in 1945 and thus subjected them to a life of misery.[34]

There was a bitter irony here. This suit was launched in the same period that elderly sex slaves and forced labourers started to make suits in Japanese courts to win compensation for their sufferings, usually without success; the grounds for rejecting the suits range from the length of time elapsed to lack of proof. Rejection of the suits has brought Japan severe embarrassment and has encouraged continuing hostility towards Japan in Korea, China, the Philippines, and other Southeast Asian countries.

Conclusion

The war was over, but the victory over Japan brought little joy to China. Instead, it was the starting point of an even more bitter war, the Civil War between the GMD and the CCP for control of China. The agonies that Chinese people had suffered during the Resistance War were only the prelude to even greater suffering to come. There are parallels with what happened after the end of World War II in Eastern Europe – which turned out to be the suffocating embrace of the Soviet Union. In China,

---

[33] Wang Huan, *Guigen: Riben canliu guer de bianji rensheng* (Beijing: Shijie zhishi chubanshe, 2004).
[34] *Guardian*, December 1, 2006.

however, the enemies were within the gates. Chinese were about to turn against each other in the bitterest of wars, a Civil War.

Readings

Reading 1: Michael David Kwan, 'The GMD Entry into Qingdao'[35]

Kwan lived as a boy in the northern port of Qingdao. After years of increasing hardship under Japanese occupation, the town returned to Chinese control at the end of the war.

A new national flag – white sun in a square of blue sky over a field of red – flew over the town. Gigantic portraits of Chiang Kai-shek appeared everywhere, and slogans on bright paper plastered every wall and lamp-post.
'Welcome, conquering heroes!'
'Down with the Imperialists!'
'Long live eight years of resistance!'
'Long live our glorious victory!'
'Long live Generalissimo Chiang Kai-shek!'
The euphoria in Qingdao was short-lived, replaced by sullen wariness that day a rag-tag collection of filthy, half-starved men straggled into town. Their uniforms were in tatters. Many were shoeless. Others had wads of straw tied to their feet. Some were without weapons; others dragged ancient hunting rifles, even bird guns, by the barrel, looking more like an army in retreat than conquering heroes. The officers riding in American jeeps were smartly turned out and well fed. American aid clearly did not filter down the ranks.
The national army descended on the town like locusts, grabbing anything, including homes and businesses, that caught their fancy on the flimsiest excuse. The people eager to curry favour with their new rulers and to ensure some degree of personal safety denounced one another as traitors, collaborators or war profiteers.

Reading 2: Ba Jin, Cold Nights[36]

This excerpt concludes a gloomy tale set in Chongqing. Tuberculosis is a metaphor for sick relationships; the wife has left her sick husband; he is cared for by his mother.

---

[35] Michael David Kwan, *Things That Must Not Be Forgotten* (Toronto, Ontario, Canada: Macfarlane, Walter and Ross, 2000), pp. 145–146.

[36] First published in 1946. This excerpt is from *Cold Nights*, translated by Nathan Mao and Liu Ts'un-yan (Hong Kong: Chinese University Press, 1978), pp. 161–162.

She shivered, the hand holding the soup bowl quaking. 'Try two more mouthfuls even though it hurts. You can't go on without food,' she said putting the spoon back into his mouth. With his mouth wide open, his eyes rolling upwards and his hands clasping the quilt, he swallowed a little more.

'Hsuan,' she whispered. Looking at her tearfully, he slowly heaved a sigh.

She tried again with the spoon. He, in pain, swallowed two or three times; then unexpectedly he spat out a mouthful. Hurriedly she put down the bowl and rubbed his chest.

He slowly closed his eyes. He wanted to take a nap but pain kept him awake. He could neither groan nor scream. Silently he wretched with the pain, somewhat soothed by his mother's massaging. He tried hard to focus his thoughts on her, hoping he could temporarily forget his pain.

Suddenly firecrackers exploded on the street, a sound rarely heard in the city during the last few years. At first, few people took any notice of it, but the noise went on unabated, from far and near, as if an important event were being celebrated. People were scrambling everywhere, many running, many singing, and others noisily chatting with one another.

He was about to ask what was going on when his mother started to speak up.

'The Japanese have surrendered! The Japanese have surrendered!' a boy's voice drowned her out, yelling the news in the street, a voice echoed by many other voices.

He shook his head in disbelief, but the sounds of the firecrackers became increasingly louder and more frequent.

Like waves, crowds gathered in the streets.

'It must be true; otherwise they wouldn't be celebrating like this,' she added excitedly.

He continued to shake his head. The news had come so suddenly!

'The Associated Press reported that the Japanese government has unconditionally surrendered to China, the United States, Great Britain and the USSR,' someone shouted in the street.

'Did you hear that? The Japanese have surrendered! The War of Resistance is over. No more suffering for us,' exclaimed his mother hysterically. She laughed, she cried, forgetting that she was in a dark room. One lone candle flickered violently, its wick leaning precariously toward one side and the wax leaking out through a small crack.

He stared at his mother, puzzled by her behaviour, tears gushing out from his eyes. Momentarily, he felt like laughing and crying, but he soon calmed down and sighed. His end was near, too, he thought.

'Extra! Extra! The Japanese have surrendered!' shouted a newspaper vendor, walking by the window.

His mother held his hand and said, 'Hsuan, are you happy? Victory! Victory!'

'Now I can die without any regrets,' he wrote on a piece of paper with his shaking hand.

Reading 3: William Hinton, Fanshen[37]

Hinton's famous book describes the early communist rule in Longbow Village, Lucheng County, Shanxi. There the CCP took over at the Japanese surrender and soon afterwards began to 'liquidate the bloody eight years' debt'

… Wen Ch'i-yung [Wei Qiyong], commander of the puppet garrison in Long Bow fort, Shen Chi-mei [Shen Jimei], head of the Fifth District police, and Ch'ing Tien-hsing [Qing Tianxing], his assistant, were brought face to face with 190 peasants from all over the district – more than ten from each village – who came together in Long Bow's square as delegates from their respective communities. These were the people who had suffered the most from puppet depredations, whose homes had been looted, whose sons and husbands had been killed, whose wives and daughters had been seduced or raped.

Hundreds of accusations were made that day against the leading traitors and all who had worked with them. A Long Bow woman told how her son, Chin-mao [Jinmao], had been killed. When she came to the part where the police threw him, gagged and bound, into a well, she broke down weeping and could not go on. Many in the crowd wept with her. …

Before the meeting ended Commander Wen and Police Officer Shen were condemned to death. They were taken to an empty field at the edge of the village and there, in the sight of the fort they had done so much to build and to defend, they were shot. While the dead Shen was still warm on the ground where he fell, a Long Bow militiaman, Yu-hsing [Yuxing], stripped a sweater off his corpse. Someone else took off his shoes. They left the body to his relatives to bury as they would.

Films

The Spring River Flows East. Director Cai Chusheng, 1947.
City of Sorrows. Director Hou Xiaoxian, 1989.
The Last Emperor. Director Bernado Bertolucci, 1987.

---

[37] William Hinton, *Fanshen: A Documentary of Revolution in a Chinese Village* (New York: Monthly Review, 1966), pp. 116–117.

7   The Legacy of the War

The war was a chasm for most.
There was one life before and one life afterwards.[1]

Deep beneath the Millennium Monument in Beijing is a vast circular chamber. On the outer wall of the chamber is laid out the orthodox version of Chinese history, carved in golden-yellow stone bas relief. The history starts with mythical culture heroes and passes through all the iconic culture figures. The last figure is Deng Xiaoping, who completes the circle. The wall carries two messages: One shows the historical inevitability of contemporary China, the unbroken march from the distant past to the present. The other shows a continuous culture whose fundamental characteristics do not change.

This is a graphic version, literally cast in stone, of the long-standing trope that China does not change – Eternal China, Unchanging China, Essential China. In this record of history, invasions, wars, and rebellions seldom appear. They are downplayed because they bring disruption and chaos but do not change the basic characteristics of the Chinese world; they are vulgar accretions to a story of culture and civilisation. Under this interpretation, the Resistance War becomes one more of these accretions, terrible but transitory, causing only temporary disruption, not touching the essence of China.

The Marxist interpretation that dominated China in the Mao era was quite different, but it too took a view that saw war as only an incidental part of history. History was divided into stages, each of which was doomed to end and in the process give rise to another stage. The demise of the old society, labelled 'feudal', was inevitable. To the Marxist revolutionaries who took over China in 1949, the fundamental problems of society were class-based – landlordism, elitism, corruption – all of which could be resolved by revolutionary struggle under the leadership of the Chinese Communist Party (CCP). The Resistance War speeded up a process that was already inexorable.

---

[1] Michael Ondaatje, *Divisadero* (Toronto: McClelland and Stewart, 2007), p. 82.

194

Western historians of China have other interpretations of China's modern history. Several start from the same premise – that China was in the grips of a process of change from the nineteenth century on. One version of this interpretation sees modern history as a grim process of decline brought about by a combination of the weakening of central authority and the intrusion of imperialism. This process was character-ised by the growth of militarism, violence, and inequality. The Japanese occupation, although more brutal than earlier stages of the decline, was not different in kind from what it replaced; that is, it was part of a con-tinuum. According to Prasenjit Duara, '[T]he effects of the Japanese regime in North China should not be too sharply differentiated from its native predecessors.'[2] Another version of history as process is more optimistic: The process of change brings with it progress and modernity, democracy, human rights, and a free economy; ideas and global trends are more important than events, even events as huge as an eight-year war. An example is a recent study of the evolution of the Chinese family that covers fifty years; in it, there is no mention of the Resistance War, only of the periods before and after the war. It is as if social changes were immune to the impact of war or, alternatively, that it had stopped for the duration of the war.[3]

This book has taken a different approach. It puts war at the centre of social change. It focuses on the tumultuous changes that the war brought to China and sees the war as a fundamental disturbance to Chinese society that produced profound and permanent change, its violence and chaos sweeping away one society without producing a new one.

The social impact of the Resistance War was different from the tradi-tional pattern of foreign conquests, in which an initially brutal occupation was followed by the reassertion of Chinese social values. The Manchu takeover in the mid-seventeenth century led to one of longest-lasting dynasties in Chinese history, 250 years. The early Manchu emperors ran the state more efficiently than their predecessors, the late Ming emperors, and although the bureaucracy was staffed largely by Chinese, military control stayed with the Manchus themselves.[4] They adopted the

---

[2] Prasanjit Duara, *Culture, Power and the State: Rural North China 1900–1942* (Stanford: Stanford University Press, 1988), p. 253.

[3] Susan Glosser, *Chinese Visions of Family and State, 1915–1953* (Berkeley: University of California Press, 2003).

[4] The first three Manchu emperors, Kangxi (1672–1722), Yongzheng (1723–1725), and Qianlong (1736–1795), are now considered to be the greatest Chinese emperors of all. See the recent exhibition at the Royal Academy in London, *The Three Emperors, 1662–1795*.

Confucian social system. There was no parallel process in the war. The Japanese were far less successful than the Manchus in imposing their rule on China. They never took over the whole country, and in the areas they held, the occupiers made few accommodations to China; instead, they regarded China as a state and society in need of transformation, not of emulation. Their rule was accepted only on the basis of fear, not willing affiliation or submission. The Japanese occupation was not the start of a renewal of traditional Chinese society, as might seem to have been the Japanese aim in the promotion of Confucianism, but instead it turned out to be a period of destruction and cataclysmic upheaval.

The war brought to Chinese society a universality of suffering. At its end, so many people had been killed or deeply injured – soldiers, their families, the victims of bombing and of scorched-earth actions, the survivors of the economic chaos, the forced labourers, the comfort women, and the orphans – that much of the whole society was suffused with loss. There were bitter recriminations against the few who had not suffered or were in better material circumstances – because their 'happy' situation was a by-product of their accommodation with the occupiers or of profiteering.

At the end of the war, Chinese society was riddled by mistrust. The natural trust between individuals and groups that had been the glue of traditional society was gone, broken by the war, eroded, undermined, and betrayed in myriad ways. The old social elites had either disappeared from the occupied areas or had lived with the Japanese in various degrees of accommodation. In the unoccupied areas, social trust had been undermined by separation, deprivation, and loss of morale.

The loss of trust was epitomised by the growth of official spying, whether the Japanese secret police or the Guomindang (GMD) and CCP spy systems. The optimistic, positive atmosphere of the early 1930s seemed to be lost forever. The atmosphere of mistrust was intensified under the early CCP in a welter of political movements that demanded victims and forced people to distrust each other – while making it easier for people to attack those with whom they no longer felt personal connections. The excesses of the Mao era had their beginnings in the Resistance War. Less than two decades after the end of the Resistance War, the cataclysm of the Cultural Revolution started to unfold. There has to be a close connection between the two – the social disintegration of the war and a widespread willingness to attack other people, one of the saddest but commonest features of the Cultural Revolution.

Social Disintegration, Social Survival

國破家亡
The country is broken, the family ruined

Michael Ondaatje compared the war in Europe to a chasm, a deep rift that demarcated two worlds. In China, the chasm of the war was just as deep. The old world was gone for good, the new one in uncertain gestation. The sufferings of the war ingrained a tough, hard survivor mentality, which put individual or small family survival ahead of the larger family and community. Eight years of war had eroded or broken down old social ties. The survivor mentality is not a benign one. It means that if one has to harm others, even relatives and friends, to secure the survival of oneself and a tiny band of closest relatives, then that is what one will do.

Social Disintegration

At the end of the war, Chinese society had lost much of its cohesion. This cohesion was already under threat in the early years of the Republic as the old order weakened under the assault of militarism, political change, and modernity. The war accelerated the process dramatically. The family declined in size. Functions that families performed for their members fell in to disuse – communal housing, the provision of financial support, and aid in times of need. Periodic tasks of ritual significance could not be performed during the war: the choice of spouses for children by their parents, the naming of children, and the proper burial of the dead. Family celebrations of the New Year or the sweeping of the graves were often impossible in wartime; the expense, the absence of key members, and the impropriety of enjoyment in war made it difficult to hold celebrations that solidified families and communities.

The greatest erosion of social security was that the constant insecurity of the war became a habit. This habit undermined the concept of mutual aid, once a key element of social cohesion. Mutual aid assumed long-term relationships and long-term repayment of obligations and debts. When the whole world became insecure, the future unclear, everything had to be short term. People had to put their own interests first, in a form of survival of the fittest. Mutual aid was almost an irrelevance.

Survival

Counterpoised against the catalogue of social losses is a loftier, transcendent conception of the impact of war that sees society uplifted by the courage and sacrifice of individuals. Warfare makes heroes. 'Baptism by fire' and 'steeled in battle' are two of the many sayings, in English and Chinese, that suggest that war and the loss and suffering it brings are positive, that people come into their own when they are faced with challenges and danger and then go on to transcend them. This is the basis of ideas of heroism, on which, in turn, are based rewards for bravery and heroism – medals, commemorations, war memorials. China has popular traditions of heroism, the knight errant tradition (*wuxia*), on which is constructed a stream of popular literature, theatre, and film,[5] and the equally popular *gongfu* (martial arts tradition).[6]

The Resistance War did not end on a heroic note; few of the people who fought in it were recognised as heroes. There were heroes in the early stages of the war, the Doomed Battalion and Zhang Zizhong, but few in the later stages. One of the most commemorated heroes of the war (with, eventually, six sites, including two grave sites) was Norman Bethune. Mao Zedong praised him for his socialist self-sacrifice shortly after Bethune died of blood poisoning in late 1939. In his essay, 'In Memory of Norman Bethune', a rather testy Mao implied that Bethune, a foreigner, had behaved better in the war than many Chinese, communist or otherwise, and that they should take his example to heart[7]:

Comrade Bethune's spirit, his utter devotion to others without any thought of self, was shown in his great sense of responsibility in his work and his great warm-heartedness towards all comrades and the people. Every Communist must learn from him. There are not a few people who are irresponsible in their work, preferring the light and shirking the heavy, passing the burdensome tasks on to others and choosing the easy ones for themselves. At every turn they think of themselves before others. When they make some small contribution, they swell with pride and brag about it for fear that others will not know. They feel no warmth towards comrades and the people but are cold, indifferent and apathetic

Few Chinese soldiers were recognised as heroes at the end of the war. There was a general reluctance to name or celebrate heroes or to

---

[5] The most famous contemporary *wuxia* writer is Jin Yong, the pen name of Louis Cha, former editor of the *Mingbao* in Hong Kong.
[6] Known in English as Kungfu.
[7] Mao Zedong, *In Memory of Norman Bethune*. The article was written in late 1939. It was kept in the forefront of attention, as one of the `commonly-read articles' until the demise of Maoism in the 1980s.

commemorate the dead. Perhaps the scale was too vast. A more likely reason is that both the GMD and the CCP, by now the only two players in Chinese politics, were preoccupied with their own internecine struggle. The war ended with the imminent threat of civil war, not with recognition of the dead or with the return of heroes to their grateful homes.

For ordinary people, there was not much to celebrate. China was not gripped by the wild joy that flooded over many of the nations that were on the winning side in World War II. At the end of the war in China, one of the most common feelings was simply relief for the people who had survived when so many had not. The reasons for survival were often mundane. Location was a critical one. People were more likely to survive if they lived in a northern city or in Manchuria or Taiwan, places where the Japanese occupation was less harsh than elsewhere and wartime survival was not difficult – the problems came afterwards, when the people who had stayed had to explain themselves to those who had fled. Age was another key reason. Young civilians were more resilient, more likely to be able to flee, to escape from the enemy. Youth was a double-edged sword. Young men were also more likely to be drafted into the army or taken for slave labour. And wealth, at least at the start of the war, was a key factor in survival. The wealthy could afford to flee; they were more likely to have connections away from home, even in the foreign concessions. Perhaps the key reason for survival was resilience, the ability to overcome hardships. The resilience that many people showed came in part from dredging deep into the Chinese tradition of endurance. This was the strength of the Chinese people. What was clear, however, even amongst those who demonstrated great resilience, was that very few people had escaped the impact of war.

There were people who assumed that they could return to their prewar life. Very few were able to do so. The course for civil war, which would be fought on social as well as military and political fronts, was already set. Whether they were adults at the start of the war and knew what they had lost or in their teens or younger at the end of the war and scarcely knew the time before the war, their lives for eight years had been lived in confusion, tension, and fear. They were survivors of trauma.

Trauma, Resilience, and Transcendence

Psychological trauma is a wound inflicted on the mind that cannot be healed as a physical wound might be. It may be the result of a single experience or of a prolonged period of suffering or abuse. The wound

7.1. Grief. (Xie Manping, 1948.)

lies hidden and may recur beyond the control of the individual.[8] Those who survive a war, whether as combatants or as civilians, have usually experienced trauma, and the trauma stays with them.

悲不自胜

Grief that one cannot overcome

The experience of trauma is often assumed to be negative. The citation of post-traumatic stress disorder (PTSD) as a cause for aberrant behaviour after traumatic experiences is commonplace. The condition, recognised since the 1970s, has been used particularly often in the context of warfare and combat as a condition to be treated. It is even used as a defence in criminal trials (though not in China).

Some psychologists are now moving away from the assumption that the effects of trauma are always negative and bring permanent psychological damage. The new approaches focus on resilience, the determination to survive damage, to be grateful for survival. The focus is less on combat-

---

[8] See Cathy Caruth, *Unclaimed Experience: Trauma, Narrative and History* (Baltimore: John Hopkins Press, 1996), pp. 2–5.

related trauma and more on the trauma experienced by civilians in war and in peace.

The leader in this field is Boris Cyrulnik, a French psychiatrist who was orphaned as a child in occupied France and maltreated for the rest of his childhood by foster parents. He overcame this tragic start in life and has made his mark as a psychiatrist and an expert on trauma. He has played a leading role in the development of the concept of post-traumatic growth. He does not deny pain: 'Inside, I still feel that lack of stability. ... I healed, but you never lose the scars.' But he talks about 'the notion of resilience, which is a person's ability to grow in the face of terrible problems'.[9] Cyrulnik's concept hangs on the availability of three things: therapy, kindness, and the experience of love.

This is a scientific version of the old adage that what doesn't kill you makes you stronger. The war was a stark revealer of character. People showed courage or cowardice, nobility or self-seeking, generosity or meanness. Those who could place themselves on the positive side of the ledger could see the war as a positive experience. They were living proof that adversity produces strength and determination.

The transcendence of trauma has been an almost commonplace feature of modern Chinese history. The endurance and toughness with which millions of people have endured terrible hardships and still kept going, with dogged determination, is something that fills foreign observers with admiration. Many millions of Chinese survived the war as proud, tough people. These were the ones who went on to be on the winning side in the Civil War and the less certain ones who stayed on in China in 1949, not quite knowing what the future would bring but assuming that it must be better than what they had just been through. The people who left the mainland in 1949 were just as determined to survive, but they were terribly battered by their experiences in the Civil War. And they were at first devastated by how much they had lost. But the worlds they created in Taiwan and Hong Kong turned out, over the duration, to be two quite different but equally successful combinations of the Chinese tradition and modernity. At the end of the Cultural Revolution, when China opened to the world again, the battered survivors of yet another cataclysm looked in awe at what Chinese people had achieved *outside* China and started down the same road of economic modernisation that Hong Kong and Taiwan had taken more than thirty years before.

A question hung in the shadows in the 1980s as China hurtled towards the future: How much would the recent past be remembered? And what would the memories be of?

---

[9] *Observer Magazine*, February 10, 2007, p. 42.

Memory

Memory is not straightforward. It is fallible, susceptible to manipulation, and may even be false. It may be inflated, especially if the memories are of success. Wartime memories for men who fought on the winning side often grow in glory the further away from the event they describe. My generation was brought up hearing of the courage and sacrifices of our fathers and grandfathers who had fought in two world wars.

Memory is sometimes instrumental, applied to a specific, current cause for group or personal benefit. It may be linked to demands for the recognition of injustice and for apologies, restitution, reparations, or compensation. Memory may be used as evidence of maltreatment, the underpinning of claims for the recent campaigns to rectify the past, from the campaigns for redress for Japanese Canadians and Americans or First Nations survivors of residential schools. So far these campaigns have been within specific states; they have not successfully crossed national borders, *viz.*, the inability of Chinese victims to win suits in Japan.

In public memory, what is remembered is selected by the authorities in charge, usually the state, to suit a particular cause. Victors may require the retrieval of memory as a confirmation of enemy guilt. When I went to school in Frankfurt am Main (Germany) in the late 1950s, we studied World War II as a project of *Entnazifikierung* ('de-Nazification'). This was a required course when that part of Germany was under US control. The aim was to make sure that children would learn about the war as a national shame, an evil period in German history. There has been no parallel in Japan. The periodic fury that grips China and Korea about Japanese reluctance or intransigence in facing issues 'left over from history (*lishi yuxialia de wenti*)' stems from a sense that the Japanese failure to recognise (*chengren*) the sufferings brought by the war amounts to a desire to bury the war, that is, to get away with past crimes. The reason why the issue of Japanese textbooks is so particularly sensitive is that there is a fear in other parts of Asia that younger generations of Japanese will have no understanding of the war other than of the damage it brought to Japan.[10]

Public memory may be entwined with victimhood and focus only on experiences of suffering. The bombing of Hiroshima is remembered at the site not as a part of World War II but as a single event. 'On August 6, 1945, Hiroshima suffered humankind's first nuclear weapons'

---

[10] Japan's Ministry of Education approves textbooks for use through the Japanese secondary school system. The history textbooks have played down the impact of Japan's armies in Asia.

tragedy.'[11] There is no mention of the war that preceded the dropping of the bombs, only of innocent victims of a horrible new plague loosed on the world.

There are valid criticisms of the fallibility or deceptiveness of public memory and its susceptibility to manipulation, but they do not negate memories themselves. They are still real, and powerful. They do not exist in a vacuum. Memory has its own structure, attached to particular places and particular times.

Memory Times

The key punctuation points of family life – births, marriages, and funerals – are occasions that stimulate social memory, times that people first store in their memories and then revive periodically, especially on anniversaries. They are the prime memory times. Personal memory has other timetables that correspond to the stages of life. Memory of the distant past becomes more acute in the latter stages of life. Older people have more to remember and more time to do it. The recognition of life drawing to a close and the fear of memory loss stimulate the process of remembering.

Public memory, in the form of commemoration, moves at a different pace. It may be dictated by anniversaries, regular times to officially remember an event. In China, the fortieth anniversary of the end of the war was commemorated throughout 1985 and the sixtieth anniversary in 2005 even more so, with a flood of ceremonies, special publications, films, and television shows. There are more wartime anniversaries than those regularly commemorated, others that are not. There have to be political decisions about which ones will be commemorated, which passed over, and here political manipulation comes in; it has much to do with China's relations with Japan and with the need to drum up popular nationalism. The wave of sometimes violent anti-Japanese demonstrations in March 2005, if not officially coordinated, certainly was sanctioned, as other popular demonstrations would not be. There are anniversaries that are taboo. It is forbidden, by the CCP, to publicly commemorate June 4, 1989 (*Liusi*). There is an official amnesia about a time that started in hope and optimism but then turned into tragedy. The official denial of memory does not mean that the tragic events are forgotten. Banning a commemoration may backfire and make it more rather than less likely that it will be remembered.

[11] Homepage of the Hiroshima Peace Museum.

Memory Places

Many societies create specific places to stimulate and promote public memory – graveyards, memorials, and cenotaphs. Confucian society put great store on remembering forebears. It kept the ancestors close to home. The ancestral cult required that the name tablets of the dead be kept on household altars, that graves be maintained regularly, and that the family dead be commemorated at annual ceremonies during the Qingming Festival, the festival in early spring when the graves of the departed are tended by the living descendants. These ceremonies took place in private family or clan burial grounds. These are family memory places. The only public burials were during epidemics or natural disasters, when mass graves (*keng*) were dug. These were places of horror, not commemoration.

In China there were few places for public memory, no public cemeteries, and for the dead of the war, no war memorials or war cemeteries. Such places were not part of the Chinese tradition, and those public memorials that there are now, such as the Martyrs' Memorial in Tiananmen Square (*Geming lieshi jinianbei*) or the Babaoshan Revolutionary Cemetery (*Babaoshan geming gongmu*), were built in a period of strong Soviet influence and mimic Soviet memory places. Mao Zedong's Memorial Hall, in Tiananmen Square, goes diametrically against the tradition of the burial of rulers outside cities (for instance, in the Ming Tombs in the Western Hills). The idea of a dead (though embalmed), body being left unburied in a city is a singular and total break with tradition.

During the 1950s, 1960s, and 1970s, there were no official memory places for the Resistance War. Over the past two decades, numerous public memory places have been opened to commemorate the war. Three major commemorative sites were opened to coincide with anniversaries: the Nanjing Massacre Memorial in Nanjing (*JinHua Rijun Nanjing dutusha yunan tongbao jinianguan*) to mark the fortieth anniversary of the end of the war, the Lugouqiao Memorial Hall (*Lugouqiao kangzhan jinianguan*) in 1987 to commemorate the fiftieth anniversary of the start of the Resistance War, and the Taierzhuang Memorial (*Taierzhuang dazhan jinianguan*) in 1993 to mark the fifty-fifth anniversary of the major Chinese victory early in the war. Individuals have been commemorated as well. Zhang Xueliang's place of house arrest in Fenghuang in Hunan has been restored, as has the tomb of General Tong Linge in the Western Hills near Beijing. There are four separate memorials to Zhang Zizhong and a major street in Beijing that has been renamed for him – *Tieshizi hutong* has become

Zhang Zizhong lu.[12] Chiang Kai-shek's compound outside Chongqing has been opened to the public – just at the time that memorials to him in Taiwan have been closing.

Memory places are designed to stimulate memory, private or public. They have little to do with the practical applications of memory, which for many people are more important.

Instrumental Memory

Memories are critical to knowing about the past; they may be the only source of historical evidence. In non-literate societies without written records, the use of memory is one of the bases for oral history. And in societies under heavy political or religious control, such as Mao era China, where to keep written records was dangerous, memory is the only place where parts of the past survive.

Memory also has a material functions. The literate may keep accurate, detailed records of their possessions, but for the illiterate, the vast majority of the Chinese population until very recently, this ability is rare. The record of one's possessions was in memory, where people stored the knowledge that was important to them. Memory can be very precise. When I interviewed elderly peasants in Shandong in the 1980s, I was impressed with the detail of their memories and of the ways they stored financial details of a time (the 1930s) when currencies fluctuated wildly. They spoke of their earnings 40 years before not in terms of cash but in terms of how much grain or beans they could buy with them.[13]

The Silence of Memory

The Resistance War has not been easy for Chinese to remember. In the immediate aftermath of the war, there was an overwhelming desire to put it away from memory, to consign the war to an *oubliette*. This was a universal reaction to the horrors of the global war. In Madeleine Thien's novel of suppressed memory, *Certainty*, Matthew Lim returned to his childhood home in Sandakan (Indonesia) a decade after the war and found that people could not talk about the war, or about the Japanese prison camp that had once been just outside the town. 'If

---

[12] Zhang Shaosi, ed., *Zhongguo kangRi zhanzheng dazidian* (Wuhan: Wuhan chubanshe, 1995), pp. 1075–1080.

[13] Thomas Gottschang and Diana Lary, *Swallows and Settlers* (Ann Arbor: University of Michigan Press, 2000).

he mentioned it, they would shake their heads, their eyes would grow distant. "Terrible times", they said. Opening and closing the memory in the same breath.'[14]

For a long time in China there was a silence about the war. The silence had its own logic. It was the silence of pain, the suppression of memories too sad to be brought out in to the light. This was the silence of victims, of people who had suffered more than they could bear. For them, silence was an essential coping mechanism. The memories were still there in subterranean streams, kept firmly below ground, their presence known but not allowed to surface. The most acute form of suppression was practised by people who had suffered the most – 'comfort women', victims of torture, and people who had survived massacres. The past was hard to remember without fear of losing one's sanity. This silence was often consensual, a mutual agreement not to talk about painful, humiliating subjects. Silence was contagious. It became a social convention to steer away from talking about the war.

There was another, localised form of consensual silence in the once-occupied cities. There memories of the war were consigned to a black hole; it seemed as if people had no memories of a long period of their lives. This was the silence of shame, the refusal to recall a period that had brought fear and humiliation to the inhabitants of the occupied areas, who were often ashamed that they had not resisted actively but who knew what the consequences of resistance would have been if they had.

As time passed, through the 1950s and 1960s, the agony of the war was displaced on the mainland by new and sometimes even more painful experiences – the Great Leap Forward, the great famine of the early 1960s, and the lunacy of the Cultural Revolution – periods to be forgotten, if at all possible.

Whatever the reasons for silence, the memories *were* there; there was no amnesia. Over the past decade or so, the memories have started to well up. Historians have conducted systematic oral interviews with survivors. One example is a group of twenty-one interviews conducted with elderly survivors in Hushan Village, just to the east of Nanjing. As children and young people, they had gone through four days of terror in early December 1937. Their memories are of the death of thirty-two people and the abduction of others. They are expressed in terse, almost dispassionate terms – but the dead are given names, ages, and relationships; they are no longer just statistics.[15] Memories have brought the past

---

[14] Madeleine Thien, *Certainty* (Toronto: McClelland and Stewart, 2007), pp. 302–303.

[15] Dai Yuanzhi, 'QinHua Rijun Hushan cun baoxing zhengci', in *Minguo dangan*, 2004, 3, pp. 48–60.

back. The recovery of memories is a key part of the recovery of a major period of China's recent past.

Recovery of the Past

Why dredge up the past? Why not leave it alone and move on? This idea might be a sensible one, if it were possible. But memories cannot be controlled so rigidly. In individuals, they well up from time to time, triggered by a sound, a smell, a casual remark, or the onset of age. In a society where many people have similar memories, they may be triggered by an event or by a change in public consciousness.

Memories cannot be submerged forever; they are also susceptible to the passage of time. The memories of the horrors of trench warfare in World War I were almost buried for nearly half a century until, in the 1960s, they were revived. The satirical show *Oh What a Lovely War* was one trigger. The show coincided with a more powerful trigger, the need for elderly survivors to reveal what happened to them, to break their silence before death made it permanent. A similar process is going on now with the Spanish Civil War. Memories that were kept locked away during the Franco regime have been pouring out in the past decades.

The submerged memories from the Resistance War surface in similar ways. The film star Vicki Zhao Wei learned a lesson about historical ignorance to her cost when in 2001 she was photographed in a sultry pose wearing the most hated of wartime symbols, a rising sun flag. A torrent of abuse came down on her head from elderly survivors of the war, and she had to apologise abjectly. She had unwittingly gone much too far and had triggered painful memories in the survivors and in her own family – her grandfather had been killed in the war.[16]

The need to release memory is often associated with the realisation that death or mental decay is approaching. Chinese survivors of the Resistance War, now in their seventies or older, feel the same need; unless they speak now, their memories will go the grave with them. The descendants of those who suffered or died may be the agents for the retrieval of memory. If younger generations have sensed the pain of their parents and grandparents without knowing where it came from, they may want to recover – or to discover – the past. They may ask the older people to tell them what actually happened to them. Iris Chang heard about the Rape of Nanjing from her parents. Her book stimulated many

[16] Vicki Zhao has since played the heroine Yao Mulan in a TV adaptation of Lin Yutang's *Moment in Peking* (2006).

other people to find out what the older generation remembered, in the process uncovering a great store of repressed memories.[17]

States have a major stake in the memory and commemoration of war. In some states, this means commemorating the dead at solemn annual ceremonies. The commemorations are an expression of national sorrow and of thanks for those who died to create a better world. A state may use commemoration as a warning of what may happen if a war is forgotten or as a means of self-glorification, a way to turn attention away from its own present failings. China does not commemorate the anniversary of the end of the Resistance War. The day of the announcement of the end of the Civil War is the most important day of the national calendar; October 1 is National Day. There is no equivalent to Remembrance Day or Memorial Day to commemorate the dead of the war.

The state recognises that there are dangers in *not* remembering. As a state under the control of the Communist Party, China's leaders know one of Karl Marx' most famous aphorisms, 'History repeats itself, first as tragedy, then as farce.' Another version of the same idea is an instrumental one, George Santayana's saying that 'those who do not learn from the past are doomed to repeat it.' The failure to remember brings the danger of repetition of past mistakes and excesses. It also means that there cannot be a recognition of what damage has been done or of correcting it or compensating for it. In the immediate aftermath of the Cultural Revolution, the Chinese government recognised what damage it had done. There was a show trial of the Gang of Four – and substantial reparations were paid in the 1980s to those who had suffered under the Policy of Restitution. This recognition made it easier for China to put the Cultural Revolution behind her, although not to close the book.

There has been no parallel process for the Resistance War. There is an irony here in that it was the war that brought the CCP to power.

War and Revolution

The most momentous outcome of the war was the communist victory, the victory of the socialist revolution. Mao Zedong was clear about this. In 1972, on the first visit of a Japanese leader to China since the war, Mao responded to Prime Minister Tanaka Kakuei's stilted efforts at a veiled apology by virtually thanking him for Japan's invasion of China. 'If Japan hadn't invaded China, the Chinese Communist Party would not

---

[17] Iris Chang, *The Rape of Nanking: the Forgotten Holocaust of World War 11* (New York: Penguin, 1998).

have been victorious; moreover, we would never be meeting today. This is the dialectic of history.'[18]

The desperation of the war set the stage for a confident, tough, remorseless revolutionary movement to take over the nation that had rejected it so decisively a little over a decade before, whose then government had harried it almost to extinction. The communists had steeled themselves after their defeat in Jiangxi and the calvary of the Long March never to be beaten again, never to be humiliated again. The war gave them the opportunity to prepare themselves to take over the whole nation.

The social damage and dislocation of the war was fodder for the CCP. The old elites had lost so much of their wealth and prestige during the war that they were virtually 'on the scrap heap of history'. Does this mean that the war was a class war as well as a war of resistance, a war in which the proletariat triumphed over the old elites? Joshua Howard suggests that it was, in his ground-breaking research on the armaments industry in Chongqing; he sees class consciousness and class formation going on during the war. A more conventional view, current now amongst Chinese historians, is that during the war, patriotism subsumed class warfare.[19] Another class-based interpretation is that the leaders of the old society were associated with abject failure during the war because they were overstretched to the point of collapse by the war, and they failed the people they were supposed to lead, at least to the extent that they could not protect them from the invading Japanese.

The war did give the CCP structural assistance in the class struggle. Beyond the losses of the war were all the things that did not happen because of the war – the loss of careers, the loss of once secure futures, the investments that were not made. These 'phantom' losses left a great number of disappointed people, whose dreams and ambitions had been destroyed by the war. They were looking for a new society – one that might well be brought about by revolution. The hardships that people had become inured to during the war made it easier for the CCP to demand sacrifices of its followers and of the population as a whole. Life had become much simpler. The war had done away with much of the luxury of the old society. The most symbolic luxury of the traditional culture almost disappeared in the unoccupied areas. Silk clothing was gradually replaced by utilitarian cotton clothing in both the Guomindang (GMD) and the CCP areas. The reasons – the silk-producing regions

[18] Quoted in Geremie Barme, "Mirrors of history: on a Sino-Japanese moment and some antecedents", *Japan Focus* (May 4, 2005).

[19] Joshua Howard, *Workers at War: labor in China's Arsenals, 1937–1953* (Stanford: Stanford University Press, 2004), pp. 3, 317.

were all under Japanese control, production declined, and supply into the unoccupied areas was negligible.

Post-war China was less divided by region than the pre-war society. The regionalism that had done so much to inhibit the creation of national unity after the 1911 Revolution was a casualty of the war. Regional interests were submerged as people moved around; the habit of separation from one's home region was ingrained during the war. The CCP at the end of the war was in north China, although its leaders were almost all from the south. Regional differences that would once have been insurmountable were gone.

The war also made it easier for the CCP to be forceful in pursuing its goals. The war brought a general rise in violence. People became inured to violence and saw it as something commonplace rather than extraordinary. This change in the attitude towards violence allowed the CCP, after 1949, to engage in more and more radical and turbulent policies; it was accepted that issues would be solved by violence, as in the tumultuous movements that racked China in the 1950s and 1960s. The survivor mentality made it easier for people to join in attacks on those they were not extremely close to. These culminated in the savage cruelty of the Cultural Revolution, a decade in which, in the midst of political turmoil, people turned on each other, on their families and colleagues, and on their friends in an orgy of violence and dissolution. After the end of that 'lost decade', with the common consent of an exhausted people, China turned to a completely new model of government and the economy.

This appeared to be the modernity that had been emerging in the 1930s and was interrupted by the war. This would make a neat sequence, but it was not what happened. The process that had been stating in the 1930s was negated rather than interrupted by the war. Movements towards the rule of law, universal education, political participation, and a free press, all processes under way in the 1930s, were aborted in the war. The changes since the start of the 1980s do not mark a return to the optimism and opening up of the 1930s. They have created a form of modernity linked tightly to the economic world, with little reference to political change – that is, economic modernisation and socialist repression, or 'socialism with Chinese characteristics'. The CCP may have changed direction in economic terms, but it has not moved very far from totalitarian control in the political world. The 1982 constitution of the People's Republic of China guarantees many rights and freedoms, amongst them freedom of speech, association, procession, demonstration, and region and the rights to vote, to privacy, to work, and to rest.[20] Few Chinese would agree that these guarantees are implemented.

The legacy of the war is still working itself out. An invasion premised on containing communism brought the CCP to power. With the invasion, the progress towards a freer China was halted. Until the legacy is worked out, the war must still be considered a disaster.[21]

---

[20] *Constitution of the Peoples' Republic of China* (1982), Articles 34–48.
[21] I am greatly indebted for this discussion to Martha Carroll, one of the most thoughtful and perceptive of global observers.

Final Words

Twenty years after the war, C. T. Hsia, a gentle, reflective literary scholar, gave this deeply personal view of the war and the connection to the communist victory[1]:

After the initial period of patriotic enthusiasm, the Chinese people, in the interior as well as in the occupied areas, by and large suffered patiently and awaited only favourable developments in the outer theatres of the war to bring about their deliverance from the enemy. Increasingly in the clutches of poverty, they sank into despondency, if not downright despair, and lost touch with the spiritual values which had sustained China in all her historical crises. They naturally blamed all their troubles on the inefficient and corrupt government, and allowed themselves to be seduced, often against their best convictions, by the propagandist wiles of the Communist party.

This sad statement was written by a man in exile in America. Mo Yan in Shandong found another way to show how futile, in the end, the divisions of the war had been. He described an event that took place in Gaomi in 1984 that is a stark reminder of the cruelty of war and of how fleeting the fatal divisions of the war were. In death, the former enemies were united – by anonymity; it was impossible to know who the dead were.[2]

Forty-six years later. In a great storm one evening, a pit of a thousand (*qianrenkeng*, i.e., mass grave), in which were buried the white bones of communists, Guomindang members, ordinary people, Japanese soldiers and the emperor's helpers [puppet troops] was split open by a bolt of lightening. The rotten bones were scattered over dozens of square meters. The rain washed them clean, and turned them all a matt white. I was at home at the time for my summer holidays. When I heard the news that the pit had been opened up, I rushed to see. ...
    There were a few people standing round the open pit, expressions of horror on their faces. I squeezed my way through them, and saw the skeletons at the

---

[1] C.T. Hsia, *A History of Modern Chinese Fiction* (New Haven: Yale University Press, 1961), p. 374.
[2] Mo Yan, *Hong gaoliang (Red Sorghum)* (Beijing: Zuojia chubanshe, 1995), I, pp. 201–202.

bottom of the pit, piles of bones looking up at the sky again. I doubt that even the provincial party secretary could have sorted out who was a Communist, who Guomindang, who a Japanese soldier, who a puppet soldier, and who an ordinary person. Each of the skulls was the same shape; they were all jammed together in one heap, each, with complete equality, washed by the same raindrops.

Glossary

Terms

anding minxin	安定民心
Banian kangRi zhanzheng	八年抗日战争
chabuduo	差不多
chengren	承认
chengyu	成语
chiku nailao	吃苦耐劳
dukou guigu	堵口归古
Ererba	二二八
Ertong baoyu hui	儿童保育会
fabi	法币
fenjia	分家
fengpai	风派
gaige kaifang	改革开放
Gongchandang	共产党
gongfei	共匪
Gou bu jiao, ji bu zhao, jingshuiku, heshui gan, shu luo ye, cao mai gu, tian wu yun, huangfengqi	狗不咬鸡不叫 井水枯 河水干 树落叶草麦枯 天无云 黄风气
gudao	孤岛
guizi	鬼子
guochi	国耻
guofei	国匪
Guomindang	国民党
guoqing	国情
hanjian	汉奸
hao nan yao dang bing, hao tie yao dang ding	好男要当兵好铁要当钉

hao tie bu dang ding, hao ren bu dang bing	好铁不当钉好人不当兵
helong	合龙
hezuo	合作
Huangfan qu	黄泛区
Huo cheng	火城
huozhe	活着
jia	家
jieshou	接受, 劫收, 接收
jiubiao	旧表
jiu guo	救国
jiu shehui dage luohua liushui	舊世界打個落花流水
Juntong	军统
kang	炕
keng	坑
ketang	客堂
kongju	恐惧
kuilei	傀儡
lamei	腊梅
lishi yuxialia de wenti	历史余下来的问题
liuli taxiang	流离他乡
Liusi	六四
luan	乱
lunxian qu	沦陷区
Luoshi zhengce	落实政策
maiguo yinmou	卖国阴谋
maitou gugan	头苦干
meiyou fazi	没有法子
minbing	民兵
Mozi jianbao	末次剪报
Nanjing da tusha	南京大屠杀
ni	逆
niangjia	娘家
nuoruo	懦弱
pantu	叛徒
Peidu	陪都
qianguan	钱馆

qianganzi limianchu zhengquan	枪杆子里面出政权
qianren keng	千人坑
qinri	亲日
qiaoxiang	侨乡
Qisanyao budui	七三一部队
qishi dashou	七十大寿
ren fanzi	人贩子
renshi	人市
Shehui bu	社会部
shengcun zhuangtai	生存状态.
shengli dongliu	胜利东流
shizong	失踪
siji ru chun	四季如春
sishi	死市
sishi tongtang	四世同堂
tongdi	通敌
waisheng	外省
wangdao	亡岛
wangguo nu	亡国奴
wei	伪
weianfu	慰安妇
wei guojia, wei minzu, wei minzhu, wei ziyou, wei ziji, wei jiaxiang, wei zisun	为国家为民族为民主为自由为自己为家乡为子孙
Weixin zhengfu	维新政府
wuju	无助
wunai	无乃
wuxia	武侠
xingcun zhe	幸存者
xingzai lehuo	幸灾乐祸
Xinminhui	新民会
yang guizi	洋鬼子
yi qiong er bai	一穷二白
yi shui dai bing	以水代兵
yuanfen	愿分
yuezha yueqiang	越炸越强
Yumi zhi xiang	鱼米之乡

zaxingcun	杂姓村
Zhonghua minguo	中华民国
zisi	自私

People

Ai Qing	艾青
Bada Shanren	八大山人
Ba Jin	巴金
Bai Chongxi	白崇禧
Bai Xianyong	白先勇
Cao Richang	曹日昌
Chen Bijun	陈璧君
Chen Da	陈达
Chen Gongbo	陈公伯
Chen Guofu	陈果夫
Chen Lifu	陈立夫
Chen Munong	陈牧农
Chen Yi	陈毅
Chu Minyi	褚民谊
Cui Jian	崔健
Dai Li	戴利
Dai Wangshu	戴望舒
Deng Yinchao	邓颖超
Ding Ling	丁零
Du Yuesheng	杜月生
Fang Zhenwu	方振武
Fei Xiaotong	费孝通
Feng Youlan	冯友兰
Feng Yuxiang	冯玉祥
Feng Zikai	封子恺
Fu Xiaoan	傅筱庵
Guixi	桂系
Guo Moruo	郭沫若
Han Fuju	韩复聚
Han Suyin	韩素音

Hao Mingzhuan	郝铭传
He Jibu	何基步
He Long	贺龙
He Siyuan	何思源
He Xiangning	何香凝
Hou Xiaoxian	侯孝贤
Hsing Fu-ying	邢福瀛
Hu Diedie	胡蝶蝶
Hu Feng	胡风
Hu Qiuyuan	胡秋愿,
Hu Shi	胡适
Hua Mulan	花木兰
Ji Chaoding	冀超鼎
Ji Chaoju	冀超铸
Jian Youwen	简又文
Jiang Guangnai	蒋光鼐
Jiang Jieshi	蒋介石
Jiang Menglin	蒋梦麟
Jiang Qing	江青
Jiang Wen	姜文
Jin Yong	金庸 (Louis Cha 查良镛)
Kang Sheng	康生
Kong Lingwei	孔令伟
Kong Xiangxi	孔祥熙
Lao She	老舍
Lee Ang	李安
Li Dequan	李德荃
Li Gongpu	李公濮
Li Meifeng	李美凤
Li Peng	李鹏
Li Zhengdao	李政道
Li Zongren	李宗仁
Liang Hongzhi	梁鸿志
Liang Qichao	梁启超
Liang Shuming	梁漱溟
Liang Sicheng	梁思成

Liao Zhongkai	廖仲恺
Lin Biao	林彪
Liu Bocheng	刘伯承
Liu Guosong	刘国松
Lu Xun	鲁迅 (Zhou Shuren 周树仁)
Luo Ronghuan	罗荣桓
Mao Dun	矛盾
Mei Lanfang	梅兰芳
Mei Niang	梅娘
Nie Er	聂耳
Nie Rongzhen	聂荣臻
Ouyang Yuqian	欧阳予倩
Pan Guangdan	潘光旦
Peng Dehuai	彭德怀
Puyi	溥仪
Qi Baishi	齐白石
Qian Duansheng	钱端升
Qian Mu	钱穆
Qu Qiubai	瞿秋白
Shitao	石涛
Song Ailing	宋霭龄
Song Meiling	宋美岭
Song Qingling	宋庆龄
Sun Benwen	孙本文
Tan Kha-khee	陈嘉庚 (Chen Jiageng)
Tan Sitong	谭嗣同
Tian Han	田汉
Tong Linge	佟麟阁
Wang Jingwei	汪精卫
Wang Kemin	王克敏
Wei Yunsong	韦云淞
Wen Yiduo	闻一多
Wu Han	吴晗
Wu Peifu	吴佩甫
Xian Xinghai	冼星海
Xiao Hong	萧红

Xu Liangguang	许良光
Xu Xiangqian	徐向前
Xue Yue	薛岳
Yang Tianshi	杨天石
Yan Xishan	阎锡山
Yang Zhenning	杨振宁
Ye Jiaying	叶嘉莹
Ye Jianying	叶剑英
Ying Ruocheng	英若诚
Yu Dafu	郁达夫
Yu Hua	余华
Yu Youren	于右任
Zeng Guofan	曾国藩
Zhang Ailing	张爱玲 (Eileen Chang)
Zhang Tianyi	张天翼
Zhang Xueliang	张学良
Zhang Yimou	张艺谋
Zhang Zhizhong	張治中
Zhang Zhongshun	张中顺
Zhang Zizhong	张自忠
Zhao Wei	赵薇
Zhao Yuanren	赵元任
Zheng Chenggong	郑成功
Zheng Zhonglin	郑钟麟
Zhou Fohai	周佛海
Zhou Zuoren	周作仁
Zhu De	朱德
Zhu Ziqing	朱自清
Zhuge Liang	诸葛亮

Songs, films, books, journals

Beijing chengshi	悲情城市
Bei Zhongguo	北中国
'Da Riben'	打日本
Dagongbao	大公报

'Dikang'	抵抗
guqu	古曲
Guizi laile	鬼子来了
gongfu	功夫
'Guoqi ge'	国旗歌
'Hengdu Taipingyang'	横渡太平洋
Hong gaoliang	红高粱
'Huang He dahechang'	黄河大合唱
Huang tudi	黄土地
Huozhe	活着
Jinian Bai Qiuen	纪念白求恩
'Jinjun ge'	进军歌
Manhua	漫画
'Manjianghong'	满江红
Mei Lanfang	梅兰芳
'Meili de Nanniwan'	美丽的南泥湾
Min ge	民歌
Mingbao	明报
Mulan cong jun	木兰从军
Mulan shi	木兰诗
'Qinfu congjun'	勤夫从军
'Qingnian g'e'	青年歌
Se Jie	色戒
'Shang shan'	上山
'Shangwu ge'	尚武歌
Sikuquanshu	四库全书
SongHu chenwang jiangshi	淞沪陈亡将士
Taibei ren	台北人
Wei renmin fuwu	为人民服务
'Wei Zuguo xingfu xiangqianjin'	为祖国幸福向前进
Wenshi ziliao	文史资料
'Xin kongjun'	新空军
'Zeng hanyi gei qianfang zhansh'i'	赠寒衣余前方将士
Yáo a yáo, yáo dào wàipó qiáo	摇啊摇，摇到外婆桥
'Yiyongjun jinxing qu'	义勇军进行曲
Yugong yishan	愚公移山

Wode muqin	我的母亲
Yijiang chunshui wang dongliu	一江春水往东流
'Zhongguo fu kangdi ge'	中国妇抗敌歌
'Zhonghua minguo wanwan nian'	中华民国万万年
Zishu	自述
Zuo zhuan	左传

Places

Anqing	案庆 (Shandong)
Babaoshan geming gongmu	八宝山革命公墓
Beijing	北京
Beiping	北平
Changchun	长春 (Jilin)
Changsha	长沙 (Hunan)
Changting	长汀 (Fujian)
Chengdu	成都 (Sichuan)
Chogqing	重庆 (Sichuan)
Dalian	大连 (Liaoning)
Ding xian	定县 (Hebei)
Dongbei	东北
Fenghuang	凤凰 (Hunan)
Fengyi	丰仪 (Longkou, Shandong)
Fenyang	汾阳 (Shanxi)
Fugou	扶沟 (Henan)
Gaomi	高密 (Shandong)
Geming lieshi jinianpai	革命烈士纪念碑
Gongxian	巩县 (Henan)
Guangzhou	广州 (Guangdong)
Gugong	古宫
Guiyang	贵阳 (Guizhou)
Guilin	桂林 (Guangxi)
Gulangyu	鼓浪屿 (Fujian)
Guling	牯岭 (Anhui)
Haerbin	哈尔滨 (Heilongjiang)
Hangzhou	杭州 (Zhejiang)

Huayuankou	花园口 (Henan)
Huanglongshan	皇龙山 (Shaanxi)
Huangxian	黄县 (Shandong)
Huludao	葫芦岛 (Liaoning)
Hushan Village	湖山村 (Jiangsu)
Jinan	济南 (Shandong)
JinHua Rijun Nanjing dutusha yunan tongbao jinianguan	侵华日军南京大屠杀遇难同胞纪念馆
Jinling daxue	金陵大学
Jinmen	金门 (Fujian)
Jinggangshan	井冈山 (Jiangxi)
Jiujiang	九江 (Anhui)
Kaifeng	开封 (Henan)
Kunming	昆明 (Yunnan)
Lanzhou	兰州 (Gansu)
Liangshanbo	梁山伯 (Shandong)
Liaodong bandao	辽东半岛 (Liaoning)
Linqu	临朐 (Shandong)
Liuzhou	柳州 (Guangxi)
Longkou	龙口 (Shandong)
Lugouqiao	卢沟桥 (Hebei)
Lugouqiao kangzhan jinianguan	卢沟桥抗战纪念馆
Lucheng	潞城 (Shanxi)
Manzhouguo	满洲国
Meishan	眉山 (Sichuan)
Minnan	闽南 (Fujian)
Nanchang	南昌 (Jiangxi)
Nanjing	南京 (Jiangsu)
Nankai University	南开大学
Ningyang	宁阳 (Shandong)
Penglai	蓬莱 (Shandong)
Qingdao	青岛 (Shandong)
Qinghua University	清华大学
Quanzhou	泉州 (Fujian)
Shandong bandao	山东半岛
Shanganning genjudi	陕甘宁根据地

Shanxitou	山西头 (Longkou, Shandong)
Shimenwan	石门湾 (Zhejiang)
Sihang cangku	四行仓库
Sishui	汜水 (Henan)
Suzhou	苏州 (Jiangsu)
Taierzhuang	台儿庄 (Shandong)
Taierzhuang dazhan jinianguan	台儿庄大战纪念馆
Taishan	台山 (Guangdong)
Tanghe	唐河 (Henan)
Tianjin	天津 (Hebei)
Tieshizi hutong	铁狮子胡同 (Beijing)
Turfan	吐鲁番 (Xinjiang)
Urumqi	乌鲁木齐 (Xinjiang)
Xiheyang	西河阳 (Longkou, Shandong)
Wanxian	万县 (Sichuan)
Weixian	维县 (Shandong)
Wuhan	武汉 (Hubei)
Xian	西安 (Shaanxi)
Xiamen	厦门 (Fujian)
Xinan Lianda	西南联大
Xinyu	新渝 (Jiangxi)
Yan'an	延安 (Shaanxi)
Yanjing daxue	燕京大学
Yantai	烟台 (Shandong)
Yichang	宜昌 (Hubei)
Yidu	益都 (Shandong)
Yongningzhen	永宁镇 (Fujian)
Zhangzhou	漳州 (Fujian)
Zhengzhou	郑州 (Henan)
Zhang Zizhong lu	张自忠路 (Beijing)
Zhongshan	中山 (Guangdong)
Zouping	邹平 (Shandong)
Zunyi	遵义 (Guizhou)

Index

CPSIA information can be obtained at www.ICGtesting.com
Printed in the USA
BVOW11s0025121213

338824BV00010B/251/P